DIMENSIONS OF COMMUNITIES

GARLAND LIBRARY OF SOCIOLOGY
GENERAL EDITOR: DAN A. CHEKKI
(Vol. 16)
GARLAND REFERENCE LIBRARY
OF SOCIAL SCIENCE
(Vol. 525)

GARLAND LIBRARY OF SOCIOLOGY
General Editor: Dan A. Chekki

DIMENSIONS OF COMMUNITIES
A Research Handbook

Dan A. Chekki
University of Winnipeg

GARLAND PUBLISHING, INC. • NEW YORK & LONDON
1989

Library of Congress Cataloging-in-Publication Data

Dimensions of communities : a research handbook / [edited by] Dan A.
Chekki.
        p. cm. — (Garland library of sociology ; vol. 16) (Garland
reference library of social science ; vol. 525)
Includes index.
ISBN 0–8240–8397–0 (alk. paper)
        1. Community organization—Cross-cultural studies. 2. Community
development—Cross-cultural studies. I. Chekki, Danesh A.
II. Series. III. Series: Garland reference library of social
science ; v. 525.
HT65.D56 1989   89-31644
307.1'4—dc20   CIP

Printed on acid-free, 250-year-life paper
Manufactured in the United States of America

TABLE OF CONTENTS

PART ONE:
INTRODUCTION

PART TWO:
COMMON INTERESTS AND ORGANIZATIONS

PART THREE:
ETHNIC COMMUNITIES

v

DIMENSIONS OF COMMUNITIES

A Research Handbook

PART ONE

INTRODUCTION

SOME NEW DIMENSIONS OF COMMUNITIES: AN OVERVIEW

Dan A. Chekki

Contemporary communities have become increasingly interdependent and complex now more than ever before. Concomitantly, community research has become highly specialized. Different facets and issues related to community life are being probed by scholars trained in various disciplines. A comprehensive understanding of community structure and dynamics, it seems, is now beyond the ability of any single researcher. It is at this juncture that the efforts of a team of scholars would be necessary to comprehend even a few dimensions of communities. This volume is the result of such an endeavor.

Sociologists have traditionally tended to focus on territorially-based human settlements. The conception of community as viewed by Robert E. Park (1929) has a spatial and geographical connotation. Sanders (1966) and Warren (1978) have emphasized both geographical and psychological aspects of communities. However, the ecological approach seems to have dominated the field of community studies. While an overwhelming majority of sociologists prefer the areal connotation when speaking of communities, William J. Goode (1957), Don Martindale (1960) and Melvin M. Webber (1963), among others, have advanced the notion of "community without propinquity."

In recent years rapid technological developments have facilitated the formation of various interest communities based on commonality of occupation, religion, ethnicity, values, or any other common activity or pursuit. It is possible to observe a stronger identification and loyalties to interest communities than to the local community.

This handbook attempts to present recent research on spatial as well as non-spatial common interest communities and their organizational structure and dynamics. Ethnic communities tend to support the concept of community when viewed in interactional terms. Various communities do persist as attachments to specific interests and goals. New communities tend to emerge from the activities which connect similar associations and networks.

Different facets of communities included in this volume refer to community organizations, ethnic community dynamics, community problems, policy, planning and development. Most of the case studies presented here happen to be descriptive, historical and comparative. We have not made an effort to bring all these contributions within a single theoretical framework. This is because of our belief that communities, like any other multi-faceted phenomena, are subject to analysis from different points of view.

Bennett Berger (1988) has noted that the concept of community has, since the nineteenth century, been contrasted with the idea of society. Community is tradition, society is change. Community is feeling, society is rationality. Community is warm and intimate, society is cold and formal. Community is love, society is business. He believes that the quest for community is very likely eternal and it reflects the fact that orderly social life is inconceivable without some shared culture. For Berger community always refers to community held values and behavioral prescriptions; and the sustenance of that common culture usually requires frequent face-to-face interaction among its members. In this sense urban communities also may provide opportunities for the formation of communities based on common interests and values.

Common interest communities have not received adequate attention by social researchers in North America. Carol Silverman and Stephen Barton think that these communities return to the neighborhood an element of Toennies "gemeinschaft" community which has largely been lost, the interdependence of a group of people united through their shared ownership and management of residential property. This study examines why despite shared space and shared ownership which normally demands involvement, most common interest community homeowners either participate very little in the affairs of their association or participate in ways that emphasize the values of individual property ownership rather than those of community interdependence. Silverman and Barton argue that cultural understandings of the meaning of private property are in conflict with the reality of common interest community living. It is observed that residents in these communities generally handle this tension by drawing on their understandings of the rights associated with private property rather than on the norms of neighborliness.

Community nonprofit organizations vary in terms of their goals, services they provide, community needs they meet, and problems they intend to tackle. Kirsten Gronbjerg focuses on those groups of nonprofit organizations that provide services in the areas of employment, housing, community organizing, advocacy, legal assistance, day care, physical and mental health, and social services. During a period of economic decline, cuts in public spending for human services, and increased hardships especially for low income groups have played a major role in minimizing community distress and anomie.

This study addresses important theoretical issues about the nature of links between communities and social institutions. What is the selective process that changes the mix of services nonprofit organizations provide to communities? Gronbjerg examines the types of missions and target groups identified by a sample of Chicago nonprofit organizations, their goals and service needs. She argues that the institutional environment within which nonprofit organizations secure their individual legitimacy may at the aggregate level prevent the nonprofit sector from making marked adjustments to changing community environments.

Nonprofit organizations exhibit a heavy resource dependency on funding organizations that may have different sets of conceptions of community needs and priorities. The analysis presented here shows how the changing community environment -- increases in poverty and welfare dependency and cuts in state spending on human services -- has posed new challenges to nonprofit organizations. The findings suggest that we should carefully examine the very complex interactions among 'public benefit' institutions, the communities in which they operate and the extra-community resources on which they depend for a better planning and provision of services and meeting community needs.

While American community studies focus on social change, in Canada the focus seems to be more on ethnic community solidarity. Leo Driedger compares American and Canadian community studies and finds that the former were greatly influenced by the process of urbanization, industrialization, and bureaucratization and the latter, primarily ethnographic rural community studies, despite change, reflect solidarity and cohesion of ethnic culture.

This review of community research in Canada reveals that the construction of ethnic communities is a complex process, influenced by many processes of change. It is interesting to know that some ethnic groups are engulfed by these changes and succumb to assimilation either voluntarily or involuntarily. Others, through constructing cultures, institutions, language, religion or because of race remain separate, some voluntarily, and others involuntarily. Driedger identifies gaps in community research and emphasizes the need to undertake in depth studies of specific distinctive ethnic communities both in rural and urban communities.

Ethnic communities happen to be important components of many American and Canadian cities. Krzysztof Frysztacki examines the evolution and trends of change of a Polish-American community in Buffalo, New York. He identifies different stages of growth of this community and speculates on some probably future trends of development of this ethnic community.

During the past thirty years there have been significant demographic and socioeconomic changes in many central cities of the United States. Changes in racial composition in urban communities have been accompanied by internal class differences. Theodoric Manley, Jr. by using the participant observation method, presents a case study of how a middle-class black urban community (Chicago's South Shore) went through a process of construction of local sentiments and values leading to a series of strategies to prevent a halfway house from locating in the community. This study, by adopting the emergent perspective, illustrates the process through which local sentiments and values were constructed by the external imposition of a policy of deinstitutionalization in mental health and by local transformation in class interest and community control.

The study of the Paris Region presented by Mary Jo Huth indicates how the national government decentralization policies coupled with demographic factors in France have contributed to changes in metropolitan community structure. After discussing the negative effects of rapid suburban expansion in the Paris

Region from 1920 to 1960, the evolution of formal
planning in the Paris Region from 1955 to 1976 is
delineated. Furthermore, there is a description of the
development of the La Defense considered to be the most
grandiose project carried out in the Paris Region since
the Second Empire over more than a century ago.

Many cities in North America have been experiencing
fiscal stress due to soaring costs of service delivery
and declining revenues. In many communities this
financial strain has resulted in increasing taxes and
reduced services. What happens when cities have limited
resources and experience escalating costs? At least some
cities are adopting innovative strategies to cope with
this urban community problem. Dan Chekki delineates how
Canadian cities have been resorting to innovative fiscal
management strategies in their attempt to maintain
existing services.

While urban governments experiencing the greatest
economic stress are more likely to have adopted more
drastic cost-cutting strategies than their more fortunate
counterparts, the diverse programs and policies
illustrate that there are few areas of urban government
responsibility being overlooked in the drive to utilize
public funds more effectively and efficiently. Despite
the seeming diversity of the specific restraint measures
introduced there is an identifiable set of factors
underlying the adoption of these innovations.

Urban communities in North America have, in recent
decades, been faced with a marked increase in the
frequency and variety of crimes. Peter McGahan attempts
to restructure the patterns of crime in Halifax and St.
John. This historical preliminary sketch, based on the
materials in the police department archives, newspapers,
journals and oral histories, focuses on the changing
nature of offenses in these cities. It provides an
interesting comparative analysis of the ecology of crime
and the nature of criminality. This study raises the
question as to how these patterns of crime relate to
community structure and change.

Despite differences urban communities in highly
developed post-industrial societies have been influenced
by national urban policies insofar as economic
development, fiscal, and political processes are
concerned. Bernd Hamm describes some trends in urban
development in the Western industrialized societies and

focuses on national urban policies in the United States, Canada, Great Britain, France, and the Federal Republic of Germany. He notes that there was a shift in national urban policies since the mid 1970's in political priorities towards economic growth, unemployment, and the problems of heavy industries. He argues that any national policy inevitably affects the cities, as eighty percent of a nation's population reside under urban conditions, decision makers faced with scarcity and austerity should aim at better urban planning.

Many communities in Third World countries are disadvantaged by poverty, illiteracy, ill health, and resource scarcity. The less developed as well as advanced industrialized countries have been promoting economic development and social change in most of Africa, Asia, and Latin America. Different development models based on varied ideologies have been used in community development. James Midgley discusses the dichotomy between 'national development' and 'community development' models of policy-planning. He believes that these different levels of intervention, although in some respects complement each other, have become antagonistic. According to him, the large scale industrial investments and urban bias of national development has tended to neglect local needs; and 'popular' and 'community' participation in development is necessary. Moreover, there is the need to synthesize apparently antithetical strategies that facilitate a balanced development.

The state sponsored macro focused interventions were paralleled by the emergence of an alternative approach known as community development espousing the ideals of citizen participation, self-help, and cooperativism. Midgley traces the historical antecedents of community development and its recent manifestations and limitations. It is important to note that the United Nations and international non-governmental organizations have facilitated the active involvement of ordinary people in the development process.

Midgley doubts whether the massive social and economic problems facing Third World countries can be solved through local efforts alone. It is observed that community development is unresponsive to needs that transcend the local level. Therefore, it is argued that there is a need to balance community and national development strategies. Two types of techniques which facilitate the harmonization of community and national development are identified and the impediments to the attainment of the decentralization ideal are discussed. It appears that the efforts to synthesize community development and national development in the Third World depends on the predispositions of political elites and their capacity to embrace ideologies committed both to national development and the involvement of people in the development process.[1]

NOTES

[1]Acknowledgements are due to Laureen Narfason who undertook the task of copy editing Chapters II to V.

REFERENCES

Berger, Benett, M., 1988. "Disenchanting the Concept of Community", Transaction/Society: 25:6

Goode, William J., 1957. "Community Within a Community: The Professions", American Sociological Review: 22.

Martindale, Don. 1960. American Social Structure, New York: Appleton-Century-Crofts.

Park, Robert E. 1929. "Sociology, Community and Society" in Research in the Social Sciences, ed. Wilson Gee, New York: Macmillan.

Sanders, Irwin T. 1966. The Community, New York: the Ronald Press.

Warren, Roland L. 1978. The Community in America, Chicago: Rand McNally.

Webber, Melvin M. 1963. "Order in Diversity: Community Without Propinquity", in Cities and Space, ed. Lowden Wingo, Jr. Baltimore: John Hopkins Press.

PART TWO

COMMON INTERESTS AND ORGANIZATIONS

II

COMMON INTEREST COMMUNITIES AND
THE AMERICAN DREAM

Carol J. Silverman
Stephen E. Barton[1]

Over the past 20 years a new form of residential development has proliferated in the United States, a form which seems to reintroduce traditional elements of community. In common-interest communities -- condominiums, planned developments, and cooperatives -- property is held in common, and owners are automatically members of an association whose elected board has the power to set and enforce rules governing common and individual property, and to raise monies to maintain that property. Thus, common-interest communities return to the neighborhood an element of the Toennies gemeinschaft community which has largely been lost, the interdependence of a group of people who do not choose each other but who are united through their shared ownership of land (Silverman, 1986). Common-interest developments also potentially resemble the early New England small town, where municipal decisions were reached through open meetings of citizen property owners.

This structure of common-interest communities makes interdependence among neighbors both explicit and unavoidable. Homeowners in the typical residential neighborhood in the United States are able to ignore their neighbors if they wish, and must rely on voluntary organizations to represent their common interests. Homeowners in common-interest communities automatically belong to a homeowners' association, own property together, and share in the use of common area facilities of the type normally provided by external agencies. In townhouse and apartment developments, they also share walls. Shared walls, shared spaces, and shared ownership mean that community standards for acceptable use and behavior must be determined and upheld (Silverman and Barton, 1984). However, despite a structure which virtually demands involvement, most common-interest community homeowners either participate very little in the affairs of the association, or participate in ways that emphasize the values of individual property ownership rather than those of community interdependence. In this article we will discuss the reasons why this is the case. We will use data gathered in a state-wide survey of associations in California, along with 12 case studies, to argue that cultural understandings of the meaning of private property are in conflict with the reality of common-interest community living. Residents generally handle this tension by drawing on their understanding of the rights associated with private property, rather than on the norms of neighborliness.

We will first briefly summarize the demographics of common-interest communities. Then we will discuss our research design. Finally, we will turn to the meaning of homeownership in the United States and the importance of this understanding to common-interest community participation.

COMMON-INTEREST COMMUNITIES

There is a tendency to think of common-interest developments as satisfying the needs of specialized portions of the population: urban apartment dwellers, young singles, and retirees. In fact, they have become an integral part of the housing stock and in some areas constitute the majority of all new residential developments.

Common-interest agreements can exist in all forms of housing, from single-family detached dwellings to apartment buildings. They are simply a means to permit ownership of common property. In cooperatives the common property includes everything: buildings, land, and all other facilities. Cooperative owners purchase a share in the common property, which entitles them to the exclusive use of a residence. In condominiums and planned developments, members own their individual units. The units encompass only the airspace in apartments and some townhouses, but include the building structure and surrounding land in single-family and some townhouse developments. Under condominium ownership members also own an undivided share in the common property, which is managed by a homeowners' association in which all owners are members. In planned developments, the homeowners' association owns the common property and members control the association. In the United States, apartments are usually organized as condominiums and single-family detached housing developments as planned developments. Both forms are widely used for townhouses.

Common-interest developments have existed in one form or another virtually throughout the history of the United States. The first were early nineteenth century developments of houses for the well-to-do, which were built surrounding a private park and streets, and protected physically by gates and legally by private covenants restricting the property to limited residential use. During the early twentieth century, cooperative ownership of apartments became common in New York City, and the condominium was established there after World War II. The federal mortgage insurance system revised its rules to include cooperatives and condominiums in 1962, after which the states passed parallel legislation creating a legal framework for this complex form of ownership. Condominiums then became widely used. In general, American homebuyers and lending institutions have been much more receptive to condominium and planned developments, which come under the familiar rubric of homeownership, than to cooperatives in which ownership is entirely shared.

Although common-interest communities are sometimes equated with affluent lifestyles, and exclusive developments have been formed to provide protection and facilities to the wealthy, most are an adaptation to the declining proportion of the population that can afford conventional housing. By building at higher densities, developers reduce land costs, while shared walls, wiring, and plumbing reduce construction costs. Common-interest developments are also an effort on the part of local municipalities, particularly in California where local governments must cope with the effects of the Proposition 13 property tax limitation, to reduce fiscal responsibilities by transferring ownership of (and therefore maintenance responsibility for) an infrastructure such as sewers, roads, and parks onto the association.

It is difficult to obtain reliable figures for the number of common-interest communities in the United States. Despite fluctuations in the housing market, they have accounted for over 15 percent of all housing starts in the United States during the 1980s (United States Construction Reports Series 20, 1987). Estimates of the number of associations range as high as 100,000, although the true figure is probably somewhat lower.

RESEARCH

The data discussed here were drawn from two sources: 1) a mail survey of associations in the State of California and, 2) 12 case studies of associations in Northern California (Barton and Silverman, 1987).

Since no frame was available of only common-interest developments, we used a keyword search to draw a sample of 1000 associations from the Mutual Benefit Corporation listing produced by the California Secretary of State's Office. A questionnaire covering a wide range of issues pertaining to association functioning was then sent to board presidents. We received returns from 77 percent of the associations for which we had valid addresses. Once the data were cleared of associations that were for some reason inapplicable -- chiefly projects that had not yet been sold, or had been sold to one owner and rented -- we had a final sample of 579 active associations.

The mutual-benefit listings only include incorporated associations. No listing is available in California of the unincorporated ones, which tend to be very small and are estimated to form about 10 percent of the population.[2] Therefore, the sample is biased towards larger associations, although small ones are certainly well represented. Some 25 percent of the sample was made up of associations of 16 units or less, while the median association size was 43 units.

The case study associations were selected to broadly represent the range of types found in our survey, and varied in size, price, type of management, and level of internal difficulties. In each association, at the minimum, we reviewed association documents, attended a board or annual meeting if the association held one, and interviewed a member of the board. In most cases, we also interviewed a number of involved and sometimes uninvolved members. In all, we conducted 50 in-depth interviews of association owners and residents.

Finally, the research was supplemented by 20 in-depth interviews with a wide range of professionals who work with common-interest developments.

COMMUNITY PARTICIPATION AND COMMON-INTEREST DEVELOPMENTS

In most residential neighborhoods there is either no neighborhood association, or membership in the association is voluntary. In some residential neighborhoods, membership in a local association is mandatory, but the powers of the association are limited to enforcement of covenants establishing uniform architectural standards and permissible land uses.[3] In common-interest communities not only is membership mandatory -- indeed, the association is established by the developer prior to the sale of any of the units -- but the powers of the association are far-reaching. The elected board and appointed committees have the right to set and enforce rules covering both common and individual property. Common-interest developments may require particular types of carpeting or other soundproofing, restrict the presence of children or pets, and regulate the color of doors and curtains, the design of porches, patios, and walks, along with the use of alcoholic beverages in public areas, parking, the use of swimming pools and tennis courts, and even the use of residences by relatives and friends of the owner. The association manages common property, which can include buildings, roads, parks, playgrounds, water and sewer lines, swimming pools, golf courses, and tennis courts. It can also provide such services as landscaping, lawn care, security patrols, and sanitation. The association further has the power to raise monies through regular and special assessments, and to punish members for rule violations by revoking voting rights and rights to use the common areas, and by levelling fines. In the case of non-payment of dues, the board can place liens and foreclose upon the unit.

Although the association's powers are broad and its activities directly affect the residents' quality of life and owners' property values, participation of residents is usually sparse. A median of 11 percent serve on boards, committees, or any other voluntary basis.[4] Virtually all of this appears based on board membership, which is mandated by the structure of the association. Looking only at the numbers who serve on committees or some other voluntary basis, the mean percentage involved .05.[5] In 21 percent of the cases, there were fewer people running for the board in the most recent elections than there were seats. In 30 percent of the cases, the association was unable to get a majority to vote or assign proxies in the previous election.[6]

In the words of one board president:

> Apathy reigns supreme: most owners want some unpaid volunteer to make decisions for them rather than attending board meetings or annual membership meetings.... We are running out of fools who will volunteer their time.

Most residents let the board make decisions, rather than becoming involved themselves. Only 16 percent of the boards reported that members gave them a lot of support, and 39 percent reported that members did not care one way or the other. (The remainder reported that at least some members argued with the board a lot, a point which will be discussed later.)

The lack of interest in association governance could be seen in many of the associations studied. In one 90-unit association, the majority of the board were absentee owners who had been on it since the founding of the association, when they themselves lived there, and who continued on because no replacements could be found. In fact, the association had not even bothered to hold an election during the past year because no one else wanted to run. A referendum on changing the pet policy, a topic of direct interest to the membership, failed to gather a necessary quorum and therefore failed.[7] In another 25-unit association a very tired board president, who essentially ran the association alone, tried to step down but was unable to find a replacement -- and indeed was told by the remainder of the board that they too would resign even if he gave up the presidency to become a less-involved board member.

Obviously, not all associations fit this pattern. We have interviewed associations wherein as much as one-third of the membership was involved in some way. However, the most frequent correlate of increased participation among the membership was dissatisfaction with the board's policies.[8] While disagreement is a normal part of politics, in these associations disagreements often took an abusive form.

We saw this type of angry and sometimes abusive behavior in several of the associations studied. In one, a group of homeowners, angered by a high but unavoidable special assessment, circulated a petition listing only a post office box as a contact point, and then put up a candidate to run against the board. In another an annual meeting we observed was beset by accusations of secret dealings and unethical behavior, as a faction, which essentially agreed with the board on the issues, attempted to elect its candidate. The meeting finally adjourned after three hours, not because of any official decision, but because there no longer was a quorum of the board present as members left in disgust, in tears, or screaming.

Individual owners also reacted angrily and sometimes abusively to board actions with which they disagreed. Thus, 44 percent of the board presidents reported that in the past year a member of the board had been harassed or subjected to personal accusations, or that the board had been threatened with a law suit. In addition, five percent of the boards had been sued by a member during the past year. Several board presidents we interviewed also mentioned they had been threatened with bodily harm by residents unhappy with enforcement of association rules. For example, one homeowner, enraged because he could not post a for sale sign on the lawn (which was common property), marched into the board meeting with the sign and threatened to hit the members with it. Many homeowners used the threat of a lawsuit as virtually their first resort, although this essentially meant they were suing themselves. In a more-than-usually substantive case, a homeowner was angered because the association would not permit him to construct a permanent ramp on common property in the front of his unit for use by a disabled friend, asking him instead to use a temporary ramp which could be removed when his friend left the unit. He refused to accept the compromise and threatened to sue for discrimination against the disabled.

Common-interest communities increase the structural interdependence among neighbors. They own property in common, and are provided with a formal apparatus which permits them to make decisions for the individual and common betterment of their lives. Yet most people do not participate in this process, and many of those who do participate are abusive in their approach to the association.

A simple explanation for the lack of participation comes from collective-action theory. O'Brien (1975), for example, in discussing the lack of participation among a neighborhood organization, refers to the free-rider problem. People who do not participate can still reap the benefits of the organization's efforts, with none of the costs. This approach, however, does not fully fit common-interest communities. It ignores the fact that owners and residents are directly and potentially negatively affected by the actions of the organization, and therefore, have an immediate interest in its behavior. This approach further does not address why participation, when it occurs, is often abusive. It also fails in a more significant way. It theoretically separates the mechanism by which people choose to become involved from the structure of the organization and from cultural understandings. The economic model which weighs costs and benefits is not sensitive to the particular nature of community in these associations. To look at these issues, we must discuss the meaning of private property and the home, particularly the tensions between the norms of inclusion associated with membership in a community and the individual rights associated with property ownership.

COMMON-INTEREST COMMUNITIES AND THE AMERICAN DREAM

One of the most strongly held values in American culture is that of home ownership. Since World War II all but the poorest Americans have come to expect that they will own their own home (Heskin, 1983). This home is far more than a shelter -- it serves symbolic purposes much greater than simple protection from the elements. Home ownership not only is a right, it is a certification that one is a respectable citizen (Perin, 1977). The home, typically the purchasers' largest single investment, provides a mark of permanence, stability, and personal success.

The home also physically maintains, as well as symbolically manifests, two of the most important American values, freedom and individuality (Seeley, Sims, and Loosley, 1956). At least within American society, the two concepts are related; one has freedom to the extent that one's actions as an individual (or member of a small group -- usually the family) are not constrained. Thus, American traditions of private property ownership emphasize the rights of the owner to do as he or she wishes with the property, rather than the obligations of the owner to use the property in a way that is responsible to the surrounding community. In general, private property is linked to freedom rather than to responsibility, limited by the rights of others rather than by a commitment to their well-being (Barton, 1985).

This tendency is reinforced when the private property at issue is a house, because the home is considered the private refuge from worldly obligations. Deeply embedded within American culture is the notion that the true self is best displayed when one is distanced from society and involved in the private world of family and selected friends (Silverman, 1983; Rakoff, 1977). Once the basic unit of an economic system based on household production, with industrialization the home has become a refuge from the competition and impersonality of the work place, as a haven in a heartless world. The home is now the space where one can best insulate against unwanted intrusions. Hence the home is the space of the greatest individuality and freedom.

However, homes are located in neighborhoods, and residents are therefore connected to each other in important ways. Shared residence means that residents share vulnerabilities to external agencies and certain aspects of their private lives, although what is shared will vary by the individual and neighborhood. Out of shared residence can come the recognition of interdependence. Neighborliness, as it is commonly used, recognizes this fact. Neighborly individuals help in times of need and offer each other those small services that make life easier (Keller, 1968).

This dual aspect of the home, its equation with property rights and individualism and its location in a larger neighborhood, can create tension. Even single-family detached dwellings in residential neighborhoods do not entirely fulfill the requirements of privacy and individualism associated with the ideal home. Neighbor's loud noises, spreading weeds, and wandering pets and children all intrude upon peoples' privacy, while sidewalks, curbside parking, and public services are shared and subject to ambiguous control by the homeowner at best. However, so long as behavior does not violate city ordinances, the homeowner has seeming control over his or her property. So long as negotiations over the appropriate use of individual and shared spaces remains tacit, residents need not directly confront the fact that neighbors represent the most immediate threat to control over property. The two ideals of the home as the site of individual freedom and the home as part of a community of neighbors co-exist, with preservation of privacy as the main shared activity of the community (Silverman, 1983).

Increasingly, particularly for first-time homeowners, the home they purchase will be in a common-interest development which incorporates neighbor interdependence into the structure of property ownership, but in a way which maintains the priority of private property ownership with its associated values over those of community.

OWNERSHIP AND RESIDENCE IN THE COMMON INTEREST COMMUNITY

Membership in the associations which govern common-interest communities is based on ownership, not residence. Absentee owners who rent their units are members of the homeowners' association, while renters are not. Renters are structurally excluded from voting, even though they are directly affected by rules governing the use of common property and are indirectly affected by financial decisions which will affect their rent. This exclusion of renters is legitimated in common-interest community law and practice. Most associations make little attempt to contact renters or even to inform them of the rules, leaving this to their landlord. Indeed, direct contact between an association and a renter, except in an emergency, may be considered illegal interference with a private contract. Many associations limit the renters' use of common areas. In one association studied, for example, renters are forbidden the use of the laundry room, while the governing documents prohibit exterior clothes lines.

The importance of ownership to membership in the community could further be seen in the manner in which those associations we interviewed discussed renters. They were seen as not keeping up the common property associated with the individual unit, a responsibility formally that of the absentee owner, and as not respectful of the rules. Perin (1977) talks about anti-renter prejudice in the United States. Few of her quotes

approached the virulence of some of the statements given
to us.

> Maybe   you   could   help   homeowner
> associations lobby legislatures to permit
> the torture of renters.
> Never let the renter get out of hand.
> Nine times out of ten the renter cares
> even less than the homeowner.

> Tenants have no pride of ownership, are
> not properly screened by out-of-town
> owners.... Renters do not read the
> [governing documents] and if the agent by
> chance should read them to the tenants,
> they do not listen or they forget.

We heard many more anti-renter statements during our
interviews than we did statements directed against
absentee owners, even though absentee owners were
structurally a larger problem. Absentee owners were more
often delinquent in paying assessments than resident
owners and were less likely to vote, which made it harder
to get a necessary quorum to pass measures proposed by
the board.   But absentee owners were still owners and,
as such, full members of the community.

While common-interest developments are based on
ownership, the association directly limits the freedoms
associated with that ownership.   In such developments,
decisions about maintenance, improvements, and finances
are made by the association rather than the individual
owner, and detailed restrictions are placed on the use
of individual and common property.   There is nothing
within a rights-based notion of ownership that recognizes
the legitimacy of these limitations imposed by the
governing documents.   For this reason, many residents
have difficulty with these restrictions. Only 14 percent
of the associations reported that they had no problems
with violations of association rules involving the use
of common and individual property.

Rules governing changes to individual units, the
limitation which most interfered with what owners
perceived to be their inherent rights to use their own
property as they pleased, proved to be more intractable
to resolution than any other form of violation. We saw

many instances of this throughout the case studies. We have already discussed the incident of the ramp. In another three-story apartment complex, an owner in an upper unit cut a skylight through the roof, ignoring the fact that the change decreased the structural integrity of the building and that the roof was the property of the entire association, rather than of the individual unit. In yet another association, a homeowner did not want the defective sheet-rock in the walls of his unit replaced, unaware that the walls were the property of the association.

Perhaps the most typical marketing strategy used to sell units in common-interest developments is stressing the "carefree living" that association life brings. A subsidiary strategy is to sell the idea that ownership brings with it the guarantee of a particular type of community -- be it one enhanced by recreational facilities, or simply one where the purchaser knows property values will be maintained because of the uniform standards of upkeep. These marketing strategies are well in accord with the cultural equation of private property with rights. They simply extend the notion of ownership into the common property, and enlarge the purchase to include maintenance service and a pleasing neighborhood.

Owners therefore feel they are purchasing the rights to control the common area as well as their individual property, and sometimes take action to enforce those rights.

> Our little group of 47 homes is in the throes of living with and without some trees.... We have spent thousands of dollars for artistic pruning and countless hours discussing who should and should not have a view of the city, the water, the mountains or whatever is just outside the window on the other side of the trees. We've had multiple discussions, some very heated, regarding individual rights, beauty in the eye of the beholder, community theme of 'Urban Forest' and what's going to happen next year and thereafter. We've had tears and tantrums, actual nocturnal pruning...and daytime pruning by unauthorized persons. Somewhere there is a happy solution to all of this.

As this example shows, strains develop when owners' notions of the appropriate use of common space are in conflict. In another association studied, residents who wished to have a play complex for their children ultimately had to concede to those who did not wish this to be a part of their exterior space, but continued to maintain ill-feelings about the issue. In some cases, residents even saw it as the responsibility of the board to supervise the behavior of the other residents in their own units. This most often occurred with renters, but board presidents were sometimes asked to talk to owners whose behavior had displeased another resident.

An understanding of property rights that recognizes only rights and not obligations contains an inherent contradiction. To the extent that any homeowner enforces his or her rights, this limits the rights of a neighbor to use property as desired. Yet to the extent that neighbors' rights are acknowledged as legitimate, this also means recognition of the legitimacy of controls over property. This contradiction creates a tension, one that in the worst case can create an inability to set or enforce rules for common behavior.

> I could get into why this is a very bad condominium project to live in. This is a very small condominium and there are 24 units and no rules and regulations were ever established. About what types of things you should do, and not do, and we really have just had a lot of problems.... That's the whole thing; a homeowners association has the power, but these people were really afraid to exert any power in any direction.... They can never solve anything, never resolve any issue.... It always amazed me, it boggled my mind that out of 24 units, 24 little units, we could never get anything together.

In the more typical case, members handle the tension by treating the association as an external body, a tendency recognized even by California law, which mandates a statement which cautions the buyer in common-interest developments that "them" is "you".

Residents and owners in common-interest developments have to directly confront that tension between the common good of the community and the individual rights of the homeowner. This confrontation is rarely as dramatic as it was in one of the associations studied, where the developer had left the complex with a large number of serious construction defects. The defects were in common property, and therefore the responsibility of the association to repair. However, the lawyer got individual settlements for the homeowners, rather than a single settlement for the association which could have been used for needed repairs. The board president was faced with arguing in court that the association needed money to fund repairs against homeowners who wished to recoup as much of their original investment as possible and then simply abandon the property. Elsewhere, even if the circumstances were not as dramatic, similar tensions occurred over the need to fund reserves to replace the common property as it wore out. Since most of the associations had been established in the past several years, there was no immediate need for large sums of money and many homeowners, assuming that they would move before the need arose, did not wish to contribute.

We interviewed numerous people throughout the study, most of them board members, who recognized the importance of the community, as well as the importance of individual rights. But they were in the minority. Most board members served to protect their investment and control the manner in which their money was spent. They most often thought of the association as a business, to be run efficiently. Some board presidents also saw the association as an extension of their own home, where they could exercise comparable levels of control. In the worst cases, they took on unreasonable powers and ignored the wishes of the other homeowners.

> The present board is composed of members of a group who rebelled against the activist fascist policies of the original group. Our motto is to live and let live. We do not believe that the behavior of our neighbors or their discretion in the use of their own property need to be supervised. We live in a beautiful neighborhood with nice folks. Keeping it that way requires vigilance, and takes more time than any of us would like but

the alternative is to let the Nazis come back.

Residents often did not understand, questioned, or even rejected the legitimacy of the collective dimension of association life. Many mistrusted the board's actions, a mistrust which was grounded in their uneasiness at letting a group (association) whose legitimacy they did not accept make what they believed should be individual decisions. The homeowners interviewed were, on the one hand, grateful to the board for volunteering time, but, on the other hand, angry at the loss of control entailed in letting the board make decisions. In turn, they believed that the board was probably extravagant with **their** money, and that they could do better if they could just make decisions for their own property. Many homeowners looked at their board as simply a group of homeowners with unfair powers over their neighbors.

There are contradictory strains, then, in common-interest communities; tendencies towards recognition of commonalities and interdependence, and towards individual rights at the potential expense of the common good. In most associations, at least some residents participate in activities that emphasize the former. For example, the proceeds from a recycling program may be used to support improvements of common areas; and residents may pick up trash and contribute time to common improvements such as road repairs. However, the emphasis on individual rights usually outweighs the tendency to recognize interdependence. Many who serve do so largely to protect their investment. Whereas many who do not serve are distrustful of the board. Neither group accepts the collective dimension of association life. Individualism is too deeply embedded in the larger culture and in the structure of the association, which recognizes ownership, not residence, as the basis for belonging.

The community in these associations is a fragile one because it is dependent upon utilitarian notions of collective action. It cannot support real differences because there is no group ethic which transcends individualistic notions. When differences arise, they then most often take a hostile form.

CONCLUSION

We have discussed a type of community that formally resembles earlier types often lauded as "true" communities. Like Toennies gemeinschaft village, residents are interdependent because of shared land ownership, and, like the early New England small town, formal mechanisms exist -- the board meeting and annual meeting of homeowners -- which can give rise to local participation and self-determination. However, we have found that this structural form and its cultural meanings lead to non-participation, hostility, and exclusion.

The common-interest development, of course, lacks much that characterized these early communities. Residents are usually not kin and they do not share workday aspects of their lives. Nonetheless, owners are economically interdependent. Decisions about the upkeep and improvement of property affect each unit's resale value and, indeed, there are cases where large special assessments have forced owners to sell their units or put them into foreclosure. Furthermore, decisions about the use and maintenance of common and individual property affect all of their private lives. For these reasons, even if the factors which should encourage collective action are weaker, they are still present and certainly cannot account for the culture we have described.

Why then do most people fail to participate? Collective action theory would have it that the important explanation is individual self-interest, that residents can collect the benefits of the association with none of the costs of participation, and therefore do not do so. There is some truth to this approach, but collective action theory does not explain why owners are often distrustful of the board and resent its necessity, yet may still not get involved or do so in disruptive ways. Unlike a voluntary neighborhood organization, the boards' actions directly affect the day-to-day circumstances of residents and owners and, if the association is mismanaged, can have significant effects on owners' finances. There are direct, often monetary, costs to not being involved, and owners are often certain that they could do the job better. Nonetheless, many residents avoid involvement, actively trying to ignore the existence of the association rather than, as collective action theory would have it, taking its benefits for granted. When they do become involved, it is often to express resentment at the association, rather than to offer to help.

The explanation for this culture of non-participation is rooted in the very structure of the common-interest development that should foster recognition of interdependence. Common-interest developments are defined by shared ownership of private property, and are therefore affected by cultural understandings of the meaning of property. So long as these focus on individual rights, rather than collective obligations, common-interest developments will contain an inherent contradiction. They will use ownership rather than residence as the basis for inclusion, and will create resentment because they represent what is seen as an abridgement of the individual's rights of homeownership. As such, the formal organization which embodies this contradiction will be resented, and people will generally either not participate or will do so in order to protect their property rights, not out of any recognition of community interdependence.

NOTES

[1]The authors share equal responsibility for this article. The Common Interest Development Governance Study was supported by a contract with the California Department of Real Estate, Contract #85-299.

[2]The estimate comes from David Warner, State of California, Department of Real Estate, March 1987.

[3]Racial and religious restrictions on residences were a major reason for the spread of such mandatory associations, but enforcement of such restrictions was held unconstitutional in 1948 (Vose, 1959).

[4]This figure is an estimate. Our survey asked for the number of people serving on the board, serving on committees, and helping the association in some informal way. Since we do not know how many board members were also committee members, we assumed that, in the case where the board did serve on committees, one-third of the total committee members were also on the board, and subtracted accordingly. Finally, we estimated that there were two adults per household.

[5]Here, since board members who serve on committees volunteer to do so the numerator was simply the number on committees or other volunteers with no correction for the presence of board members.

[6]All point estimates are plus or minus 4 percent at the 95 percent confidence level.

[7]In order for such measures to pass, some specified percentage of all owners, not just of those owners who vote, must approve.

[8]When a partial correlation is run between whether members had argued with the board and whether there were more candidates than seats in the last election, controlling for the other correlates of increased participation (size of association and people's understandings of their association responsibilities), the r was .18 (sig. .000).

REFERENCES

Barton, Stephen E., 1985. "Property Rights and Democracy: The Beliefs of San Francisco Neighborhood Leaders and the American Liberal Tradition." PhD Dissertation, Department of City and Regional Planning, University of California, Berkeley.

Barton, Stephen E., and Carol J. Silverman, 1987. Common Interest Development Homeowners' Associations in California: Report to the State of California Department of Real Estate. State of California Department of Real Estate, Sacramento.

Heskin, David A., 1984. Tenants and the American Dream. New York: Praeger.

Keller, Suzanne, 1968. The Urban Neighborhood. New York: Random House Books.

O'Brien, David, 1975. Neighborhood Organization and Interest Group Processes. Princeton: Princeton University Press.

Perin, Constance, 1977. Everything in Its Place: Social Order and Land Use in America. Princeton: Princeton University Press.

Rakoff, Robert M., 1977. "Ideology in Everyday Life: The Meaning of the House." Politics and Society, 7(1), pp. 87-104.

Seeley, John, R. Sims and E. Loosley, 1956. Crestwood Heights. Toronto: University of Toronto Press.

Silverman, Carol J., 1986. "Neighboring and Urbanism: Commonalities Versus Friendship." Urban Affairs Quarterly, Dec., pp. 312-328.

_____, 1983. "Neighbors and Neighbors: A Study in Negotiated Claim." PhD Dissertation, Department of Sociology, University of California, Berkeley.

Silverman, Carol J., and Stephen E. Barton, 1986. "Private Property and Private Government: Tensions between Individualism and Community in Common

Interest Developments." Presented at the annual
meeting of the American Sociological Association,
August 1986, New York: Working Paper No. 451,
Institute of Urban and Regional Development,
University of California, Berkeley.

_____, 1984. Condominiums: Individualism and Community
in a Mixed Property Form. Working Paper No. 434,
Institute of Urban and Regional Development,
University of California, Berkeley.

United States Department of the Census, 1987.
Construction Reports, Series 20, Washington, D.C.,
U.S. Government Printing Office.

Vose, Clement, 1959. Caucasians Only: The Supreme Court,
the NAACP, and the Restrictive Covenant Cases.
Berkeley: University of California Press.

III

COMMUNITIES AND NONPROFIT ORGANIZATIONS:
INTERLOCKING ECOLOGICAL SYSTEMS[1]

Kirsten A. Gronbjerg

All nonprofit organizations see themselves as serving important community functions and receive official recognition of that claim when they are granted special tax privileges.[2] However, the missions, goals and activities of nonprofit organizations[3] vary greatly, as do the particular community needs they serve. Some nonprofit organizations pursue "community needs" that reflect largely the interests of broad constituency groups: arts, culture, recreation, education or research. Other nonprofit organizations pursue community needs more closely linked to the problems of the poor and lower income groups.

I focus on this latter group of organizations. They provide services in the areas of employment, housing, community organizing, advocacy, legal assistance, day care, social services, and outpatient health and mental health care. Ordinarily these community-based organizations which are thought to stand on the front lines, answering to the most difficult of human needs. The role of such organizations gains importance during a period of regional economic decline, such as the one Chicago has experienced since the late 1960's. The recent recession and cuts in public spending for human services have also hit the region hard. As a result, both the magnitude and range of human hardships has increased. For this reason, one might expect the post-1980 period to have been one of innovation among nonprofits, or at least a period of ferment and heroic effort.

The timing of this study provides a unique opportunity to address important theoretical issues about the nature of links between communities and social institutions. It relates to two key questions: First, what is the selective process that changes the mix of services nonprofit organizations provide to communities? Second, what is the selective process which creates the mix of needs they are confronted with? Necessarily, this paper addresses primarily the first of these processes, although I will briefly review the changing economic structure of the Chicago region, the impact of the 1981-2 recession, and the reduced public human service efforts in the city.

To document the response of human service nonprofit organizations to these major changes in their community environments, I examine the types of missions and target groups identified by a sample of Chicago nonprofit organizations, the service needs these agencies state as the most important for their target group, and the way in which goals and service needs are selected.   I distinguish between the adaptations made by individual organizations in their separate efforts to maintain legitimacy and the aggregate effects of these individual organizational adjustments.   I argue that the institutional environment within which nonprofit organizations secure their individual legitimacy may, at the aggregate level, prevent the nonprofit sector from making marked adjustments to changing community environments.   At the very least, these processes insure some time-lag in such adjustment, but they may also threaten the long-term legitimacy of the sector itself.[4]

As semi-official public benefit organizations, nonprofit organizations "should" respond to changing community circumstances, not simply move away as might a business firm that has lost its market. But nonprofits operate in an exceedingly complex environment, where competing definitions of "community needs" are more common than not.   These definitions of need constitute an important institutional resource for nonprofits.[5] They not only form the raw material from which organizations select their missions, but impact on critical organizational resources because funders also have their own definitions of community needs.

Nonprofit organizations, then, exhibit an exceptional form of resource dependency, which makes them highly vulnerable to threats to their legitimacy. The ability of nonprofit organizations to obtain government contracts, corporate or individual donations, United Way support, or foundation grants, depends very much on whether they can convince both the community and funders that they are doing "good work" that is "important to the community." Community relevance, therefore, becomes of primary importance to nonprofit organizations. They must somehow demonstrate that they have it, while at same time guarding themselves against appearances to the contrary.

Trapped between provincial "markets" and remote and often cosmopolitan funders, nonprofit organizations must remain mindful of their own organizational maintenance. In one respect, their situation resembles that described by Meyer and Scott (1983), who emphasize the importance of broad institutional belief systems that shape organizational structure and provide legitimacy. In another respect, however, they are like the separate firms experiencing community transition, such as those studied by Aldrich and Reiss (1976). Neither of these approaches is entirely adequate, although each helps to reveal some of the variations among nonprofits.

For the particular set of nonprofits I studied, there does seem to be an ecological process at work that selectively moves some of them in the direction of serving changing community needs. However, by far the most important finding in this study is the 'stasis' of these localized nonprofits and their reliance on outside "institutional" actors to help them define community needs, reach potential clients and determine their program content. It is not simply that they are preoccupied with the demands of "organizational maintenance" (a frequent scholarly criticism), but that they do not have the flexibility or organizational culture to transform themselves. While a direct knowledge of this may not penetrate general public awareness, the lack of notable innovations may leave the sector itself relatively defenseless in a broader climate of crisis.

CHALLENGES FROM A CHANGING COMMUNITY ENVIRONMENT

Chicago is a good place to undertake a study of this sort. The region has experienced a major restructuring of its local economy and demographic composition since the mid-1960's. It was hit particularly hard by the recession and farm crisis of the early 1980's, and cuts in federal spending were aggravated by even larger cuts in spending for human services. As a result, the region has experienced major increases in poverty and a large proportion of households now suffer major hardships and needs.

ECONOMIC RE-STRUCTURING AND RECESSION

Chicago, like most other cities in the Midwest, was
considerably affected by the recession of 1982-83.
Industrial investment (current dollars) in the Chicago
Region[6] declined 29 percent between 1979 and 1982, and by
1984 still had not returned to the 1979 level. Were
these figures adjusted for inflation the decline would
be even more dramatic. Industrial investments in the
city itself declined more rapidly (down 89 percent
between 1979 and 1982), but also recovered faster (up 376
percent between 1982 and 1984). The area's index of
industrial productivity (adjusted for inflation) showed
a loss of 18 percent between 1979 and 1982, and a modest
gain of only 8 percent between 1982 and 1984. Similarly,
the region lost almost one-fifth of its manufacturing
sector employment between 1979 and 1984, and just kept
even in non-manufacturing sector employment.

For the Chicago metropolitan area, the unemployment
rate stood at 5.2 percent in 1979, 7.7 percent in 1980,
8.1 percent in 1981, 10.5 percent in 1982 (Comptroller's
Report, March 30, 1983) and 1983, and finally declined
to 8.1 percent in the summer of 1984 (U.S. Department of
Labor, various).[7] As a result, the number of unemployed
in the region more than doubled from 194,000 in 1979 to
415,000 in 1982. Similarly, the number of mortgage
foreclosures in Cook County increased from about 3,100
per year in 1979 to 6,100 in 1982, 6,700 in 1984 and
7,000 in 1985. Thus, while the region probably turned
the corner sometime during 1983, the area was suffering
from considerable economic hardship during the first half
of the 1980's.

These recession effects compounded the long-term
decline of the "Old Urban Heartland," stretching from
Milwaukee to Boston and Washington, D.C., as a center for
economic activity and population growth (Suttles 1981).
For the entire state of Illinois, employment levels have
grown less during economic upturns and declined more
during economic downturns compared to national trends.
As the Illinois Economic and Fiscal Commission concludes
(1982, p.6), the Illinois economy no longer "merely
reflects national recessions, it magnifies them to such
an extent that national recovery may be of little
immediate relevance to state economic activity."

The movement of jobs and population from the Midwest
and Northeast regions to the sunbelt, especially since

the early 1970's, is well documented. The impact of
these changes on older, industrial cities, such as
Chicago, is more complex. Kasarda (1983) concludes that
there has occurred a:

> .... functional transformation of our larger
> older cities from centers of material goods
> production to centers of information exchange
> and higher-order service provision. In the
> process of urban functional transformation, may
> blue-collar industries that once constituted
> the economic backbone of cities and provided
> ready employment for lesser educated residents
> have vanished. These blue-collar industries
> have been replaced, in part, by knowledge
> intensive   white-collar   industries   whose
> requisites   for   employment   entry   entail
> substantial education or technical training
> and, hence, are unavailable to large segments
> of minority populations residing in these
> cities. The outcome has been simultaneous
> rising rates of unemployment, labor force
> nonparticipation, and dependency among central
> city minority residents.[8]

These trends have also occurred in the Chicago
region. The restructuring of the region's economy away
from manufacturing and towards service industries[9]
significantly increased the need for employment
retraining and education. The decline of large firms
and growth of small businesses[10] reduced the number and
"quality" of jobs in terms of wage levels, fringe
benefits, and job security (Portes and Sassen-Koob 1987).
The differential city-suburban growth rates[11] created
problems in both areas: lack of jobs in the city, lack
of low-wage employees in the suburbs, while problems in
public transportation and lack of suburban low-cost
housing prevented city residents from benefitting from
the suburban booms.

The result has been a significant increase in
poverty and economic dependency in the city. Census data
reveal that more than 600,000 persons in Chicago fell
below the poverty line in 1979, up 25 percent from
482,000 in 1969. For families, the increase was even
steeper, up 36 percent from one in ten to one in six,
almost two-thirds of them headed by women. The increase
in poverty was especially severe for Hispanics (up 131
percent from 44,000 to 101,000), and blacks (up 37

percent from 273,000 to 375,000). The increase of 118,000 poor persons between 1969 and 1979 occurred in the same period that the city lost 362,000 of its total population, primarily whites. Moreover, of the more than 600,000 Chicagoans living in poverty in 1979, three-fourths, or more than 454,000, were living in extreme poverty (less than 75 percent of the poverty level), people for whom hunger and lack of basic needs was a virtual certainty. The recession that occurred subsequent to 1979 only aggravated these conditions.

SERVICE NEEDS AND PROBLEMS

As these figures suggest, the welfare system became increasingly important after 1970. Data presented by the state suggest that most of the increase in the Chicago region's economic base during 1965-77 was due to transfer incomes (Illinois Department of Business and Economic Development 1978, p. 79). That trend is likely to have been accentuated between 1977 and 1982. Similarly, an analysis of census data shows that the number of families receiving public assistance increased 180 percent between 1970 and 1980, or by 100,000 families in the city alone. By 1980 public income transfer payments accounted for 6.1 percent of all family income in the SMSA, up from 2.7 percent in 1970. For the city, the increase went from 4.4 percent to 10.6 percent.

Welfare dependency continued to increase in the 1980's. The number of General Assistance recipients in Cook County increased from 70,000 in 1980 to 117,000 in 1983, while AFDC recipients increased much more modestly from 150,000 to 160,000. Both programs would have grown more considerably if the federal and state governments had not tightened eligibility requirements. Inflation adjusted average assistance payments declined: General Assistance payments by 48 percent to $161 per recipient, and AFDC payments by 28 percent to $448 per recipient in 1984. The payment declines reflected both tighter limitations in counting available income, and the failure of maximum payment levels to keep up with inflation. Maximum payments declined 16 percent between 1980 and 1985 for an AFDC family of four with no other sources of income.[12]

It should come as no surprise that economic hardships in Chicago have reached the point of threatening the basic necessities of life. The best indication of hardship comes from a survey undertaken by Cook et al. (1986) in the fall of 1983 and again in 1985. The first survey found that substantial proportions of Chicago's population had experienced serious hardships: major problems in getting enough food, meeting housing costs, or obtaining needed medical or dental care for lack of money. Overall, more than one-third of all families reported one or more such problems. These hardships were heavily concentrated among the city's minority, low-income and female-headed families, of which two-thirds reported such problems. More than twice as many households said their standard of living had declined over the previous two years as had improved. Blacks, poorly educated whites, and mothers without husbands were especially likely to report declines. In spite of the economic recovery between 1983 and 1985, the second survey in 1985 found the overall incidence of hardship virtually unchanged: lack of food declined slightly, while lack of medical care increased slightly.

Among welfare recipients, the great majority (72 percent) complained of a serious lack of money to meet basic needs, major problems finding work (34 percent), and problems with housing (26 percent) or getting food (22 percent) (Stagner and Richman 1986). The low levels of welfare payments pose severe problems for recipients, and one would expect them to turn to other institutions such as public human services or nonprofit organizations for help. Surprisingly, however, a large number of welfare recipients (43 percent) didn't know of any organizations that could help them, or didn't know where to go (31 percent). As a result, only about half the welfare recipients sought help from a service provider for their most important problems. These service providers were mainly public human service agencies (33 percent), and, less frequently, nonprofit organizations (23 percent) or churches (17 percent).

PUBLIC SPENDING TRENDS AND EFFORTS

While these trends present a major challenge to all Chicago human service institutions, one further development increased the challenge for the nonprofit sector. The level of public human service spending in Chicago has been quite low compared to that of other metropolitan areas, at least in the early 1980's.[13] Thus, total spending for social services, employment and training, housing and community development, health care (exclusive of Medicare), and arts and culture from all sources (federal, state, and local funds) stood at slightly less than $500 per capita in 1982 in Cook County. This was about 54 percent of the per capita level in New York City, 58 percent of that in San Francisco, 83 percent of that in Minneapolis, and even slightly below the levels in St. Paul, Atlanta, and Providence, Rhode Island (Salamon et al. 1986, p. 4).

Moreover, low as public human service expenditures were in the early 1980's, they again declined considerably between 1981 and 1984, down 14 percent (adjusted for inflation), resulting in a cumulative loss of $733 million in public investments for human services. The cuts in public spending were severest in the areas of employment and training (down 51 percent), mental health (down 21 percent) and Medicaid (down 20 percent). Although federal cuts were important (down by 11 percent by 1984), state spending cuts were more significant (down 23 percent). These trends point to continued future constraints in meeting human service needs through public efforts in Chicago, since federal spending accounts for about half of all human service spending in that region, and the state controls almost two-thirds of the spending.[14]

ROLE OF THE NONPROFIT SECTOR
IN MEETING COMMUNITY CHALLENGES

The trends outlined above have an obvious impact on individual residents of the region and the demand for services. However, the trends extend beyond that to the nonprofit sector, since public funding constitutes almost half of the total revenues of this human service sector in Cook County. The growing service needs also raise specific questions as to how appropriate the nonprofit definitions of their purposes and goals are, and how responsive nonprofit organizations are to the changes in community needs.

THE STUDY

The data presented here were derived mainly from personal interviews with the executive directors of 128 nonprofit organizations in Cook County, completed during the summer of 1985.[15] The interviews asked the executive directors how they define the role of their nonprofit organization, what service needs they saw existing, and what changes had occurred in the program activities of the organization over a three year period. This information could be linked to other information on the organization (e.g., size and sources of revenues).[16]

The nonprofit organizations looked at were part of a random sample of 1,008 such organizations in the Chicago metropolitan area identified in 1982 for a mail questionnaire conducted by The Urban Institute in that same year. They were surveyed again in 1984.[17] A total of 419 organizations responded to the first mail questionnaire, and 304 of these also responded to the second mail questionnaire.

Only a subsample of these organizations were interviewed. We excluded organizations located outside of Cook County, in order to focus more directly on those providing services in Chicago and its closely linked older suburbs, where social change is concentrated and needs most acute.[18] We also excluded organizations which devoted most of their service efforts to arts, culture, recreation, and research activities[19], because they fall outside our major focus on human service needs and changing community conditions.

Of the original 419 organizations included in the first wave of data collection, 206 met our geographic and service restrictions and 149 (72 percent) of these also responded to the second mail questionnaire. We interviewed 130 of the 149 second-round respondents,[20] but eliminated one interview for technical reasons. There are very few differences between the final set of 128 interviewed organizations and the 76 organizations that dropped out of the study between 1982 and 1985 (see Gronbjerg 1986, Ch.1 and Appendix A.)

This paper, then, is based on data from the sample of 128 nonprofit organizations in Cook County that survived the 1982-85 survey period and devote most of their services to employment, housing, community organization, advocacy, legal aid, the social sector (including day-care), health (other than nursing home and hospital-care) and mental health. They can be thought of as fairly representative of those nonprofits which are most likely to see themselves as "responding to community needs." Our failure to include new emerging organizations is a weakness, and probably means that we are understanding the extent to which the nonprofit sector, as a whole, is responding to these needs.

DEFINITIONS OF COMMUNITY NEEDS BY NONPROFIT ORGANIZATIONS

Mission/Target of Nonprofit Organizations. The charter of a nonprofit organization usually states its official goals and, by implication, the specific community needs the organization aims to meet. We classified organizations along two dimensions: The types of clients it had targeted for special attention, and the types of activities the organization had selected as its main purpose. As Table 1 shows, the largest number of nonprofit organizations, or agencies, (40 percent) target general population groups. These agencies split into two types of missions: 17 percent focused on a variety of social services, while 23 percent emphasized more specialized services (e.g., health services, drug rehabilitation, legal counselling, housing referrals, etc.). An additional 18 percent identified day-care services for young children as their special mission. Thus almost three-fifths of the organizations focus on providing services to the general public.

The remaining two-fifths of the interviewed agencies come closest to directing their attention to low-income residents and local community needs. About a quarter of the agencies focused directly on low-income or "powerless" clients (e.g., victims of domestic violence, youth offenders, the disabled, etc.). Some of these agencies (16 percent) focused on social services, while others (12 percent) emphasized more specialized service programs. An additional 15 percent defined their special mission as providing community development or community organizing services to a particular geographic area (e.g., a residential neighborhood). Clearly, nonprofit organizations are quite diverse, and do not **simply** serve the poor or minority clients.

Table 1

Client Target/Service Goals of Interviewed Organizations

Client Target/Service Goals (n)*	Number of Organizations	Percentage
Children:		
Day-care/child development	23	18
General Population:	51	40
General social services	22	17
Specialized services	29	23
Geographic Neighborhood:		
Community development/organizing	19	15
Powerless:	35	27
General social services	20	16
Specialized services	15	12
ALL AGENCIES	128	100

*(n) denotes the number of organizations in this category.

Note: The term "powerless" refers to low income persons, victims
of domestic violence, ex-offenders, and others
traditionally seen as in need of special assistance.

SOURCE: Urban Institute Nonprofit Sector Project, Personal
Interviews.

Making the Targeting Decisions. About three-fifths of the interviewed organizations indicate that their targeting decisions were made at the time the organization was established (see Table 2). In other cases, targets were reconfirmed or changed as part of a revised charter when an agency spun off from a parent organization (19 percent) of the agencies) or merged with another organization (5 percent) of the cases). The prominence given to the organization's charter indicates how integral, or fateful, this decision is to the organization's mission or purpose.

Table 2

Occasions for Selecting Target Groups
(n=128)

Types of Occasions	Percent of Organizations
At Establishment of Organization	
Original charter of organization	60
At Restructuring of Organization	
Spin-off from other organizations	19
Merger of organizations	5
After Establishment of Organization	
New staff or board	2
Other reasons	8
NO TARGET GROUP	6

SOURCE: Urban Institute Nonprofit Sector Project, Personal Interviews.

Pressure from community and clients plays a major role in defining an agency's target focus. Fifty-six percent of the agencies said that community or client pressures were important in shaping their original mission. For an additional 16 percent of the agencies, pressure from the community or clients was instrumental in modifying an existing target focus. Our data are not refined enough to show how extensive these modifications were, or in which directions they occurred.

Funders also influence the target focus of nonprofit organizations, but not so extensively or clearly as community or client factors. Overall, about two-fifths of the agencies reported that funder priorities affected their targeting decisions. Funder **initiatives** are most important. About 17 percent of the agencies in our sample said that they had modified or changed their target goals after direct contact with or appeals from, potential funders. Direct contact with funders usually occurs only after the organization is established, and is as important as community or client pressure in modifying an existing target focus.

Two conclusions can be drawn from these findings. First, it appears that most targeting decisions are made at the time an organization is founded, and that this initial decision is seldom altered except through mergers or major reorganizations. The role of community leaders and client groups appears to be quite influential during the early stages of organizational development.

Second, the relative importance of funders in shaping the target focus of nonprofit organizations highlights the complex environment in which these organizations operate. The priorities of funders, particularly those of government agencies and private givers,[21] constitute "available" definitions of community needs, as does pressure from community leaders and clients. Both types of available definitions carry incentives for nonprofit organizations; funder definitions because they come with potential sources of funding, and community definitions because they provide nonprofits with available clients and documentation that they are responding to community needs.

The selection of special target groups is only the first step agencies take to position themselves in meeting community needs. They must also develop service strategies to serve these groups. This is a complex process and not easily measured. Each organization must determine the needs of its target groups, and develop and operate the bulk of its services accordingly.

Service Needs of Target Groups. Most of the nonprofit executive directors described their client's service needs in broad terms. Their definitions of service needs ranged from "social and emotional room to grow up," "support to learn to cope," and "chronic disease management," to "career orientation" and "preschool and nursery services in a Christian environment." Table 3 groups these definitions of service needs into seven service categories.

Table 3

Agency Perceptions of Most Important Needs of Target Groups
(n=121)

Type of Need	Percentage of Organizations
General social service needs	37
Day-care/Early child development	19
Health-related needs	14
Community development/Organization	8
Primary material needs	7
Employment-related needs	5
Other	10
ALL AGENCIES	100

Note: Primary material needs refers to food, clothing, shelter, etc.

SOURCE: Urban Institute Nonprofit Sector Project, Personal Interviews.

The three most frequently cited needs were general social services (37 percent), day-care and early child development services (19 percent), and health-related services (14 percent). Primary material needs (such as food, clothing, shelter) and employment-related needs were identified as the most important needs of targeted clients by only seven and five percent of the agencies, respectively.

This rank order of service needs closely matches the expenditures organizations devote to different service efforts.[2]2 As shown in Table 4, more than 40 percent concentrate on providing social services. Nearly one-quarter were classified as multi-service organizations because they offer a range of services that cut across the designated service categories. Only 16 percent of the sub-sample focus on health-related services[2]3 and another 20 percent specialize in either employment and training programs, housing and community development services, or legal services and advocacy activities.

Table 4

Service Areas of Interviewed Organizations: 1982

Service Area*	Number of Organizations	Percentage
General Social Services:	52	41
Social Service	46	36
Residential/shelter programs	6	5
Health-related Services:	20	16
Health	12	9
Mental Health	8	6
Other Specific Services:	26	20
Employment/training/income support	6	5
Housing/community development	10	8
Legal services/advocacy	10	8
Multiservice	30	23
ALL AGENCIES	128	100

*Majority of service expenditures devoted to area.

Note: Percentages may not add to 100 percent because of rounding.

SOURCE: Urban Institute Nonprofit Sector Project, Personal Interviews.

These perceptions of service needs, and the related distribution of nonprofit service efforts, stands in contrast to indications of service needs in Chicago. Stagner and Richman (1984), 1986) and Hemmens et al. (1986), for instance, found an overwhelming need for jobs and employment and training programs

These perceptions of service needs, and the related distribution of nonprofit service efforts, stands in contrast to indications of service needs in Chicago. Stagner and Richman (1984), 1986) and Hemmens et al. (1986), for instance, found an overwhelming need for jobs and employment and training programs among the low-income groups they surveyed. These studies also document extensive material needs, such as a lack of food, medical care, or housing. Similar material needs were also revealed for the general Chicago population by Cook et al. (1986).

Service Strategies. On the surface, these findings show a broad mismatch between the needs identified by nonprofit service providers as essential for their clients, and the needs identified by either Chicago's general population or its low-income population. This, however, may overstate the range of mismatch. Individuals often define their needs in terms of their inability to purchase the basic items they know they need, such as health-care, food, clothing, and housing. Nonprofit organizations, however, may adopt a professional service model and see these material needs as reflecting different underlying problems, such as family conflict, apathy, and lack of job skills.[24]

We found some indication of this perspective when we asked the directors whether they thought the service needs they had identified were related to poverty. As Table 5 shows, slightly more than half of the executive directors felt that poverty was either directly or indirectly related to the service needs they had identified. This was especially so for those organizations that target powerless groups. Still, almost two-thirds of those which target the general population, and more than three-fourths of single-purpose day-care centers, saw no link between the needs of their target group and low-income.

It would appear that only about half of the organizations we interviewed state that their activities meet the needs of low-income families. A small minority of these agencies see the types of problems people identify as being serious for themselves (i.e., basic needs) as the most important services to provide. Although a large proportion of Chicago's population has extensive material needs, meeting these needs directly is not a **primary** concern of most of these nonprofit organizations. Furthermore, the types of organizations

we excluded from the interview study would presumably be
even less involved in meeting such needs.

Table 5

Agency Perceptions of Links Between
Poverty and Service Needs of Target Group

Organization Focus(n)	Direct Poverty Link	Poverty Related	Poverty Not Important
ALL ORGANIZATIONS (120)	18	35	48
Client Target Focus			
Child day-care (23)	9	13	78
General population (48)	-	38	62
Neighborhood (16)	19	38	44
Powerless groups (33)	48	46	6

SOURCE: Urban Institute Nonprofit Sector Project, Personal
Interview.

One reason for this lack of attention to basic
material needs is that many nonprofit agencies appear to
pursue an "intervention" strategy in dealing with
problems of poverty, rather than an "ameliorative"
strategy. The intervention strategy makes more effective
use of the professional skills nonprofit organizations
possess, while the ameliorative strategy is expensive if
widely pursued. Both service strategies are grounded
within the historical development of a public/private
division of labor, in which the public sector
increasingly provided basic income maintenance support
and material services to low-income persons, while the

nonprofit sector provided more specialized services or limited material help in special emergency circumstances. However, public income maintenance benefits have not kept up with inflation and fall short of the economic needs of Chicago families. Our findings suggest that many nonprofit organizations would need to undertake major changes in both their goals and basic orientations if they are to play a significant role in alleviating these needs directly. Such changes are possible, but unlikely, because they would require these organizations to abandon many of the purposes they currently pursue.

In fact, our findings show that direct nonprofit concern with the poor and their most important needs (as defined by the poor themselves) appear to lie outside of the nonprofit organizational culture in Chicago. As shown in Table 6, multiple regression analysis suggest that those organizations which most directly target low-income clients, see the closest links between client service needs and low-income, or pursue most clearly an ameliorative anti-poverty strategy, are also least closely linked to other nonprofit organizations. Scales measuring the degree of nonprofit inter-organizational,[25] membership in lobbying or umbrella organizations, and reliance on other nonprofits or funder priorities for determining client needs, are negatively related to one or more of the anti-poverty orientations. These relationships change somewhat if single purpose day-care centers, the most fee oriented of the nonprofit organizations, are excluded from the analysis.

Table 6

Stepwise Regression Results for
Nonprofit Antipoverty Orientations

Analyses	Standardized Regression Coefficients in Final Equation	
	All Agencies (n=76)	w/o Day-Care (n=67)

Poverty Composition of Target Group

Average dependence on fee income (1981-84)	-.42***	
Log of average size (1981-84)	.38***	
Public policy involvement	.35***	.31*
Involvement in lobby or umbrella organization	-.20*	
Efforts to recruit board members with business or professional expertise	.27**	
Involvement in nonprofit organizational network	-.29**	.38**
Contact with corporate funders and foundations		.33*
Multiple R	.67***	.57***
Total adjusted variance explained	.40	.22

Extent to Which Identify Link Between Service Needs and Poverty

Average dependence on fee income (1981-84)	-.37**	
Proportion of board members who are minority	.24*	.43***
Extent to which executive director is involved in community activities	.26*	.26*
Log of average size (1981-84)	.23*	
Average dependence on donation income (1981-84)		.38**
Multiple R	.54***	.51***
Total Adjusted variance explained	.25	.22

Extent to Which Pursue Antipoverty Service Strategies

Average reliance on fee income (1981-84)	-.27*	
Frequency of contacts with foundations or corporate funders	.28**	.42**
Proportion of board members who are minority	.24*	
Reliance on nonprofit organizations or funder priorities for determining service needs	-.22*	
Average dependence on donation income (1981-84)		.24*
Multiple R	.53***	.43**
Total adjusted variance explained	.24	.15

NOTE: * p<.05, ** p<.01, *** p<.001

SOURCE: Urban Institute Nonprofit Sector Project, Personal Interviews.

CHANGES IN NONPROFIT ORIENTATIONS

To understand more fully the nature of the link between community and nonprofit organizations, it is necessary to examine also the extent to which nonprofit organizations change their service orientations and the conditions under which such changes take place. If such changes take place easily and rapidly, the nonprofit sector, as a whole, may require only a relatively short period of adjustment to reorient itself to the poor.

Extent of Changes in Target Groups. On the whole, the target focus of our subsample of agencies tends to be stable. The Urban Institute Round 2 questionnaire (fall of 1984) asked the organizations whether they had increased or decreased their emphasis on certain client or target groups over the past two years. Between one-fifth and one-quarter shifted their attention at least slightly towards particular disadvantaged groups (such as the poor, single-parent families, the unemployed or blacks) over the two year period. Although these shifts are notable, they were reported by only a minority of agencies and usually did not involve major shifts. Very few indicated that they placed **much more** emphasis on the poor (12 percent), single parents (8 percent), the unemployed (8 percent), or blacks (7 percent).

These shifts were probably not cumulative for the period we looked at. The multiple regression analysis of anti-poverty orientations summarized in Table 6 above shows consistently that reliance on fee income is negatively related to nonprofit concern with the poor and their needs. On the average, organizations experienced a steady growth in fee income when year to year fluctuations are separated out.[26] On the other hand, donation income is positively related to nonprofit poverty concerns when single-purpose day-care centers are excluded. In fact, on the average, private donations did increase over the period for that group of agencies.[27]

However, the best single predictor of an index measuring the extent to which nonprofit organizations increased their emphasis on the most vulnerable target groups (the poor, single-parent families, the unemployed, or blacks) was the amount of increase in government support (r=.36, p< .005); the only variable to enter the multiple regression equation, even when single-purpose day-care centers are excluded from the analysis. This particular finding is confirmed by results from the

first wave of data collection (1982), in which 62 percent
of the nonprofit organizations indicated that government
funding caused them to direct more services toward the
disadvantaged. However, government funding declined over
the 1981-84 period.[28] These trends in nonprofit revenues
suggest that the nonprofit sector, as a whole, probably
did not succeed at the aggregate level to reorient itself
to the needs of the city's low-income population. This,
probably because of the importance of the organization's
original charter in determining target groups.

Examining Service Strategies. Nonprofit organizations
pursue service strategies that they believe will meet the
types of needs they detect among their target groups.
To examine what types of factors influence how service
strategies may change, we looked at whether these
organizations (according to reports from the executive
directors) used any of eight different methods in
determining the service needs of their target groups.

As Table 7 shows, some of the most common methods
used were those based on internal rather than external
sources of information. The most popular procedure, used
by 90 percent of the agencies in our study, was to hold
formal staff meetings to discuss client needs. In
addition, seven out of every ten agency directors
indicated that they reviewed client files, or surveyed
their current clients, to determine service needs. These
methods have the potential of reinforcing internal values
or objectives. They also focus on existing clients,
rather than potential ones.

Used almost as frequently were methods that provide
the organizations with information as to what other
important actors in their organizational environment
thought of as important service needs. Many of the
nonprofit executive directors said that they talked to
local leaders (89 percent), used reports from other
organizations (78 percent), or examined funder priorities
(64 percent) as ways of determining service needs.
These methods allow nonprofit agencies to see how closely
their own definitions of service needs match
institutionalized definitions. By using such external
definitions of service needs, they increase the
likelihood of being perceived by these other actors as
performing valuable services. Hence, these methods are
important tools for nonprofit organizations in
documenting their legitimacy and worthiness of support.

Table 7

Methods of Determining Client Needs
(n=121)

Method	% of Organizations	Rank Order
Internal		
Discussion with staff	90	1
Reviewed client files	72	4
Surveyed own clients	71	5
Average Rank		3.3
External--Legitimacy of Needs		
Talked to local community leaders	89	2
Used reports of other organizations	78	3
Priorities of funders	64	6
Average Rank		3.7
External--Measurement of Needs		
Held public hearings or workshops	50	7
Performed Special Needs Assessment Studies	49	8
Average Rank		7.5

SOURCE: Urban Institute Nonprofit Sector Project, Personal
Interviews.

For some nonprofit organizations, such institutionalized definitions may, in fact, be quite appropriate. Many of these organizations do not have the capacity to undertake the extensive research required in needs assessments studies.[29] Carefully prepared reports and well-researched funder priorities may identify service needs and strategies that many nonprofit agencies might only imperfectly perceive otherwise. However, not all studies or statements of funder priorities reflect careful assessments of needs and service strategies. Also, Hemmens et al. (1986) and Stagner and Richman (1986) found considerable geographic variations in service needs and trends in Chicago, limiting further the applicability of these broad methods for determining such needs.

Other more formal means of determining local service needs, such as public hearings or formal needs assessment studies, were mentioned by about half of the agencies in our study. These methods may also be employed selectively by organizations. Thus, most of the literature on evaluation research emphasizes the extent to which such research is easily subverted into reinforcing existing perceptions and program orientations, and often avoids asking hard questions about different approaches to particular problems. However, these methods do allow for a more independent assessment by nonprofit organizations about their actual service needs.

Less formal evidence also indicates that needs assessment studies easily pose potential threats to the legitimacy of nonprofit organizations. Thus, recent Chicago efforts to link data on service needs among the poor to their use of nonprofit service providers and the service orientations of nonprofit agencies (Gronbjerg 1987) have been met with some resistance from key nonprofit leaders, apparently in part because the findings pointed to a potential mismatch between needs and nonprofit service efforts.

The relative importance of legitimizing methods, as opposed to assessment methods, in determining service needs is consistent with the peculiarly dependent relationship nonprofit organizations have with their community and organizational environment. As Meyer and Scott emphasize, organizations which depend heavily on institutional environments, such as nonprofit organizations do, tend to use external or ceremonial criteria to assess the values of their structural elements (1983, pp. 30-31), and operate in ways to minimize evaluation and control (1983, pp. 38-40).

The minor use of evaluation methods for determining needs is consistent with the behavior of organizations that face higher demands for their services than they can easily meet. Eighty-two percent of the executive directors felt that their organization was limited by its level of funding in meeting the needs of its target group. As Glennerster (1975) argues, organizations which face the need to ration their services may avoid directly acknowledging the rationing process. Instead, they operate existing programs on a first-come, first-serve basis. Given the lack of knowledge among the poor about available sources of support, the result is a priority system based on ignorance and isolation. Those who are part of a network know about services and get them, while those who are more isolated don't get access.

NONPROFIT PROGRAM ACTIVITIES

At one level of analysis, Chicago nonprofit organizations were extremely active during the early 1980's. Thus, between one-quarter and one-third of the interviewed organizations reported a substantial increase in demands for their services in each two years of the study (1982 and 1984). As a result of these demands, Chicago nonprofits engaged in a flurry of program activities. Almost all (95 percent) undertook some program change over the 1982-85 period, and program expansions or starts outnumbered program curtailments or cuts by a ratio of almost 4 to 1. It is likely that a good proportion of these program changes simply reflected the constant shift in funding that nonprofit organizations have to contend with.[30] However, only 8 percent of the new or expanded programs involved meeting basic needs, while 9 percent involved employment and training. Thus, by far the greatest amount of program change involved the more standard social service activities (29 percent of all program expansions) and health and mental health related programs (19 percent).

SUMMARY AND DISCUSSION

Our findings clearly indicate that the types of nonprofit organizations we interviewed rely heavily on institutional definitions of community needs in making their targeting decisions and in devising service strategies. In addition, since most targeting decisions appear to be made at the inception of the agency, the nonprofit sector would seem to most easily adopt new targets through the establishment of new organizations designed to serve emerging definitions of needs. They may help to explain the relative youth of the sector[31] and points to the need for a careful examination of organizational ecology, i.e., the selective birth and death of nonprofit organizations.

Within this general picture of continuity, marginal changes are made to accommodate highly visible instances of community deprivation or to obtain funds. The general nonprofit ideology of "intervening into the poverty cycle", and of maintaining the division of labor between government and "private" organizations, appears to impede any dramatic effort to directly confront community needs and material deprivations.

However, our interviews left us with the impression that many nonprofit organizations do not chart their courses of action in pursuit of their own definitions of high priority community needs very aggressively. In fact, relatively few seem to actively look for funding that directly suits their mission. Thus, a large proportion of executive directors expressed their appreciation of the interview experience because it had forced them to think of the larger picture and the options available to them, something they rarely did. In addition, the high level of community needs in Chicago provide no market test of how "well" these organizations meet community needs. There is almost always a sufficient enough demand for their services to leave them with the impression that they are doing a good job, if not one of the highest priority.

Of course, many nonprofits are not large enough, or resourceful enough, to mount the persuasive studies needed to convince themselves or funders of changing priorities. And those that are may resist efforts to institutionalize needs assessments efforts beyond their immediate control. For these organizations, the greater freedom and advantage is in their ability to use their own considerable resources to present the data their way and use their own documentation to make a case for funding. In addition, the loss of government funding has clearly made it more difficult for the Chicago nonprofit sector to devote more attention to the needs of the poor.

These lags in shaping goals and service strategies assume greater importance if dramatic shifts occur in service needs (e.g., population transition, recession). Lags may also be notable if nonprofit organizations are asked to take on a different, more extensive role in the public/nonprofit partnership. The economic restructuring of the Chicago region, the major economic recession of the early 1980's, and the withdrawal of public spending for human service efforts constituted such a challenge for the nonprofit sector. My findings suggest that the sector, as a whole, was not able to respond effectively to the challenge, although individual organizations engaged in a great deal of activity and program development.

The overall picture is that of a series of organizations which have been doing much the same thing, or making only incremental changes, for some period of time. The extent of local primary needs must have outpaced their efforts some time ago, and the weakness of the intervention strategy has been apparent for at least as long.

To a considerable degree these findings bear out Meyer and Scott's (1983) argument that institutionalized belief systems and organizational dependency shape the behavior of nonprofit organizations. That approach, however, does not fully anticipate the very local and "archaic" importance of organizational charters. More importantly, it seems to imply that subscription to these beliefs and organizational directives will confer legitimacy on these organizations. This may be the case for legitimacy within the nonprofit agency community itself, but does not necessarily extend beyond that community to the general population of donors.

At a more general theoretical level, the findings point to the need for the ecological perspectives in the study of communities, and of organizations, to be linked more directly in the future. The findings that have been presented here do not constitute a formal test of any particular theory; they were not designed to do that. They do suggest, however, that we need to pay much closer attention to the very complex interactions that exist among "public benefit" institutions, the communities in which they operate, and the extra-community resources on which they depend.

The community literature has paid a great deal of attention to community transitions, the links between public institutions and local communities, as well as the patterns of leadership and sources of influence that operate within both. The organizational literature has increasingly examined the extra-organizational factors that influence the structure and operations of formal organizations. To conclude, a more systematic attention to the interactions between these two sets of forces could contribute greatly to our understanding of community and public benefit institutions.

NOTES

[1]Revised version of paper prepared for presentation at the Annual Meeting of the American Sociological Association, New York, N.Y., August 30-September 3, 1986. Portions of the data presented in this paper were originally published in Gronbjerg (1986) prepared under The Urban Institute Nonprofit Sector Project, Lester M. Salamon, Director. Washington, D.C. The conclusions presented in this paper are those of the author and do not necessarily reflect the positions of Loyola University of Chicago, The Urban Institute, or oganizations that have supported the Nonprofit Sector Project. I want to thank Lyn Lofland for her helpful comments on an early draft of this manuscript. I am particularly grateful to Gerald Suttles for his comments, support and willingness to bear with me during the last several years when this project occasionally threatened to get the best of me.

[2]Exemption from paying several types of taxes, such as income, real estate and sales taxes; lower postal rates; and eligibility to receive tax deductible donations.

[3]These basic goals reflect how the organization's current or past board members conceive of community needs, and how they perceive the role of nonprofit organizations in meeting existing needs.

[4]These are concerns about such a threat to the legitimacy of the nonprofit human service sector in Chicago. Major Chicago foundations and nonprofit sector leaders reacted with considerable distress to The Urban Institute's Nonprofit Sector Project, finding that fee income has grown significantly and more than compensated for lost government support and declines in private donations for the sector, as a whole.

[5]I am relying extensively on Meyer and Scott's (1983) concept of institutional organizational environments, which emphasizes the importance of institutionalized belief systems originating outside the organization and which shape its structure and provide a measure of its legitimacy.

[6]"Chicago Region" here refers to the 6 county SMSA area plus Lake and Porter counties in Indiana. The term "Chicago SMSA" will be used in the standard meaning, while "Chicago" will refer to the City of Chicago. Data

on trends in industrial activities and other economic indicators come from **Chicagoland Development**, various February issues, unless otherwise indicated.

[7]Unemployment in the city of Chicago stood at about 17 percent during 1982 and 1983.

[8]Although Kasarda's detailed argument is based on an examination of New York, Philadelphia, Baltimore, St. Louis, Atlanta, Denver and San Francisco, he also provides evidence that similar patterns persist for the regions those cities represent.

[9]Between 1969 and 1985, the Chicago Region lost almost 344,000 manufacturing jobs (a decline of 32 percent) and had only 737,000 such jobs by the end of 1985.

[10]Most of the manufacturing losses were due to declines in the number of large manufacturing establishments, while most of the growth in employment (manufacturing as well as other industries) has been in small businesses (see Illinois Department of Business and Economic Development 1978).

[11]The suburbs also gained most of the new non-manufacturing jobs. Thus, while the number of employed persons in the Chicago SMSA increased from 2.9 million in 1970 to 3.2 million in 1980, or by 14 percent, the number of employed persons in the city itself declined from 1.4 million to 1.2 million during the same period.

[12]The maximum payment level had already declined by 42 percent (adjusted for inflation) between 1970 and 1980 (computed from Testa and Lawlor 1985, p. 22).

[13]In addition, income maintenance payments in Illinois have traditionally been substantially below most other industrial states, although substantially above many southern states.

[14]Illinois has experienced continuous fiscal problems since 1982, and a succession of budget cuts that have affected the human services fields particularly severely.

[15]The interviews were designed in conjunction with a larger study of nonprofit organizations and public spending in Chicago and other metropolitan cities in the U.S., conducted by The Urban Institute and its Nonprofit Sector Project. The personal interviews also

complemented a series of other studies on hardship and service needs in Chicago (see Cook et al. 1984, 1986; Hemmens et al. 1985, 1986; Stagner and Richman 1984, 1986).

[16]Some of these findings are presented in greater detail in Chapters 2 and 3 in Gronbjerg (1986). Additional portions of that report focus on the extent and types of program changes undertaken during the 1982-84 period, the factors executive directors of nonprofit organizations see as important in making those program changes, the impact of program changes on the organizations and their clients, the extent to which directors see their organization as being limited in its capacity to meet service needs, and the activities the organizations pursue to reach potential clients. Finally, the report examines changes in funding levels and sources of support over the 1981-84 period.

[17]Results from these two waves of mail questionnaires are reported in Gronbjerg et al. (1985) and Salamon et al. (1986).

[18]These were also the areas looked at most comprehensively by our companion studies.

[19]Nursing homes and hospitals were also excluded, the former because they were too distinct but too few to provide reliable information, the latter because their size and complexity made it difficult to use the same interview instruments we used for the remaining nonprofit organizations.

[20]The remaining 19 organizations either refused to participate in this third phase of data collection or could not be located.

[21]About one-third (34 percent) of the executive directors reported that the availability of government funding had been important in shaping the targeting decision of their organization. Almost as many (32 percent) reported that the priorities of private givers (e.g., foundations and corporations) had been important.

[22]The Nonprofit Sector project classified organizations into service categories by identifying a designated service area to which the organization devoted half or more of its service expenditures in 1982. Those organizations which did not have a single service area

that received 50 percent or more of the agency's funding were classified as multiservice agencies (see Gronbjerg et al. 1985, Ch. 2).

[23]Since we have excluded nursing homes and hospitals from our study, this proportion seriously underestimates the amount of health services nonprofit organizations provide.

[24]There is considerable debate about the relative merits of the two service strategies implied in these perspectives, i.e., providing for the direct needs and problems of people v. pursuing an intervention strategy by providing professional services. The former is criticized for providing only surface remedies without getting at causal factors. The latter is seen as not really providing the help that people really need, and is sometimes accused of being self-serving and reflecting an over-commitment to the professional service model. A final strategy, namely the restructuring of the U.S. economy to provide adequate employment income, and income maintenance programs to provide adequate income support, is generally seen as beyond the capacity of the nonprofit sector to pursue effectively.

[25]Sharing resources, having mutual board members, participating in joint activities or programs, engaging in referrals or information sharing, or participating in joint networks or umbrella organizations.

[26]The average slope of fee income regressed on year is about 2.6 percent of total average revenues, even when single purpose day-care centers are excluded.

[27]The average slope for donation income regressed on year is 2.1 percent of total average revenues when single-purpose day-care centers are excluded.

[28]The average slope of government funding regressed on year is -1 percent of total agency revenues.

[29]Half of the interviewed agencies had revenues of less than $220,000 in 1981, and almost two-thirds had incomes of less than $500,000.

[30]Each year, about one-third of the interviewed organizations reported a shift in at least one major source of funding that amounted to 25 percent of their total revenues.

[1]Almost half (49 percent) of the organizations in the subsample were established after 1970.

REFERENCES

Aldrich, Howard E. and A. J. Reiss, Jr. 1976. "Continuities in the Study of Ecological Succession: Changes in the Race Composition of Neighborhoods and Their Businesses." American Journal of Sociology 81 (January):846-66.

Cook, Fay Lomax, Christopher Jencks, Lorraine Kramek, and Susan Mayer. 1984. Economic Hardship in Chicago: 1983. A Research and Policy Report, Center for Urban Affairs and Policy Research, Northwestern University, Evanston, IL.

Cook, Fay Lomax, Christopher Jencks, Susan Mayer, Ernesto Constantino, and Susan Popkin. 1986. Stability and Change in Economic Hardship: Chicago 1983-1985. A Research and Policy Report, Center for Urban Affairs and Policy Research, Northwestern University, Evanston, IL.

Glennerster, H. 1975. Social Service Budgets and Social Policy. London: Allen & Unwin, Ltd.

Gronbjerg, Kirsten A. 1987. "Hardship and Support Systems in Chicago: A Synthesis of Recent Findings and Policy Implications." Department of Sociology-Anthropology, Loyola University of Chicago.

_____. 1986. Responding to Community Needs: The Missions and Programs of Chicago Nonprofit Organizations. With Sheila Nelson (CSA), Tammy Jones and Ramola Joseph. Prepared under The Urban Institute Nonprofit Sector Project, Washington, D.C.

Gronbjerg, Kirsten A., Madeleine H. Kimmich, and Lester M. Salamon. 1985. The Chicago Nonprofit Sector in a Time of Government Retrenchment. Washington, D.C.: The Urban Institute Press.

Hemmens, George, Charles Hoch, RoJean Madsen, and Wim Wiewel. 1985. Households' Needs and Community Response in Three Chicago Neighborhoods. School of Urban Planning and Policy, University of Illinois at Chicago.

Hemmens, George, Charles Hoch, Donna Hardina, RoJean Madsen, and Wim Wiewel. 1986. Changing Needs and Social Services in Three Chicago Communities.

School of Urban Planning and Policy, University of Illinois at Chicago.

Illinois Department of Business and Economic Development. 1978. Illinois Data Book: State and Regional, 1978 Ed. Illinois Department of Business and Economic Community Development.

Illinois Economic and Fiscal Commission. 1982. "Revenge Estimate and Economic Outlook, FY 1983." Mimeographed.

Kasarda, John D. 1983. "Entry Level Jobs, Mobility and Minority Employment." Department of Sociology, University of North Carolina.

Meyer, John W., and W. Richard Scott. 1983. Organizational Environments: Ritual and Rationality. Beverly Hills: Sage Publications.

Portes, Alejandro, and Saskia Sassen-Koob. 1987. "Making it Underground: Comparative Material on the Informal Sector in Western Market Economics." American Journal of Sociology 93 (July):30-61.

Salamon, Lester M., David M. Altschuler, and Carol J. De Vita. 1986. Chicago Nonprofit Organizations: The Challenge of Retrenchment. An Urban Institute Research Report.

Stagner, Matthew, and Harold Richman. 1984. General Assistance in Chicago: Findings of a Survey of New Recipients. Social Policy Research Center at the National Opinion Research Center, The University of Chicago.

_____. 1986. Help-Seeking and the Use of Social Service Agencies by Welfare Families in Chicago. Chapin Hall Center for Children at the University of Chicago.

Suttles, Gerald D. 1981. "Changing Priorities for the Urban Heartland." In J. John Palen (ed.), City Scenes: Problems and Prospects. Boston: Little, Brown.

Testa, Mark, and Edward Lawlor. 1985. 1985: The State of the Child. University of Chicago: The Chapin Hall Center for Children.

U.S. Bureau of the Census. 1972. 1970 Census of Population and Housing. PC(1)-Volume 15, Illinois. Washington, D.C.: U.S. Government Printing Office.

_____. 1982. 1980 Census of Population and Housing. PC(1)-Volume 15, Illinois. Washington, D.C.: U.S. Government Printing Office.

U.S. Department of Labor. Various. "Monthly Employment Statistics for the Midwest." Washington, D.C.

PART THREE

ETHNIC COMMUNITIES

IV

ETHNIC COMMUNITIES:
THE CANADIAN RESEARCH CONTEXT

Leo Driedger

In this paper we suggest that while American community studies focus on social change, in Canada the focus is more on ethnic community solidarity. We think this is due to the greater American sociological emphasis on assimilation and the melting pot, in contrast to the Canadian concern with bilingualism and multiculturalism, where pluralism is more acceptable. First, we shall briefly review community studies in the United States summarized by Stein (1960), and then we shall seek to do a similar summary of community studies in Canada, which to our knowledge has not been attempted before. Interestingly, a review of Canadian community studies usually involves ethnic communities, which is not the case to the same extent in America.

THE ECLIPSE OF COMMUNITY

Some years ago, Maurice Stein (1960) wrote **The Eclipse of Community**, in which he summarized some of the classic community studies done in the USA, stimulating us to try the same in Canada. Stein (1960:1-93) suggests that the laying of the foundations of American sociology was begun sixty years ago by Chicago sociologists who were studying a series of urban communities in that city to better understand the urbanization process. Other community studies were done by the Lynds, who explored the impact of industrialization on small town America, and still other community studies took place in the east with Lloyd Warner's publications on Yankee City, which focused on class and bureaucratization. According to Stein (1960), these community studies were all process-oriented, revolving around urbanization, industrialization and bureaucratization. Let us briefly review these American studies to see how they compare with Canadian community studies. The title of Stein's book suggests that these processes endangered American communities, so that these communities were being eclipsed.

STUDIES OF AMERICAN COMMUNITIES

Stein (1960) traces the urbanization, industrialization and bureaucratization processes in three sets of classical community studies, beginning with Chicago in the 1920's. He writes:

> There is no more comprehensive approach to the study of American communities than that developed at the University of Chicago during the twenties. Here is a group of scholars completed a set of empirical studies that leave us with more sociological knowledge about the city of Chicago than is currently available for any other single American community.... On the scene during this period were men like William I. Thomas, George Herbert Mead, Robert Park, Ellsworth Faris, Ernest Burgess, Roderick McKenzie, William Ogburn, Harold Lasswell, Charles Merriam and T.V. Smith. Students, assistants, and occasional faculty included Louis Wirth, Herbert Blumer, Everett Hughes, Leonard Cottrell, Franklin Frazer, Emory Bogardus, Herbert Gosnell, Samuel Stauffer, Francis Merrill, Pauline Young, Ruth Cavan, Clifford Shaw, Frederick Thrasher, Harvey Zorbaugh, Paul Cressey, Norman Hayner, and Robert Redfield" (Stein, 1960:13, 14).

The list of well-known sociologists is astounding, and the dominance of the Chicago School is also reflected in "nineteen of the thirty-five presidents of the American Sociological Society who received their doctorates at Chicago, most of them during the twenties and thirties" (Stein, 1960:14). Many of these scholars spent their early years in small town America, so they were most interested in the influence of urbanization on social communities. Interestingly, sociologists of the Chicago School are more known for their urban studies than for their ethnic and minority studies, even though Park, Thoms, Wirth, Hughes, Frazier, and Redfield all published volumes on ethnic groups. Their interest in the process of urbanization seemed to eclipse their focus on ethnicity. Their theories of assimilation and secularization loomed so large that ethnic pluralism seemed to fade into the background.

"There is no question that Park was seriously influenced by Durkheim. Both were aware of the precariousness of organic solidarity" (Stein, 1960:18). Like Durkheim, Park saw that freedom from group restraints could also entail freedom from group supports, and both were concerned with the potential for anomie or personal and social disorganization. "Personal disorganization was seen by both as the result of exposure to conflicting standards; insofar as cities provided much opportunity for living 'on the margin' between different subcultures, the likelihood of disorganization was maximized" (Stein, 1960:18). However, Park was always conscious of both the creative and disorganizing potentialities of marginality. Human potentialities could also be released in heterogeneous communities, which was less the case in homogeneous ones. The city of Chicago became the laboratory for the study of the influences of urbanization on community.

In the twenties Chicago was booming and masses of immigrants from Europe, along with Blacks from the deep South, converged on the city, making it a very dynamic, heterogeneous place. Here, Park developed his conception of "natural areas" - subcommunities with distinctive mixes of social class, religion, race and ethnicity. He saw a mosaic of subcommunities developing within Chicago, and viewed these "natural areas" as building blocks, both to managing the research of such a large urban heterogeneous complex and understanding the social relationships in a form of 'Verstehen', or depth understanding in Weber's terms. Park was also greatly influenced by Georg Simmel, whose writings on urban Germany greatly influenced sociologists of the time in their understanding of the important place of conflict.

Chicago scholars proceeded to study the natural areas in Chicago. Shaw published several books on juvenile delinquents in urban areas; Thrasher studied gangs; Zorbaugh, the Gold Coast and the Slum; and Wirth, the Jewish Ghetto. The University of Chicago bordered on a large Jewish community, which Wirth studied and published **The Ghetto** in 1928. This study included an historical context of where the Jews migrated from to

Chicago, and showed how their ideology, social patterns, and personality types provided a basis for ethnic solidarity; it also lessened observances of kosher foods, religious ritual, Hebrew education and the like. It revealed increased differentiation and the potential for conflict, social mobility, and the establishment and re-establishment of communities as they moved. Interestingly, although Wirth's study was on ethnicity, he emphasized the change elements of the Jews more than their ethnic identity and their community solidarity.

While the Chicago sociologists published a number of community studies on urbanization in the twenties, Helen and Robert Lynd published their two studies of **Middletown**, (the small town of Muncie, Indiana) in 1929, and a restudy, **Middletown in Transition**, in 1937, comparable in depth to many Chicago studies. Since the Lynds studied this town in two time periods, they were able to document the effects of industrialization. Although this town reached a population of 35,000 in 1924, most of its growth involved migrants from the farms, rather than foreign immigrants. They traced the effects of industrialization on Middletowners making a living, along with their families, education, leisure, religion and community activities. They found that the greatest changes took place in the job market, which changed from craft labor to a more technological skill orientation. However, these changes were gradual and involved such things as trying to get ahead and concerns with status. These two in-depth studies provided a basis for the comparison of rural small towns with larger cities like Chicago. Again, there was little concern with ethnicity; rather, the processes of change through industrialization were primary.

The third classic study of an American community, ranking with those of Chicago and Muncie, is Lloyd Warner's study of Newburyport, Massachusetts. The field work for this study was completed between 1930 and 1935, and four volumes were published in the forties. Warner was interested in bureaucratization and this study became an important basis for his study of the familiar six level social class system. The third volume, **The Social System of American Ethnic Groups** (1945), focused on ethnicity in this New England community of 17,000. This volume provided greater historical context, and focused on eight ethnic groups (Irish, French Canadians, South Italians, Greeks, Poles, Jews, Armenians and English), their internal organization, and how they fit into the status hierarchies. The complexity of eight ethnic groups and six strata provides us with an early community study which takes ethnic diversity seriously, and links it to the process of upward mobility in industrial society.

Stein (1960) has very helpfully summarized three classical community studies that deal with the processes of urbanization, industrialization and bureaucratization. The Chicago studies and Warner's Yankee City series have greatly influenced and shaped much of the sociological literature that has been written over the past sixty years, literature which grew out of careful community studies. Stein (1960) also proceeds to discuss other community studies of the slum (Whyte's **Street Corner Society**); Caroline Ware's **Bohemian Greenwich Village**; John Dollard's **Caste and Class in a Southern Town** (1957), which focused on ethnicity; and Seeley's, et al, **Crestwood Heights** (1956), a study of one of Toronto's suburbs, including a large Jewish population. In various ways Stein fits the many studies into his classical model, showing some of the fine efforts made in the study of community in the USA.

The major reason behind our review of these American studies is: 1) to show how rich the study of communities in the United States has been, 2) to show the extent to which community studies have influenced general sociological work in America, 3) to illustrate the extent to which these studies have focused on the processes of change, and 4) to review to what extent these studies have focused on ethnicity. Our task in the rest of this paper is to see whether similar community studies have been done in Canada, and explore the extent to which they focus on ethnic solidarity. What we have found is that some very fine community studies have been done and that most of them have focused on ethnicity. We turn now to these Canadian studies.

DAWSON AND SECULARIZATION ON THE PRAIRIES

While the Chicago School of the twenties was dominant in the development of sociology in the United States, it also had its influence upon early sociology in Canada. As Canadian sociology began later, early sociologists in Canada, such as C.A. Dawson, Everett Hughes and Horace Miner, were Chicago graduates. Dawson and Hughes especially carried the Chicago tradition to

Canada, and since they were both at McGill where early Canadian sociology began in the thirties and published studies of ethnic importance, we shall begin with their contributions. Located in Quebec, which has a very different ethnic milieu than the rest of Canada, they may have modified their Chicago inclinations toward assimilation and considered ethnic pluralism more.

Dawson's **Group Settlement: Ethnic Communities in Western Canada** (1936) was the seventh volume in a nine volume Canadian **Frontiers of Settlement** series, edited by historians Mackintosh and Joerg. To be a sociologist in Canada in the thirties, to do research on ethnic groups, and to do so in western rather than eastern Canada, was rather astounding. Indeed, the short preface by editor Mackintosh clearly shows the early British bias when he refers to western minorities as "peculiar peoples" who have "formed 'cultural islands' which have retarded the progress of assimilation," and adds Dawson will present them as groups rather than as "foreigners". Few today would dare to include even one of the words "peculiar," "retarded," "assimilation progress," or "foreigners" in any sentence today, let alone in a preface to a book on western pluralism.

The Chicago influence clearly shows when Dawson frames his study with the statement "the main characteristics of sects which have been set forth with insight by Professor R.E. Park" (Dawson, 1936:xiii). The main writings of the "sect cycle" and the sect-church continuum were actually introduced by the German sociologist Ernst Troeltsch, and then were adopted and applied by Park in Chicago. The sect cycle implies a secularization process of religious groups (especially Christian groups), where a new group may spring forth out of a larger church, because the new believers think the old church does not observe the original intent rigorously enough. However, as this new sect practices greater fervor, follows the Scriptures more intensely, and its concern with purity ages, this commitment again wanes. Slowly it once more becomes an established sect, a denomination, and finally a church-like organization more concerned with structures than original beliefs and practices.

In this sense Dawson was a typical Chicago School sociologist, concerned more with the process of change, assuming that solidarity or concern with The Sacred would give way to secularization. All indicators of change were seen as decline, rather than as change expressed in forms more adapted to the new social milieu for the sake of survival.

Since Dawson (1936) was interested in the change of ethno-religious sects, he chose to study the Dukhobors, Mennonites, Mormons, German Catholics and French Catholics of western Canada. He and his associates made extensive studies of these five groups at the beginning of the depression (1930-32) and their findings were published in 1936. The West had been settled by European immigrants only some fifty years earlier, and many were first and second generation immigrants, so their ethnic origins were still very salient. Dawson was one of the first sociologists to study this new frontier. Many of these groups had settled in block communities, therefore they could easily be studied as distinct segregated ethnic groups.

Dawson (1936) also chose to study five ethno-religious groups for comparative purposes, much in the style of Max Weber, but this has not been sufficiently recognized in Canada as one of the first comparative studies.   Methodologically these five groups were studied, using a combination of ethnographic, survey, interview, community and census sources, both qualitative and quantitative means of data collection. Although he describes each group in 60-100 pages, these are not community studies in the sense of having lived with them or having done participant observation in a more qualitative way.

Dawson was mainly concerned with the process of secularization, and used the Dukhobors and Mennonites as a segregated, sacred, sect group baseline, to see how they had changed; change is usually interpreted as secularization. He also looked at the German and French Catholics as nonsect religious groups, comparing the sect and church groups to find the differences in secularization and assimilation. As expected, he found that the sects had distinguishing features, such as a greater concern with segregation, the maintenance of sect institutions of their own, a reluctance to associate with the outside world, and keeping themselves distinctive and apart by using different dress, language, morals and the like.

Dawson saw the Dukhobors, Mennonites and Mormons as more "sacred" groups, and the German and French Catholics

as   more   secularized.   However,   their   plural
differentiations are clearly evident.

As illustrated in Figure 1, Dawson carefully plotted
eleven block settlements of the five groups, and then
proceeded to discuss each one in detail.   Generally he
outlines how each group came to the prairies, and from
where, the locale in which they settled, the institutions
and organizations they formed, the process of invasion
of the area, how the groups were invaded by others, and
the general social adjustments which were involved, as
well as their resistance to secularization.   This is
enormously useful data because it describes these multi-
ethnic groups in a very plural region more than fifty
years ago, a treasure which can no longer be duplicated.
The study of these five groups also provides a baseline
of religious practices, customs, traditions and values
which can be compared to those today to see how means of
solidarity have changed, how some groups have indeed
since integrated, and the extent to which community
distinctiveness is still present albeit in changed forms.

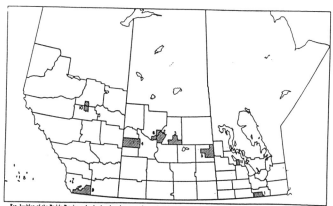

Fig. 1—Map of the Prairie Provinces showing location of group settlements included in the present study: 1, Mennonite West Reserve (Dutch-German); 2, Rosthern Mennonite colony (Dutch-German); 3, St. Peter's colony (German); 4, St. Joseph's colony (German); 5, North and South colonies and Devil's Lake colony (Doukhobor) (also called Yorkton and Swan River colonies); 6, Saskatchewan (Blaine Lake and Saskatoon) colonies (Doukhobor); 7, Cowley colony (Doukhobor); 8, British Colum-bia colonies (Doukhobor); 9, Mormon country (Anglo-Saxon); 10, St. Albert settlement (French-Canadian); 11, Ste. Rose settlement (French-Canadian).

Figure   1.   Location of the Eleven Ethno-Religious Reserves and Settlements Dawson Studied.

Source: C.A. Dawson, Group Settlement: Ethnic Communities in Western Canada.
Toronto: Macmillan Company, 1936. p. xviii.

HUGHES AND INDUSTRIALIZATION IN QUEBEC

Like Dawson, Everett Hughes was among one of the few sociologists in Canada located at McGill. He too was trained in Chicago, and they each acknowledged the other for the support given in their respective 1936 and 1943 publications. And, like Dawson, Hughes, as would be expected of a Chicago School sociologist, was interested in the industrialization process in Quebec. This was well illustrated in his **French Canada in Transition**, published in 1943. Thus, we have two McGill sociologists, one who studied sectarian communities in the West, and the other British-French relations in the industrial Quebec town of Cantonville. While Dawson's study involved the comparison of five ethno-religious groups, Hughes' study explored charter French-English relations.

Hughes (1943:x) chose Cantonville for his study because "it stands in between the two extremes" of Horace Miner's community study of the traditional rural French St. Denis parish prototype (which we shall review shortly), and Montreal, the largest metropolis in Quebec. Industries had both "enlivened and disturbed" Cantonville, and all had been started and managed by English-speaking people. In 1941 Cantonville had a population of 20,000, 95 percent of whom were Catholic and French. This was the first of a series of French towns which he had planned to study (Hughes, 1943:xv). The industrial invasion of Anglophones was in many ways alien to French Quebec, and the fact that the English held the top positions, while the French in their own territory filled in as lower-class workers, created potential conflict in French-English relations. This ethnic relationship resulted in Hughes exploring minority-majority relations more than many of the other sociologists at that time.

Hughes (1943:21) begins his book by sketching the rural Quebec context, including the French-Canadian family farm, the centrality of the Catholic parish (historically the first institution of local self-government) the rural village and parish populations, and the homogeneity of the French population -- especially in eastern Quebec. Then, in contrast, Hughes (1943:22-28) shows how farming had declined, how new industries had invaded the rural areas; how, by the forties, forty percent of Quebec's adult workers were engaged in industry; and, as a result, how intensely family life, work patterns and French society were changing due to this industrialization.

The ethno-religious symbolism of the huge Roman Catholic church of the French overlooking the public park, and "the 1911 Anglican church, a time-weathered monument of the English past," illustrates the predominance of the 95 percent of the residents in Cantonville who were French. Politically the French also dominated. Furthermore, while language and religion separated the two ethnic communities, the schools were also separated into Catholic and Protestant, and children were educated in their respective languages, whether French or English.

Socially the French and English were equally segregated:

> When English and French Women meet socially, there is something of a barrier between them. Golf club and other semipublic bridge parties furnish the chief occasions for female mixing. Most of the English women cannot converse in French and accuse the French women of chattering away among themselves: 'The French are much freer. They laugh and giggle, while the English sit quietly and talk......' These apparently trivial complaints reveal a wide and deep gulf between French and English manners. It is a difference which appears in men's sports as well..... (Hughes, 1943:166).

While socially, politically, demographically and in business the French predominated, the English had the highest positions in industry. These managerial positions paid well, so their families were well-housed on streets of tall elms and maples which shaded their spacious comfortable homes. In contrast, ramshackle tenements, where poverty was evident, belonged to the French blue-collar workers who toiled in the factories. The wide newly-paved streets led to the larger factories. Since the higher managerial and technical staff salaries allowed for more conspicuous living, it was clear where the money was. Thus, two ethnic solitudes lived side by side, each in its own place.

Table   1.   French Catholic and English Protestant Affiliation with Voluntary Assocations.

Religious Affiliation	Ethnic Affiliation						
	French by Definition	French in Fact	Mostly French	Mixed	Mostly English	English in Fact	English by Definition
Catholic by definition	Insurance*(1) Fraternal(1)	Church** Savings and loan** Drill corps(1) Insurance(1) Fraternal(1) Charity** Youth(3) Labor(1)					
Catholic in fact	Political(1) Insurance(1)	Business (2) Drama and music(3) Political(1) Insurance(1) Drill corps(1) Fraternal(2) Sports(3)					
Mostly Catholic			Sports(3) Musical(2				
Mixed					Business(1) First-aid(1) Sports(1)		
Mostly Protestant						Business(1) Sports(1	
Protestant in fact						Sports(1) Drama(1) Boys(1)	Frater- nal(2)
Protestant by definition						Church	

  * The insurance associations are all fraternal insurance orders.
 ** Parochial organizations found in some or all ofthe Catholic parishes.

Source: E.C. Hughes, _French Canada in Transition_.   Chicago: University of
          Chicago Press, 1943, p. 124.

The two Canadian studies do not cover as wide a range of social change as the American ones, but Hughes' small town study of industrialization is similar in some respects to Warner's Yankee City studies, although Warner focused more on social-class and Hughes more on industry. Also, while Dawson's prairie studies focused on farming communities, similar to the Lynds rural Indiana study, the ethnic content of each was quite different.   In Canada we do not have the extent of urban community research done in Chicago, although a number of studies have been done in Toronto and Montreal.

In this section we have tried to show that the influence of the Chicago School reached into Canada, where Dawson and Hughes studied the effects of secularization and industrialization on rural communities.   In the next section we intend to examine some Canadian ethnic community studies.

CONTRIBUTION OF RURAL ETHNIC COMMUNITIES

Earlier we discussed the processes of urbanization, industrialization and bureaucratization which were of interest to sociologists of the Chicago School. Here the focus shall be on various anthropological community studies done in Canada. Canadian ethnic classics such as Miner's French habitants in Quebec, Henry's Blacks in Nova Scotia, and Francis' Mennonites in Manitoba shall be highlighted. These are all in-depth community studies which focus on ethnicity, in three different regions. Almost all community studies done in Canada focus on ethnic groups, illustrating the multicultural reality in Canada. Rex Lucas' **Minetown, Milltown and Railtown** would be an exception.

MINER'S FRENCH HABITANTS IN ST. DENIS

One of the earliest community studies in Canada was done by Horace Miner and published in 1939, three years after Dawson's western sectarian community studies. Miner was a student of Robert Redfield of Chicago, and casts his study in Redfield's peasant or folk-society mode. Redfield wrote the introduction. Miner (1939:ix) states his objectives as being an ethnographic description of the old rural French-Canadian folk culture, an analysis of the social structure, and finding factors of social change with respect to urbanization and anglicization. The first two aims are that of an anthropologist, and the last one, on urbanization and assimilation, a major focus of the Chicago School. Miner did participant observation for a year (1936-37). Two chapters of his study were published in **The American Sociological Review** in 1938. In 1949 Miner revisited St. Denis and published his findings of change in the **American Journal of Sociology** (1950).

St. Denis is a rural French-Canadian parish located on the lower south side of the St. Lawrence River between Montreal and Quebec City. When Miner studied St. Denis in the thirties, it was one of many "sacred" communities symbolized by the steeple of the Roman Catholic Church, which was located in the center of each parish like a hen with her brood of chicks. Miner briefly describes some of the historical context, however it was elaborated more fully by French scholars such as Rioux and Martin (1964), and Rioux (1969, 1973). St. Denis, a parish on the St. Lawrence shore, is located in the center of the agricultural range system, where narrow strips of land begin at the river and extend inland with farm buildings bordering the river, forming a long snake-like village.

In typical anthropological fashion, Miner (1939) describes kinship and the family cycle, the role of religion, the agricultural means of making a living and patterns of community organization. The appendix includes a description of folk medicine: traditional cures and remedies for bad colds -- using pine gum and maple syrup, or eating service berries for constipation; cures for burns, bedwetting, hemorrhoids, earaches and the like. Also included in the appendix are: the autobiography of a Habitant as a child, at school, first communion, family reunions, marriage, death in the family, land improvement and travel. These ethnographic insights help to provide a feel for the peasant's lifestyle.

Miner compares the changes that had taken place between life in the 1800's and 1936 when he studied St. Denis. Flail threshing had been replaced by mechanical tools, hand bucksaws by circular saws, local bean and barley coffee by store-bought tea and coffee; while kerosene lamps had replaced candles; washing and sewing machines, handbraided rugs and blankets; store-bought shoes and clothes, homemade ones; and bobsleighs and buggies, traineaus and carrioles.

When Miner returned to St. Denis in 1949 to look at
the changes made since 1936, he found a considerable
change in the thirteen years since World War II. "Life
is now less 'like a turning wheel"; as an old habitant
described it, "for the repetitive cycle of life no longer
returns to the same point with each succeeding
generation" (Miner, 1936:255). By 1949 television had
spread to many households, "a number of gravel roads were
surfaced; many more automobiles had appeared; and easier
communication by means of buses, trucks and telephones
had been made possible. In addition, on farms tractors
had replaced horses and electricity had made electric
washers, milking machines, refrigerators, electric pumps
and running water possible, and store-bought furniture,
as well as packaged food and clothes, no longer required
as much home woodwork, cooking and sewing. It is a
classic ethnographic study of one French Canadian parish,
an important means of traditional reference.

While Miner's (1936) community study of St. Denis
was one of the first, and Hughes (1943) study of French-
English relations in Cantonville was among the earliest
to document the effects of industrialization on a
community, we have several more to add to a better
understanding of French communities.   In 1975
anthropologist Gerald Gold of Laval studied St.
Pascal, another French-Canadian parish adjacent to St.
Denis.   In Figure 2 we see that St. Pascal is just
southeast of St. Denis, located not on the river, but in
the second tier of inland rangs. The small map shows a
full dozen of the Catholic parishes named after saints,
which clearly emphasizes "the sacre l" milieu that we are
dealing with.   Paul Charest (1975:iv) in his forward
writes "the non-Quebecois reader, familiar with the now
classic works of Hughes and Miner, will here find an
image of Quebec that is not only different but also much
more contemporary and realistic."   Gold (1975) focuses
on the changing leadership and social organization of St.
Pascal, showing the social structure of the town and the
influences of industry, combining the interests of both
Miner and Hughes.   More local French control of the
economic welfare of the community has developed since
Hughes' study, and more important linkages have developed
with the larger networks outside. Small-town St. Pascal
has prospered and joined the larger scene. The French
are no longer as economically dependent as they were in
Cantonville in the 1940's.

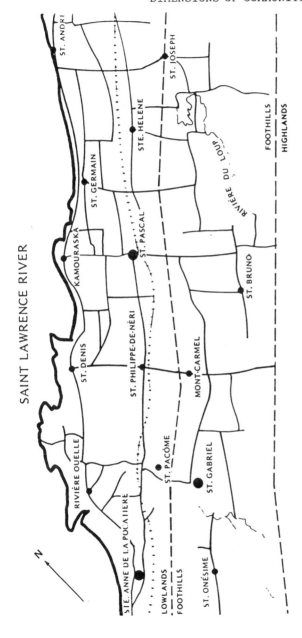

Figure 2.   St. Denis and St. Pascal Parishes on the South Shore of the St. Lawrence in Quebec.

Source: G. Gold, St. Pascal.   Toronto: Holt, Rinehart and Winston, 1975, p. 23.

While the St. Denis, Cantonville and St. Pascal studies focus on French communities in the Quebec heartland, John Jackson (1975) made a community study of French-English relations in Tecumseh, near Windsor, in English-speaking Ontario. His research focused on the conflict between the Francophones and Anglophones over language. While in 1921, 86 percent of the population in Tecumseh was French, by 1971 it had declined to 48 percent. Thus, the French were still the largest ethnic group (Jackson, 1975:9). Religion also added to the complexity. While, in 1921, 94 percent were Roman Catholic, by 1971 this had declined to 75 percent. The French-Ontarians were mostly Catholic, while the British and other groups were either Catholic or Protestant. Ethnic origin, language, religion and social class were all factors that influenced the amount of conflict generated, especially on social issues such as French language education and Catholic schools. Jackson concluded that highly intense conflict reduces the level of assimilation, and that an institutionalized conflict mitigates the force of assimilation. Jackson (1975:173) also concluded that "using language as an index, they saw that Tecumseh Francophones, though not as strong as their conferees in the Ottawa Valley and northwestern Ontario, have maintained an amazing viability against the extreme pressure of anglicization in the Detroit-Windsor metropolitan complex." These four ethnic studies document French community solidarity. The French-Canadian community studies reveal the importance of language and culture for Canada's minority charter group. Let us turn next to the Atlantic Region.

HENRY'S BLACKS IN NOVA SCOTIA

We wish to highlight the Blacks in Nova Scotia, representing visible minority communities in the Atlantic Region. Black studies are numerous in the USA, where there are as many Blacks as the total population of Canada. In comparison, there are relatively few Blacks in Canada, less than one percent. They first settled in Nova Scotia, and a large proportion are still there, especially around Halifax. Blacks have been in Canada since 1628, at least, when a young slave was brought to New France. By the mid-18th century there were about 4,000 Black slaves in New France (Winks, 1970:26). The United Empire Loyalists also brought some slaves with them, but slavery was soon abandoned because it was not too profitable in Canada. Slavery was practiced in

British North America until 1833, when all slaves within the British Empire were freed. While the first Blacks went to Nova Scotia, more recently Blacks have entered Toronto and Montreal in larger numbers (Calliste, 1987:1-20).

Frances Henry (1973) researched thirteen Black rural and urban communities in Nova Scotia, which are located on the map in Figure 3. Interviews were conducted by a team of Black students in each of these thirteen communities in 1970. In her volume **Forgotten Canadians: Blacks in Nova Scotia**, Henry could provide a general context of the Black communities, showing the rural and urban diversity in the province. Interviews in each of these communities showed that 42 percent of the Blacks had less than grade school education, their incomes were very low, they were engaged in the lower-class occupations, many were unemployed, they were pessimistic about chances for upward mobility and often reported prejudice and discrimination (Henry, 1973).

Figure 3.   Location of Thirteen Black Communities in Nova Scotia, Studied by Henry.
Source: F. Henry, Forgotten Canadians: The Blacks of Nova Scotia. Don Mills, Ontario: Longman Canada, 1973, p. 17.

Henry and her associates selected two Black communities for in-depth ethnographic study. Vale Haven is a small depressed rural community located in southeastern Nova Scotia, 300 miles from Halifax, and Far Town is an upper-lower-class semi-urban Black community about ten miles from Halifax, also an economically depressed area. These two ethnographic studies demonstrate the life of a visible minority in the Atlantic Region.

The small rural Black community of Vale Haven lies along a dirt road, or extension of one of the streets of Sea View, with a small primary school, two churches and a community hall. It is entirely dependent upon Sea View's services, which include five grocery stores, a clothing store, bank, post office, funeral parlor, two garages, hospital, courthouse, pool hall, schools and churches (Henry, 1973:38). On the provincial map Vale Haven is simply denoted as a "Black settlement." Most of Vale Haven's children attend the small local school with other Black children.

In 1970 Vale Haven had a population of 294. Very little use was made of the land, except for a few planted gardens. A few kept a horse and cart; there were only twelve cars and three or four trucks in the town. Most of the houses were ramshackle, unpainted and neglected, although two had inside plumbing and running water. A third of the houses had no electricity. Few appliances were found, and the furniture was old and sometimes broken. A few had telephones, radios and television. Most of the people wore poor-quality clothes, often torn (Henry, 1973:42-43).

Many were out of work, and disillusioned about finding work. Younger people tended to leave for jobs outside the community, leaving the children and the old in Vale Haven. The Baptist church was served by a rotating minister who came in occasionally, and church attendance was small and sporadic (Henry, 1973:40-45). Vale Haven residents went for supplies to Sea View, but there was little interaction between the Blacks and Whites. Men in Vale Haven tended to meet in the evenings for joking, drinking and storytelling, and privacy was almost non-existent. Vale Haven is a segregated rural Black community, tucked away from general Nova Scotian life and activity.

Far Town, a second Black community was a semi-urban string of houses located along an unpaved road ten miles out of Halifax (Henry, 1973:53-69). Three Black communities (Far Town, New Town, and East Town) combined represent the most dense population of Blacks in Nova Scotia, estimated to be about 3,000 in 1970. Almost all had radios, television, and a third owned cars. Far Town's population of 700 was comprised of 52 households with fairly stable families (Henry, 1973:57). Recently women were able to get jobs more easily than men, primarily as domestics in Halifax.

Support for the Baptist church in the community was declining. Politicians tended to visit the area mostly during election time, when they needed Black votes, but did little for the community. However, the Blacks were keenly aware of expecting little. There were few militants among the Blacks agitating for change and the community was generally conservative, unwilling to directly confront the White power structures. Blacks and Whites were seldom in contact, even when they worked in the same place. Semi-urban Far Town was similar to rural Black Vale Haven only larger, with a few more conveniences and opportunities for work in Halifax.

These two ethnographic studies are good rural and semi-urban samples of most of the Black communities plotted in Figure 3. These communities all face a life of poverty, at the periphery of White society. They are usually segregated, services are lacking, and schools, churches and social institutions are limited. Blacks in Nova Scotia are marginalized and discrimination against them is evident, all because of the racial factor. Let us now turn to a metropolitan Black community which was likewise a marginal community.

Donald Clairmont and Dennis Magill (1974) have documented the life and death of a Canadian Black urban community, which no longer exists. It was called Africville. "Africville was a Black enclave within the city of Halifax, inhabited by approximately 400 people, comprising 80 families, many of whom were descended from settlers who came over a century ago" (Clairmont and Magill, 1974:19). It was referred to as "shack town", and was relatively invisible, tucked away in a corner of the city. The dwellings were located beside the city dump, and were cut in half by the railroad tracks, without sewage, lighting or public services. Most of the

Black families had squatter rights while others rented. The ghetto was isolated from the rest of Halifax located behind the railroad and city dump, with an undeveloped area between the city and the Black enclave. In 1964 the entire Black community was moved into project housing elsewhere and all buildings were razed, so that this Black community is no longer in existence. This former urban Black community, like Vale Town and Far Town, was poor, isolated, unserviced and neglected. Having examined racial communities, we shall now look at a religious community.

FRANCIS' MENNONITES IN MANITOBA

E.K. Francis came to Canada from Austria in 1945, where he did a major two year (1945-1947) community study of the Mennonites in Manitoba for the Manitoba Historical and Scientific Society. Later, he took positions at Notre Dame in the USA and the University of Munich; however he continued to publish using his Mennonite data for a decade, culminating in a major volume entitled **In Search of Utopia: The Mennonites in Manitoba** in 1955. During this decade (1945-55) Francis published 15-20 articles using his Mennonite data, many of which appeared in major sociological journals such as **The American Journal of Sociology** (1947, 1948, 1950, 1954), **Die Kolner Zeitschrift** (1954), **The British Journal of Sociology** (1950) and **Rural Sociology** (1950).

The Mennonites originally settled in 100 villages on the East and West Reserves of southern Manitoba that were reserved for Mennonite rural block settlement. The West Reserve was also studied by Dawson, and is marked in Figure 6-1. It is located on the west side of the Red River, and on the American border; the East Reserve is located on the east side of the Red River, and is centered by Steinbach, forty miles east of Winnipeg. In 1881, seven years after the first group arrived in 1874, the Mennonites represented 13 percent of Manitoba's population, its fourth largest ethnic group. By the time Francis studied these two reserves in 1945-47 there were 40,000 Mennonites in Manitoba, and they represented 5.4 percent of the provincial population, the sixth largest ethnic group.

The Mennonites originated during the Protestant Reformation in Switzerland, Holland and Germany, beginning in 1525. They were severely persecuted and

migrated eastward into Poland and Russia. The earliest
immigrants came to North America 300 years ago, first to
the eastern USA and Ontario, and then to the West in
1874.

Although a sociologist, Francis used ethnographic
as well as other methods of collecting oral traditions,
by means of interviews with eyewitnesses, historical
material and participant observation common to social and
cultural anthropologists. Since the Mennonites were
highly concentrated and segregated in two main original
reserves, Francis could also study in-depth the community
institutions, culture, values and traditions of the
Mennonites. Some Mennonites were beginning to settle
elsewhere, including the city of Winnipeg, but the heart
of their activity was still located in the two reserves.

Almost all Mennonites in 1955 spoke the Low German
dialect at home and in the villages and towns, but used
the High German in church. Families were highly
endogamous, the schools on the reserves included mostly
Mennonite children and teachers, and the business
activity in the towns of Steinbach, Winkler, and Altona
was done mostly in German. Since the Mennonites selected
some of the best soil for farming they had a very good
rural economic base, so many soon prospered, resulting
in expanded farms and new industry in the towns and
villages. Supporting institutions, such as Waisenamts
for orphans and estates, co-ops, private bible and high
schools, and various forms of fire and other insurance
developed.

When Francis submitted his manuscript **In Search of
Utopia: Mennonites in Manitoba** to the Manitoba Historical
Society, they demanded extensive revisions because they
wanted a more anglo-conformity, assimilationist volume,
not such a favorable bent toward multiculturalism and
pluralism. In a sense the manuscript was ahead of its
time; assimilationist thinking would not yet allow for
the plural versions which were to come later. **In Search
of Utopia**, published in 1955, is clearly one of the first
Canadian ethnocultural community studies done in the
West. It shows the early beginnings of one ethnic group
on the prairies and the various challenges to their
religious tradition, the educational and rural conflict,
as well as the social changes which took place. Since
then urbanization has set in, and all the ethnic groups
have greatly changed. This thorough ethnographic and
historical study served as a data base, launching the

author into numerous conceptual and theoretical questions which Francis dealt with more fully in the scholarly sociological journals.

At the same time that Francis reported his historical and community understanding of one ethnic group, he kept working on in-depth conceptual and theoretical publications which appeared in the sociological journals of the day. He asked serious sociological questions on progress and utopia, the nature of religious and ethnic groups, the role of tradition in modern society, the inadequacy of minority concepts, the adjustment of peasant groups to the capitalist economy, related educational and social institutional problems and the need for new typologies. Francis' work later culminated in his major volumes **Ethnos and Demos** and **Interethnic Relations. An Essay in Sociological Theory** published in 1965 and 1976 respectively (Driedger, 1987:23-29).

One of Francis' first articles on Mennonites dealt with tradition and progress. The issue was private versus public schools, an issue which tended to divide the various Mennonite groups. Contrary to Dawson, who predicted eventual assimilation of prairie groups, Francis began to separate the various Mennonite groups, some of whom clung to their traditional private schools while others were beginning to acculturate, willing to accept the English language and public schools. Francis saw this as a shift and accommodation, not assimilation, akin to the later findings of Glazer and Moynihan (1963) in New York.

The articles which appeared in the **American Journal of Sociology** (1947, 1948, 1950, 1954) best illustrate Francis' quest for a pluralist theory. Francis' contributions were among the first to plough new ground with the ethnic group as a focus. First of all, Francis directed his attention to "the Nature of the Ethnic Group", thinking of it as a subtype of the Gemeinschaft. He stressed that once the ethnic group had reached a certain maturity, the ideology which had led to its formation, as well as the other conditions present in its early stages, could later change without affecting its identity. He concluded that an ethnic group is a mature form of the gemeinschaft. He traced how the Russian Mennonites changed from a religious to an ethnic group as a form of mutation. Despite migration Mennonite identity and cohesion did not suffer materially. He saw sacred institutions as crucial to the group's survival.

Francis continued the quest for clarification of concepts and working with categories. He examined the "peasant group" type using the Manitoba Mennonites as an example, showed the adjustments Mennonites made to capitalist economy. He rejected Dawson's (1936) prediction that they would assimilate, and documented that Mennonites adjusted by developing selectively, by forming new institutions and behavior patterns. By 1954 he began four works (1954, 1957, 1958) based on concepts of a theory of ethnicity, which appeared in **Die Kolner Zeitschrift fur Soziologie.** This later led to his two major theoretical volumes on ethnicity.

There are several supplementary community studies which elaborate on the Mennonite community and social change on the prairies. These are by Driedger (1955), Redekop (1969) and Kauffman and Harder (1975). Driedger's (1955) Chicago thesis was a study of the Old Colony Mennonite community north of Saskatoon, described by Dawson as the Rosthern community. Redekop's (1969) study of the Old Colony Mennonites, with a forward by Everett Hughes, studies these Mennonites in a dozen localities throughout the world, including the three prairie provinces and British Columbia. A more recent survey study done by Kauffman and Harder (1975) looks at Mennonites in both the USA and Canada, documenting some of the changes which have taken place recently. The Mennonite community continues to grow, but half of them in Canada are now urban as so much movement into the cities has occurred, and many have now entered business and the professions (Driedger, 1975, 1977, 1980, 1982, 1983, 1986). Even so, they have retained their Mennonite identity.

We were not able to find the same kinds of urban ethnographic community studies that we were able to find on the rural French, Blacks and Mennonites. However, a great deal of literature is available on the Chinese, who came at the turn of the century, the Italians, who came after World War Ii, and the Portuguese, who have come primarily since the seventies. So far, we have sampled ethnic communities in Quebec, the Atlantic and the western regions, but there has been little focus on the Portuguese in Toronto, the Italians in Montreal, and the Chinese in Vancouver, who represent urban ethnic community segregation. However, we do not have space to elaborate on this here. A review of urban ethnic literature does show that intensive urban ethnographic community studies are needed.

SUMMARY

To begin, we used Stein's American community study investigation as a guide to examine community change processes. We then turned our focus to three rural community studies that had been done in Canada. Durkheim, especially, was interested in cohesion; and the construction of ethnic communities seemed like a good test of the extent of ethnic solidarity. Stein reviewed community studies in Chicago, Middletown in the Mid-west, and the Yankee City series in the northeast, and concluded that they were greatly influenced by the processes of urbanization, industrialization and bureaucratization, respectively. With this social change frame of reference, Stein placed various other rural and urban communities into this change model.

Although fewer community studies have been done in Canada, we found that Hughes documented the process of industrialization in Cantonville, a small Quebec town. The change processes mentioned above greatly affected these Canadian ethnic communities, similar to the findings in the U.S. We also found three typically ethnographic rural community studies that had been done in three separate regions of Canada, which seemed to demonstrate solidarity and cohesion very strongly. Miner's French habitants in St. Denis illustrated the strengths of ethnic culture and language despite change, and more recent studies of the French have illustrated that solidarity can be maintained effectively under considerable change.

Henry's Black communities in the Atlantic region show that race is an effective means of separating and segregating minorities, in that they find it difficult to compete with the larger society from the periphery in which they are ghettoized involuntarily. Lastly, Francis' study of the Mennonites in the West clearly demonstrates that cultural boundary maintenance, institutional completeness and spatial segregation can very effectively keep a minority separated voluntarily.

The construction of ethnic communities is a complex process, influenced by many processes of change. Some ethnic groups are engulfed by these changes, and succumb to assimilation either voluntarily or involuntarily. Others, through constructing cultures, institutions, languages, religion, or because of race, remain separate, some voluntarily, and others involuntarily.

In our review of the literature, the gaps, and what still needs to be done, become fairly obvious. We were not able to find any in-depth community study of an Indian reserve, which was surprising. A study of a series of Indian community reserves on the West Coast, on the prairies, in the Northwest Territories, and in Ontario and Quebec needs to be done. More studies of distinctive ethnic communities on the prairies, such as the Icelanders, Ukrainians, Germans, British, French and others should be done while they still have some of their original traditional characteristics (like Miner did in St. Denis), so that later the change can be documented with replications, such as the Lynds did in Middletown.

Unfortunately, we could not include a review of the urban community literature, but here too there are enormous gaps. While there are several studies of the Chinese in Canada, we could not find an in-depth community study of the largest Chinese communities, which are located in Vancouver and Toronto. While Anderson studied the Portuguese community in Toronto, many more in-depth studies, like Suttles' study of the slum in Chicago, need to be done in the larger cities like Toronto, Montreal and Vancouver, in addition to others. While Shaffir studied the Lubavitcher Chassidim Jews in Montreal, larger urban Jewish communities need to be studied in depth. And newly formed urban Indian, East Indian, Greek, Phillipine, and Mennonite communities along with many others, need greater in-depth study. The British community in Montreal should also be studied. While early scholars, such as Dawson, Miner, Hughes and Francis, have given us a fine start, there is too little evidence that modern scholars are continuing this fine in-depth community study tradition.

REFERENCES

Calliste, Agnes. 1987. "Sleeping Car Porters in Canada: An Ethnically Submerged Labour Market." Canadian Ethnic Studies 19:1-20.

Clairmont, Donald H. and Dennis W. Magill. 1974. Africville: The Life and Death of a Canadian Black Community. Toronto: McClelland and Stewart.

Dawson, Charles A. 1936. Group Settlement: Ethnic Communities in Western Canada. Toronto.

Dollard, John. 1957. Caste and Class in a Southern Town. Garden City, N.Y.: Doubleday.

Driedger, Leo. 1955. "A Sect in an Industrial Society: The Old Colony Mennonites of Saskatchewan." Unpublished M.A. thesis, Department of Sociology, University of Chicago.

Driedger, Leo. 1975. "Canadian Mennonite Urbanism: Ethnic Villagers or Metropolitan Remnant." Mennonite Quarterly Review 49:150-162.

Driedger, Leo. 1977. "The Anabaptist Identification Ladder: Plain-Urban Continuity in Diversity." Mennonite Quarterly Review 51:278-291.

Driedger, Leo. 1980. "Fifty Years of Mennonite Identity in Winnipeg: A Sacred Canopy in a Changing Laboratory," in Harry Loewen (ed.), Mennonite Images, Winnipeg: Hyperion Press, 341-356.

Driedger, Leo. 1986. "Community Conflict: The Eldorado Invasion of Warman." Canadian Review of Sociology and Anthropology 23:247-269.

Driedger, Leo. 1986. "Mennonite Community Change: From Ethnic Enclaves to Social Networks." Mennonite Quarterly Review 60:374-386.

Driedger, Leo. 1987. Ethnic Canada: Identities and Inequalities. Toronto: Copp Clark Pitman.

Driedger, Leo and J. Howard Kauffman. 1982. "Urbanization of Mennonites: Canadian and American Comparisons." Mennonite Quarterly Review 51:269-290.

Driedger, Leo and Calvin Redekop. 1983. "Sociology of Mennonites: State of the Art and Science." Journal of Mennonite Studies 1:33-63.

Francis, E.K. 1947. "The Nature of the Ethnic Group." American Sociological Review 52:393-400.

Francis, E.K. 1948. "The Russian Mennonites: From Religious to Ethnic Group." American Journal of Sociology 54:101-106.

Francis, E.K. 1950. "Tradition and Progress Among Mennonites in Manitoba." Mennonite Quarterly Review 24:312-328.

Francis, E.K. 1950. "The Russian Mennonites: From Religious Group to Ethnic Group." American Journal of Sociology. 101-107.

Francis, E.K. 1951. "The Mennonite Commonwealth in Russia, 1789-1914: A Sociological Interpretation." Mennonite Quarterly Review 25:173-182, 200.

Francis, E.K. 1951. "Minority Groups -- A Revision of Concepts." British Journal of Sociology 2:219-229.

Francis, E.K. 1952. "The Adjustment of a Peasant Group to a Capitalisitic Economy." Rural Sociology 27:218-228.

Francis, E.K. 1954. "Variables in the Formation of So-Called Minority Groups." American Journal of Sociology 60:6-14.

Francis, E.K. 1955. In Search of Utopia: The Mennonites in Manitoba. Altona, Manitoba: D.W. Friesens Publishers.

Glazer, Nathan and Daniel P. Moynihan. 1963. Beyond the Melting Pot. Cambridge, Massachusetts: MIT Press.

Gold, Gerald L. 1975. St. Pascal: Changing Leadership and Social Organizations in a Quebec Town. Toronto: Holt, Rinehart and Winston.

Henry, Frances. 1973. Forgotten Canadians: The Black of Nova Scotia. Don Mills, Ontario: Longmans.

Hughes, Everett. 1941. French Canada in Transition. Chicago: University of Chicago Press.

Jackson, John D. 1975. Community and Conflict: A Study of French-English Relations in Ontario. Toronto: Holt, Rinehart and Winston.

Kauffman, J. Howard and Leland Harder. 1975. Anabaptists Four Centuries Later. Scottdale, PA: Herald Press.

Lynd, Robert and Helen Lynd. 1929. Middletown. New York: Harcourt Brace.

Lynd, Robert and Helen Lynd. 1937. Middletown in Transition. New York: Harcourt and Brace.

Miner, Horace. 1939. St. Denis: A French-Canadian Parish. Toronto: University of Toronto Press.

Miner, Horace. 1950. "A New Epoch in Rural Quebec." American Journal of Sociology 56:1-10.

Redekop, Calvin. 1969. The Old Colony Mennonites: Dilemmas of Ethnic Minority Life. Baltimore: Johns Hopkins Press.

Richmond, Anthony. 1972. "Ethnic Residential Segregation in Metropolitan Toronto." Ethnic Research Programme, Institute for Behavioral Research, Toronto: York University.

Seeley, John A., Alexander Sim and E.W. Loosley. 1956. Crestwood Heights. Toronto: University of Toronto Press.

Stein, Maurice R. 1960. The Eclipse of Community. Princeton: University of Princeton Press.

Warner, W. Lloyd and Leo Srole. 1945. The Social System of American Ethnic Groups. New Haven, Conn.: Yale University Press.

Winks, Robin. 1970. Blacks in Canada. Montreal: McGill-Queens Press.

Wirth, Louis. 1928. The Ghetto. Chicago: University of Chicago Press.

V

TRANSITIONS OF POLISH-AMERICAN COMMUNITIES

Krztysztof Frysztacki

The purpose of this paper is to examine an ethnic community of Polish origin in an American city, Buffalo, New York. Its aim is to investigate the origins of this community, its growth and trends of change. This study is based on two main premises. First, that territorial agglomerations, primarily those of metropolitan character, produce specific conditions of social life. Second, there is a connection between the character and development of the whole urban community and the various ethnic groups of which it is composed. Thus, an ethnically distinct urban population -- like the Polonia of Buffalo[1] -- are described according to the characteristics of the whole cities and metropolitan areas.

This study is representative of the general history of Polish immigrants in the USA: most of them have tended to settle in towns and cities, find homes and jobs, and take part in community life there, thus starting on a new chapter in their existence (Brozek, 1985, Znaniecki Lopata, 1976). At the same time, this pattern of the Polonia settlement in the USA is consistent with the vital importance of big cities and the areas adjoining them in both the history and contemporary life of American society. It is in the cities that most of the population and the prevailing part of their resources are concentrated, and ideas and models of behavior are created. It is also in the cities that most of the nation's domestic problems and difficulties arise (Bollens, Schmandt, 1970). Buffalo, N.Y., is one of the cities in which the ethnic factor exerts a markedly strong effect. The presence of citizens of Polish descent has had a strong impact on this city.

The main bulk of my research was carried out in the USA. The research program was sponsored by the State University of New York at Stony Brook, although I spent most of my time in Buffalo, where I was affiliated with the local State University College.

The sources and the materials collected were twofold in nature. The major part consisted of previously existing materials: various sociological publications of the subject under examination, statistical data, papers published and unpublished, and other studies concerned with American cities and their Polish communities. In addition, there were the results of the surveys I carried out: notes made of talks I had with some forty local representatives of the Polonia community in Buffalo, and fifty written answers to my mailed questionnaire.

In this study I concentrated mainly on defining the characteristics of the Polonia group as a local ethnic subcommunity; i.e. a relatively autonomous and internally integrated unit of the whole metropolitan structure, a unit whose characteristic traits correspond to the more general phenomenon of the local community. These traits occur principally in two dimensions. One is the grouping of population and material conditions in a limited area. This means that the given territory is taken over, developed and utilized by a population with specific, distinctive properties, such as national origin.   On these grounds communities are formed. They arise and exist with the support of social organization and connecting links within the community.

Social organization is based on preferred and established forms of activity, leading to regularities in the conduct of individuals and groups. It involves a dynamic process of social actors being integrated into social relations. The connecting link has to do with the awareness of the local community, which manifests itself under four different aspects.   They are, from the simplest to the most complex: the everyday, the identifying, the personal, and the normative, -- the latter referring to the most developed, positively experienced attitude to the same traditions and values; identification with the prosperous growth of one's own community, its future, and the need for collective effort on its behalf.

Whereas the city, as a whole, is thought of as a local community, a given ethnic group in this city should be conceived of as a local ethnic subcommunity, with generalized characteristics consistent with those of the whole.   Nevertheless, an ethnic subcommunity has some additional specific traits.   In this paper, the main stress has been put on the situation of the Polish subcommunities as minorities -- where their inferior and

underprivileged position has been more or less
pronounced. Supplementarily, based on L. Wirth's
suggestion, it has been hypothetically assumed that the
reaction of that particular subcommunity was mainly
pluralistic and assimilative in character.

II

The main theoretical conception of this paper
involves the idea of local transformation. As suggested
by E.K. Francis (1976: passim), the Polonia subcommunity
has passed through four principal stages.

The first stage involves the emergence of a
territorial community, and its transformation into a
strictly closed ethnic community with an homogeneous and
relatively simple manifestation of inner organization and
integration. This is displayed mainly in an
organizational and conscious manifestation of direct
social relations and the integrating functions performed
by the parish and related groups. This period has been
labelled the primary ethnic subcommunity.

The second stage involves the strengthening and
consolidation of this subcommunity, with a simultaneous
growth of internally differentiating factors. These
manifest themselves both on the demographic-spatial level
and a sociologically conceived whole; on the latter
level, it is mainly the network of institutions and
associations that becomes markedly enriched. This period
has been the stage of a "closed" secondary ethnic
subcommunity.

During the third stage, when spatial grouping still
continues to be prominent, the previous rules of internal
functioning within the subcommunity become gradually more
and more entwined with those governing the surrounding
environment. There, the progression and consequences of
the outwardly oriented relations exert a stronger
influence upon the internal order than vice-versa. This
period has been called the stage of an "open" secondary
ethnic subcommunity.

During the fourth stage the demographic and spatial
basis is weakened. This is accompanied by a simultaneous
weakening of the previous manifestations of social
integrity and distinctness. This regression is
comparatively more pronounced in the formal traits of

social organization. As a result, informal phenomena of community life as well as manifestations of national realization (identification) become relatively more important. This period has been called the stage of the neo-community, an ethnic category.

III

The extensive and highly varied process of empirical verification cannot be fully described in this paper. Thus, only some of the major processes shall be presented. These, depict, first of all, the situation of the Polonia in Buffalo between the 1870's and the 1970's, and compare it with some others in the context of what has already been discussed.

The historical background that conditioned the Polish newcomers was the general situation of the American society and its political structure at that time. During several decades in the late 19th and early 20th centuries, the intense flow of immigrants was due to the liberal approach to the problem of immigration. This policy created some practical opportunities for economic expansion and urban growth. The Polish immigrants were allowed to seek permanent residence, although only under certain conditions putting them in an inferior position. On the other hand, the local community accepted the immigrants' prevailing readiness to consolidate their individual and family existence in America. Neither the Polish immigrants nor their descendants were mere "birds of passage". In spite of a temporary lack of equilibrium between the sexes, and the desire of some of the immigrants (mostly the earlier ones) to return to their native country, the majority stayed.

The Polish population rapidly acquired marked spatial properties. In fact, throughout its history this population has lived in a situation of spatial concentration, at first almost complete, and then gradually loosening, but never quite dissolving. Concentration on "their own area", a separate part of the city's space, was the starting-point, and a permanently active factor in their "togetherness". The zones occupied by these families had comparatively well-delineated and constant borderlines. However, within them it was easy to discern the central outposts, among which pride of place was given to the parishes and

servicing shops, as well as the linear forms of spatial
organization. Both of the particular components, (for
example, "Stanislawowo" and "Broadway-Fillmore" in
Buffalo), and broader areas (such as "Polish East Side"
in the same city) found a reflection in social
consciousness. They were also an object of recognition
and appraisal by the members of the Polonia, as well as
the other groups that came from the outside.

Let us now consider another aspect of this specific
property that has become manifest, especially during the
last two decades. The fact that, for example, the
Polonia of Buffalo, along with other groups of the same
background, have always been so strongly connected to the
area inhabited by them seems to have made them very
susceptible to any changes occurring in it. These
changes have already come to a head and, in all
probability, will evolve, following two interrelated
trends. First, large groups of the population have left
the cities proper to settle in the suburbs. Second,
there has been a strong pressure from other groups
(mainly black) to occupy the areas hitherto occupied by
immigrants of Polish origin.

These changes markedly undermine the traditional
community forms of the Polonia organizations and their
interconnections. Hence, a further reduction of
territorial specificity may result in either the
withering away of the local subcommunity of the Polonia,
or the traditional elements of local identification and
co-existence will be consolidated and some new ones will
arise; these will not be so closely correlated with the
spatial divisions of the city and metropolitan area.
This shifts the major stress of this paper to problems
more strictly sociological in character.

To sum up, we can state that the patterns of
behavior, and forms of relations within the subcommunity,
were of a fairly lasting character. In addition, the
members of this subcommunity, in their multiple
activities, made it practically almost self-servicing,
with most of the needs and requirements met within its
frame. Of the various forms of community life, the most
consolidating effect on the internal patterns of
functioning was exerted by the Polonia's own institutions
and associations. In particular, the parish institutions
were distinguished by their unchangeable character and
the constant abundance of functions offered to those
within their respective ranges of activity, while the

parish priests played prominent leading roles among their members.

The associations, both those closely connected with the parishes and those independent of them, constituted a network which was somewhat less permanent. Some of these associations underwent a process of transformation, and some were replaced by new ones, but, generally speaking, they did exert a markedly consolidating influence within the Polonia subcommunity. Another influential factor was the founding of various business enterprises in which the owners, the employees, and most of the clientele were all members of the Polonia. Moreover, daily life favored the development of informal social relations between families, friends and acquaintances living the same neighborhood and/or working for the same employers.

It should be borne in mind, too, that, from the very beginning, there were marked manifestations of centralized leadership; that within the Polonia subcommunities it was possible to obtain aid and support guaranteed to the needy; and that the subcommunities under discussion gave their members a sense of security greater than would be found outside them. All this demonstrates that the process of integration was fairly advanced. When due reference is made to the spatial aspect the integrating influence of the Polonia "ghetto" appears more well-founded. This statement can be extended beyond the lifetime of one generation. On the other hand this trend towards internal growth, though strong and long-standing, has been modified and weakened by two other trends, at least.

The first refers to the fact that almost since the very beginning, apart from a short-lived initial period, the Polonia groups have not been homogeneous. The tendency to establish a number of highly diversified institutions and associations carrying out different forms of activities, arose very soon, even in the course of the first stage of immigration of Polonia's history. In later years it became even more pronounced. This tendency, though not necessarily inconsistent with the general integrating trend discussed above, exerted a rather restraining influence on it and, at some particular moments, stood in marked opposition to the more extreme centralizing and unifying measures. Let us point out, as an example, competition between different fraternal benefit organizations.

The second trend refers to the general evolution towards weakening of the various factors which, co-existing and interconnected, compose the Polonia. A general feeling of "togetherness" with that which is Polish, the number and vitality of the local group initiatives, the unwritten "rules" according to which spouses are selected and new families are formed, are classical tokens of this phenomenon. It is hard to establish, for certain, when this evolutionary weakening actually began. Nevertheless, three successive turning-points can be distinguished, namely: the "macrosocial" restraining of the flow of Polish immigrants to the U.S. after the First World War, the "microsocial" loosening of endogamy in the inter-war period, and the "local" transformations between the central city and the remaining part of the metropolitan area after the Second World War.

In conclusion, this research has confirmed the occurrence of the previously discussed first three stages, and the onset of the fourth, as discussed. However, this fourth stage, which has been labelled the "neocommunity" stage, also presents a separate issue.

Why separate? Because, in the light of empirical data, this is but a hypothetical projection at this particular stage, if it really will develop in time, still lies largely ahead. In fact, the Polonia is faced with three main alternatives for the years to come, namely: (a) either the process of change will slow down and the previous forms of activity, though reduced, but modelled on the past, will be carried on; (b) the old structures will almost entirely disappear - "almost entirely", for in the foreseeable future there can hardly be a question of "total disappearance"; or (c) a qualitatively new structure will arise: a new Polish-American ethnic category.

The latter may be characterized, above all, by the following:

1. in the spatial aspect, the basic factor will be the whole metropolitan area and only to a minor degree, its particular subareas, including the central city;

2. with respect to the reduced daily organizational manifestations of community life, the self-realization factors will grow

in strength, hence it will be less a
subcommunity of people who "co-exist" than one
of those who are "aware" of one another and
associate favorable states of consciousness
with that awareness;

3. these states of consciousness will continue to
be derived from the common identification with
Polish national descent, while at the same time
they will definitely concern local
circumstances;

4. this subcommunity will probably continue to
exist for a long time, though it will be
greatly reduced in numbers.

It seems that it will be just that third alternative
which will be adopted ultimately by the Polonia in the
years to come, as a group of people representative of an
American metropolitan subcommunity of ethnic character.

NOTES

[1]Polish-American ethnic community and other Polish communities outside of Poland are called Polonia.

REFERENCES

Bollens, J.C., H.J. Schmandt. 1970. "The Metropolis.
     Its People, Politics, and Economic Life", New York.

Brozek, A. 1985. "Polish Americans 1854-1939", Warsaw.

Francis, E.K. 1976. "Interethnic Relations. An Essay
     in Sociological Theory", New York, Oxford,
     Amsterdam.

Znaniecki, Lopata H. 1976. "Polish Americans, Status
     Competition in an Ethnic Community", Englewood
     Cliffs, N.J.

VI

CONSTRUCTION OF SENTIMENTS AND VALUES
IN A
MIDDLE-CLASS BLACK URBAN COMMUNITY[1]

Theodoric Manley, Jr.[2]

INTRODUCTION

Research on the black American class structure and the class relationships between middle-class and lower-class blacks has generated a great deal of controversy over the years, especially among black scholars (Frazier, 1957; Sowell, 1975; Wilson, 1980). The present study delineates the construction of local sentiments and values that led to the opposition of a half-way house for black rehabilitated mental patients in a middle-class black urban community. My analysis emanates from the current theoretical debate on the occurrence of class bifurcation in black communities (Wilson, 1981; Kilson, 1981).

In the 1960's, most of the research on black communities focused solely on race, very little attention was devoted to internal class differences and the construction of local sentiments and values in black urban communities (Hannerz, 1969; Wilson, 1981). These differences were overlooked as researchers investigated local black/white urban community differences (Duncan, 1957; Taeuber and Taeuber, 1965) The movement of black workers from lower paying to higher paying positions, however, resulted in the formation of a diverse set of class interest among middle-class and lower-class blacks in urban communities. These diverse class interest are inextricably tied to the changing structure of the American economy and have manifested the construction of local sentiments and values in black urban communities.

This analysis will focus on the social process involved in the construction of local sentiments and values in a middle-class black urban community. The author intends to show how the interpenetration of social policies of the larger urban complex constructed these local sentiments and values. This construction of local sentiments and values led to a series of strategies to keep a halfway house for rehabilitated black mental health patients from locating in the community.

My analysis is based on one and a half years of participant observation in Chicago's South Shore, one of the original 75 Chicago "communities" identified by Burgess and his students in the 1920's. An attempt is made to demonstrate how residents within South Shore came together because social policy changes in mental health institutionalization clashed with their shared sense of their neighborhood; and also encouraged them to articulate those feelings in a way that had not been necessary before. This case study describes the process through which local sentiments and values in South Shore were constructed by the external interpenetration of social policies from the larger urban complex and by local transformations in community control and class interest.

DATA COLLECTION

I used data gathered during one and a half years (January 1984 through August 1985) of participant observation in the community, particularly in the neighborhood area most involved in mobilizing to prevent a halfway house from locating there. Data are presented from recorded open-ended interviews with local residents, community organization leaders, and the local political leader, and from systematic observation and participation in community and block club meetings that involved residents concerned about and opposed to the halfway house. Also presented are newspaper accounts and conversation data from meetings held at the local community organization office and aldermanic ward service office, where I was employed during the research project as a part-time "housing conservationist."

WHY DO BLACK COMMUNITIES ACT?

From slavery to freedom, black communities have been forced to act and react to external societal forces of economic inequality, political disenfranchisement, and social isolation--all of which have been commonly considered race subordination (Genovese, 1972; Franklin, 1980; McAdam, 1982; Morris, 1984). These structural conditions in several local urban communities from the 1930's until the present have

been viewed as the central social forces that motivated
black communities to act in the past.   The mobilization
of local southern black urban communities during the
Civil Rights Movement has been greatly discussed--
especially by resource mobilization and political process
theorists (cf. McAdam, 1982; Morris, 1984).   This
analysis, however, is based on a rather peculiar
transformation in a local Midwest middle-class black
urban community: the transformation of middle-class
blacks in a local urban community into powerful actors
controlling the fate of a group of black rehabilitated
mental health patients.

RACIAL CHANGE IN SOUTH SHORE, 1950-1980

South Shore, in a twenty year period, underwent
rapid racial change (see Table 1).   The migration of
blacks into the community in 1960 resulted in the
simultaneous out-migration of whites.   Whereas in 1960,
whites were 89.6 percent of the population by 1970 this
percent had plummeted to 29.9 percent and was a meager
3.6 percent in 1980.   During the early period of racial
change in South Shore several blacks, whose socioeconomic
status was comparable to their white counterparts, had
been forced to rent under-maintained housing (mostly
multi-family) because of the local bank practice of
denying blacks conventional mortgages (Molotch, 1972;
Manley, 1986).   However, in 1970, when blacks became a
majority in South Shore (69.0 percent), the local bank
attempted to move from the community.   The move by the
bank was stopped short by the mobilization efforts of the
black in-migrant group.   Upon hearing of the local bank
decision to move from the community the in-migrant group
of middle-class blacks petitioned the Federal
Comptroller, who is in charge of granting banks
permission to move, to deny the bank the right to move.
The middle-class blacks of South Shore presented to the
Federal Comptroller the past racist actions of the local
bank and argued that the result of a move by the bank
would be catastrophic to the overall stability of the
community.   Indeed, the Federal Comptroller went along
with the community and for the first time in banking
history denied the bank the right to move and mandated
that the bank become a local neighborhood bank (Manley,
1986).

Racial change in South Shore was also accompanied
by internal class differences.   As Table 1 shows, the

population of South Shore decreased during the 1970's, but more importantly, as median school years and median family income increased, so too did families headed by females, income below poverty, and the unemployed civilian labor force. This data begins to show a bimodal stream of in-migrants into South Shore. That is, the blacks who moved to South Shore in the beginning of the in-migration stream (1960 migrants) were, on several social indices, equivalent to their white counterparts, but the blacks at the tail-end of the migration stream tended to be less so (1970 migrants). Thus, the mobilization efforts of the early black in-migrants to keep the bank in the community was based on their class interest to control and stabilize a community that whites were fleeing from because of racial invasion.

The percentage of residents in white collar jobs decreased from 62.6 percent in 1960 to 29.1 percent in 1970 because of rapid white flight, and although the white collar percentage went back up to 59.0 percent in 1980, families with percent incomes over the median family income in South Shore declined throughout the racial change period (see Table 1). But if all the blacks who migrated to South Shore were equivalent socioeconomically to their white-flight counterparts, there should have been little reduction in percent of income over the median family income for South Shore. However, although middle-class blacks in South Shore tended to have educational backgrounds similar to those of the displaced whites and although in 1980, after the community had become predominantly black, the median education increased, the relative increase in younger age groups was concomitant with the national trend of black adolescent unemployment and out-of-wedlock births. This trend in the migration stream of the black in-migrants had a role in reducing the percent of income above the median family income in South Shore.

Although racial change in South Shore produced a bimodal stream of migrants, the early in-migrant blacks had begun to construct local sentiments and values in the community by the formation of their class interests. The formation of their class interests was similar to the historical internal class distinctions among blacks in urban communities (Frazier, 1957; Zunz, 1982). This process of constructing local sentiments and values by the formation of middle-class black class interest in an urban community was clearly manifested when a group-home for rehabilitated mental patients was purchased in the O'Keefe neighborhood area of South Shore.

The O'Keefe neighborhood area has a strong component of middle-class and working-class residents (see Table 2). Indeed, on the block where the group home was purchased single family homes and two and three flat family units surrounded it. O'Keefe, like South Shore in general, resembled the bimodal distribution of the population that migrated to the community.

The O'Keefe neighborhood in 1980, had the highest percent of male workers in white-collar occupations, 67.8 percent, coupled with the highest percent of families headed by females 53.6 percent, in the community. Aware of these internal class differences in the O'Keefe neighborhood of South Shore the middle-class blacks in the community came together to ward off the interpenetration of social policy changes in mental health institutionalization.

SOCIAL POLICY CHANGES IN MENTAL HEALTH INSTITUTIONALIZATION

The advent of "deinstitutionalization" in the middle of the 1970's with its core ideal of phasing out mental hospitals had been a subject of continuous policy debates since the early 1950's (Mechanic, 1969). The social policy of deinstitutionalization was thus part of a cycle of social reform movements aimed at alleviating the problems of overcrowding, understaffing, and the permanent institutionalization of "mental" patients in state mental health hospitals (Morrissey, 1982). It was specifically implemented to remove from overcrowded and understaffed state hospitals patients who seemed capable of coping outside. Deinstitutionalization involved an effort to dismantle and close state mental hospitals and to relocate their clientele in a new network of community-based mental health services (Bachrach, 1976, 1978).

For example, between 1955 and 1980 the resident population of state mental hospitals was reduced by more than 75 percent. During this period, over 700 community mental health centers (CMHCs) serving catchment areas representing 50 percent of the U.S. population were created in local community areas (Morrissey, 1982).

In Chicago, a psychiatric rehabilitation center, "Thresholds", founded in 1958, pioneered the process of deinstitutionalization. Thresholds was considered by the Illinois Department of Mental Health to be "one of the best of its kind in the country" (Koehler, 1984:2). In 1984 Thresholds received a six-month interim loan ($225,000) from the Illinois Department of Mental Health and Developmental Disabilities (DMHDD) to complete the purchase of two residences--one for the mentally ill and deaf, and the other, a halfway house for rehabilitated mental patients on the southeast side of Chicago in the community area of South Shore. If Thresholds was successful in South Shore, DMHDD officials argued, it could have a wide-ranging impact on other agencies' abilities to secure funding to build, rehabilitate, or expand facilities. The following discussion focuses on the local process involved in establishing the halfway house in the community under consideration.

ANALYSIS AND FINDINGS

The loan Thresholds received from the Illinois Department of Mental Health and Developmental Disabilities (DMHDD) allowed it to purchase a two-flat home in the O'Keefe neighborhood area of South Shore at 6941 South Paxton Avenue (Figure 1). The intent of the purchase was to move black mental patients who were able to function normally in the community into South Shore. But residents of the O'Keefe neighborhood and surrounding areas of the community were uninformed of this development. The president of the community organization of South Shore expressed the residents' concerns as follows:

> From what I can understand the community was not informed about this particular development. In other words, the community would not have found out. Not it is true that Thresholds has done the same thing in other communities, where it has gone in, not informed the community--just moved them in. In some places it has worked, in other places it has not (Interview with President of Community Organization, October 3, 1984).

Table 1

South Shore Population Characteristics, 1950-1980

	1950	1960	1970	1980
Total Population	79336	73086	80660	77743
% Male	45.7	45.3	46.0	45.3
% Female	54.3	54.7	54.0	54.2
% White	99.8	89.6	29.9	3.6
% Black	0.2	9.6	69.0	95.1
% Other Non-White	0.0	0.8	1.1	1.3
Age Structure				
% Under 5 Years Old	7.7	6.7	7.9	8.7
% 5-19 Years Old	15.0	16.4	20.3	24.0
% 20-44 Years Old	36.8	27.8	40.0	43.3
% 45-64 Years Old	30.5	33.4	20.3	17.5
% 65 Years and Older	10.0	15.7	11.5	6.5
% Families Female Headed	-	-	20.5	49.3
Median School Years	12.3	12.2	12.3	12.3
Median Family Income, 1959/1969/1979 ($)	-	-	7,888	15,969
% Income Below Poverty	-	-	7.8	20.8
% Income Above Median Family Income	-	34.1	24.4	19.1
% White-Collar Workers	-	62.6	29.1	59.0
% Civilian Labor Force Unemployed	-	3.5	4.2	13.1

Source: Local Community Fact Book, Chicago Metropolitan Area, 1980.

Table 2

O'KEEFE NEIGHBORHOOD AREA POPULATION CHARACTERISTICS, 1960-1980

	1960	1970	1980
Total Population	11,392	13,388	12,735
% Male	-	46.0	44.8
% Black	0.3	73.6	95.4
% Other Nonwhite	0.1	0.8	0.7
% Of Spanish Origin	-	0.6	0.4
% Foreign	49.6	4.6	1.4
Age Structure			
% Under 13 Years Old	-	18.6	21.7
% 14-20 Years Old	-	7.4	9.2
% 21-64 Years Old	-	62.9	61.0
% 65-74 Years Old	-	7.0	4.9
% 75 Years and Older	18.1	4.1	3.1
% Families with Female Head	-	22.3	53.6
Median School Years Completed	12.5	12.5	13.0
Median Family Income, (1959/1969/1979 $$)*	8,861	11,063	16,199
% Income Below Poverty	-	7.0	19.9
% Income Above Median Family Income	41.6	28.2	21.4
% White-Collar Workers	80.8	33.8	67.8
% Civilian Labor Force Unemployed	2.1	3.7	11.3

Source: Local Community Fact Book, Chicago Metropolitan Area, 1980.

FIGURE 1.--MAP OF SOUTH SHORE COMMUNITY

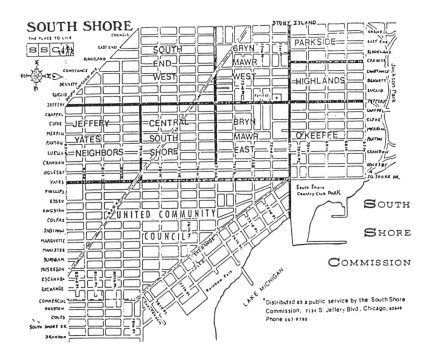

A resident of the O'Keefe neighborhood who lived next door to the building that had been sold to Thresholds called a meeting of the local community organization. Incidentally, this local resident of O'Keefe contacted the Alderman's office for advice on how to find out who had recently bought the building. After the neighbor became aware of the intentions of Thresholds, a community meeting was held with a representative of the Thresholds organization to address this concern. The following data are from field notes I recorded after attending this meeting.

Mr. A. (director of the South Shore Commission [community organization]) opened the meeting:

Mr. A.: Today we have with us a representative from Thresholds who will address the concerns we have for locating a halfway house for rehabilitated mental patients in our community. Let me first describe Threshold's plans. Threshold plans to place nine discharged residents of their facility into 6941 South Paxton. This was never brought to the attention of South Shore's block clubs or other community groups. The community learned of these plans accidentally. With this brief statement let me introduce Mr. M. (representative from Thresholds).

Mr. M.: I feel the gap Mr. A. speaks of concerning lack of communication can now be bridged. Thresholds works on psychosocial rehabilitation. The people being placed at 6941 South Paxton are able to function normally in the community.

Ms. L. (resident of O'Keefe): I am concerned about the increased danger and violence in the community as a result of the nine new residents entering South Shore.

Mr. M.: Most literature on this concern shows that mental patients are the least likely to commit crime.

Mr. C. (resident of O'Keefe): Mr. M., will you respect the wishes of the community and keep this residential facility out of the South Shore area?

Mr. M.: The land has already been bought, and plans have been made for the use of this property by Thresholds. I believe the people of this community need some education on mental health. Let me refer you to a group home at 431 East 48th Street as proof that these people can function normally in a community setting. Although we placed them there without the community's knowledge, the residents, once they found out, stated they really didn't notice a difference. Most claimed that they were the best neighbors on the block.

Ms. F.: (resident of O'Keefe): Why doesn't Thresholds rent the housing space to someone besides Thresholds patients?

Mr. M.: Thresholds is not a real estate agency. [Mr. M. comments that he feels very antagonized by the people at the meeting.]

Ms. F. (standing up and shouting): I believe the reason South Shore was chosen for this project is because Thresholds sees it as a marginal community. This is a middle-class black community, and you cannot come in here violating our right as a resident of the community to speak out against this project!! We are not pushovers!

Mr. M. (calm but nervous): South Shore is a good community. We feel that the nine people can benefit from the concerns you have about your community and the values you place on a good neighborhood.

The residents of the community continued to discuss how the safety of the neighborhood would be affected if the project was carried through. At this point, Ms. W. (aldermanic assistant) stated that "Some zoning regulations will have to be checked out regarding this project. There may be a problem with the type of facility that is planned for this building." The residents of the O'Keefe neighborhood began to gather around the aldermanic assistant for further information on the issue of zoning. This would become a key strategy for the middle-class blacks in South Shore to prevent the halfway house from locating in the O'Keefe neighborhood and to preserve their class interest and control over the local sentiments and values in the community. The meeting continued:

Mr. A.: Mr. M. will you explain the difference between a group home and an independent living facility?

Mr. M.: Group homes are made up of many people together with in-house staff 24 hours a day. An independent living site would have only one person, to act as an apartment manager, who would not necessarily live in the building.

Mr. C.: What!? You mean an absentee landlord in South Shore if the staff person did not live on the property; this is another problem.

More discussion followed, but many residents had become hostile towards Mr. M. At this point, Mr. A. adjourned the meeting.

These data from the community meeting reflect several themes regarding the "defended neighborhood" concept (Suttles, 1972). Thresholds, as an external urban organization, became a threat to the ability of middle-class blacks to control the construction of local sentiment and values in the community. That is, Thresholds was perceived by middle-class residents as a threat and violation of their economic and social class interest in the O'Keefe neighborhood because of the "type" of community Thresholds chose for its halfway house for rehabilitated mental patients. But the situation not only threatened their ability to control the construction of local sentiments and values in the community, but also transformed the local mobilization efforts of middle-class blacks who had been confronted with similar prejudicial (racial) opposition from white ethnic groups when they migrated to South Shore in the early 1960's. One resident who attended the community meeting spoke of the unintended consequences of the construction of local community sentiment and values among middle-class black residents of South Shore.

> It really shamed me to hear black people talk so badly about other black people when our tradition has always been that we made room for everybody and that we went through so much that when people are using the same argument about not letting other blacks move into the neighborhood that we should have learned from our prior experiences not to inflict the same kind of selfish argument (Interview with Resident of O'Keefe neighborhood, October 15, 1984).

For many of the black middle-class residents of South Shore, however, a major social cleavage existed between Thresholds and the residents' construction of local sentiments and values. This cleavage resembled the utilitarian and purposeful approach some issue-oriented community groups, of diverse race, ethnic, and class backgrounds adopt when confronting governmental bodies about problems related to the allocation and distribution of public housing, police and city services (Clark, 1975:305-359).

The reactions of the residents of South Shore fit an ongoing pattern of the effect of urban institutions on community solidarities. As Suttles (1972: 49) makes clear, "the general trajectory of American society has been toward large-scale and specialized organizations which make extreme demands on consensus and collaboration of groups previously unrelated to one another." Black middle-class residents of South Shore fit this pattern because they continued to bear an unavoidable social responsibility of controlling and maintaining their class interests within their community boundaries. The demands of an external organization on a local community constructed local sentiments and values. These constructed local sentiments and values are connective and similar to larger value systems in other communities (e.g., white opposition to blacks in-migrating to their neighborhood), but they are also crucially disconnective (e.g., the denial of the entry of rehabilitated black mental health patients into the neighborhood).

The social policy of deinstitutionalization is in conflict with the values of middle-class black residents when their class interest and sense of community control are dependent on a collective image of each other's "cognitive map" of the local community. Furthermore, the construction of local sentiments and values in South Shore were similar to the past class interest of both the middle-class white residents of South Shore and the local bank--even though these particular class interests were acted out through racial prejudice.

This process of constructing local sentiments and values in South Shore led to the bifurcation of the community along mental health characterizations. Local community sentiments and values held by blacks in the 1960's, during racial change in the community, might have allowed such processes as locating rehabilitated black mental health patients to be integrated into the neighborhood's social fabric. But the transformation in local economic and political power--from denial of mortgages to black home ownership--constructed (in this instance) the middle-class black residents local sentiments and values in the South Shore community.

The middle-class black residents' commitment to collectively opposing the external organization resembled a "conscious community" (Hunter, 1983: 186). This is a subcomponent of the emergent perspective approach to urban neighborhoods. The development of a "conscious community" is described by Hunter (1983: 186):

> The primary structural ingredient of the conscious community is the development of a more formal community organization that provides critical internal and external functions for maintaining local solidarity and sentiments. Internally, such groups provide a structure within which primary bonds of neighboring may be developed and within which the common community interests may become expressed and translated into specific organizational goals. Externally, the organization becomes the 'legitimate' representative of the community, an identifiable vehicle or corporate body that may more easily interact with outside agencies and institutions.

O'Keefe residents of South Shore requested that the Alderman provide them with more information on the legal approach to preventing the halfway house from locating in their community. At this meeting, the residents of South Shore became politically active and formally organized for local collective action. The alderman informed the community that the zoning of the building at 6941 South Paxton had been researched by office staff. "According to the Department of Inspectional Services, City of Chicago, if three or more unrelated adults were to occupy this building it could be considered a special-care facility. It is a special-care facility, Thresholds must acquire a special permit, which could be blocked by a restraining order. The community could determine this by having the Department of Inspectional Services inspect the building once the Thresholds people move in." The alderman went on to say that the community had three options:

1. Have the city file a suit. This would be a free service, but the suit could take a long time to come to court.

2. The community could hire their own lawyer to file a suit. This could be expensive but the suit would go through the system more quickly, and the community would have more control over the suit.

3. The community could wait and see what it is like to have Thresholds in the community.

The residents of the community decided to hire a lawyer who would use the city's zoning department as a legal tool to prevent the halfway house from locating in the O'Keefe neighborhood area. The O'Keefe neighborhood council hired a lawyer to represent them and to inform the director of Thresholds of their actions. A letter from the lawyer to the Director of Thresholds was explicit in stating the community's present construction of local sentiments and values in their area:

> The size of the building and the interior alterations made will accommodate many more than the limit of two unrelated persons per unit, which city ordinances sets as the maximum to avoid imposition of the requirement of obtaining a special use zoning variance. The neighbors of the building are aware of the legal remedies available to them should your organization attempt to occupy the building in violation of the law. They hope that no such violation will occur but are prepared to oppose it if it does.[3]

This strategy of using the legal process to prevent the halfway house from locating in the neighborhood resembles actions taken by governments and communities throughout the country who have used zoning regulations to block the establishment of halfway houses (cf. Odenwald, 1985; Paterson and Craig, 1985). It also resembles attempts used by local urban whites in the 1960's to prevent public housing from being built in

their communities and blacks from moving into their
neighborhoods (Rossi and Dentler, 1961; Goodwin, 1979).

The alderman provided the community with information
that could be used to substantially increase their
chances of controlling their emotional, social, and
economic interest in the community.   That is, the
Alderman provided the community a political   resource.
The community's connection with municipal
government, through the alderman, allowed residents of
South Shore to determine the most effective course of
action and the degree of economic and social investment
needed to produce the desired outcome for constructing
local sentiments and values in the community and
preserving their class interest.

The director of Thresholds, after being notified of
the community's position through their lawyer, responded:

> I have received your letter and, of
> course, will refer it to our attorney
> for a more formal reply. We have,
> of course, no desire to utilize the
> building in violation of the law and
> will not do so. The response of the
> neighborhood, however, in immediately
> hiring an attorney without first
> trying to sit down with us and talk
> about the situation puts us in an
> adversarial relationship which I do
> not desire.[4]

The director went on to state:

> In the early 1960's, I was Chairman
> of the Fair Housing Committee in
> Teaneck, New Jersey. The object of
> that committee was to insure that
> black people could buy houses in
> white neighborhoods and that real
> estate brokers should show such
> houses. It was my modest effort at
> that time (before I was involved with
> Thresholds), to demonstrate that fair
> housing is for everyone, regardless
> of race or disability. The arguments
> as, "our property value will go
> down," "we don't want 'them' in our
> neighborhood," "our neighborhood will

go down in ruins," etc. It is all
nonsense, of course, and indicates
unnecessary fearfulness at its heart.
In 1963, I fought like a tiger for
the right of the black people to move
into white neighborhoods. It's 1984
now and the clientele has changed,
but my attitude has not.[5]

This appeal to the sympathies of middle-class blacks
in South Shore did not reduce the conflict. Residents
of South Shore largely ignored the appeal and awaited
Thresholds' next move.

The black middle-class residents of South Shore
constructed these local sentiments and values not only
because of their attachment to the geographical area and
their emotional, social, and economic interests in the
community, but also because of the external constraints
imposed on the local community by the interpenetration
of social policy in mental health institutionalization.
The social organization of South Shore did not rest on
the assumption of community deterioration, but on the
concerted effort, on the part of local residents, to
maintain and control within South Shore's boundaries
external organizations that would directly affect its
cultural and social identification of residential
stability, its status, and its self-respect.

DISCUSSION

The construction of local sentiments and values in
South Shore can be understood in terms of the "emergent
perspective" on urban neighborhoods (Hunter, 1983). This
perspective considers local community sentiments and
values as either the "product of new and emerging
reconstructions or see neighborhoods as occasionally
playing a critical role in the organization of modern
urban life" (Hunter, 1983: 185). Earlier versions of
this perspective were grounded in the concept of
"community of limited liability" (Janowitz, 1967).
Although this concept offered insight into why certain
residents had limited attachments and orientations to
their community--a question best viewed from an exchange
perspective (Blau, 1967)--it did not take into account
the internal class diversity of local urban relationships
and the form in which those relationships would manifest
themselves in material and social resources that could

increase the effectiveness of residents in warding off social policy interpenetrations of the larger urban structure.

The social policy change in mental health institutionalization that eventually produced the policy of deinstitutionalization are confounded by the local people who must confront such a policy at the level of the urban community. Indeed, policies that emanate from larger forces in urban society are not isolated from the local social forces that may determine their success or failure. The middle-class blacks in the urban community of South Shore were willing and able to construct local sentiments and values that challenged a state-level policy which directly affected their conception of community and their class interests at the local neighborhood level.

The emergent perspective on urban neighborhoods shows that the basis for constructing local sentiments and values directly affects the class interests of middle-class residents and does not lead to positive outcomes for external urban institutions. In fact, what appeared on the surface to be "limited involvement" was in reality a middle-class group of individuals maintaining and constructing their emotional, social, and economic interests in the community. These constructed local sentiments and values were constituted by the larger urban constraints of deinstitutionalization and the local conditions in which such a policy was introduced.

Local middle-class black residents of South Shore are not bound by ideological appeals, but by what they perceive to be of immediate concern to their local community and class interests. Indeed, the social processes that generate the construction of local sentiments and values in urban communities within larger urban areas will continue and are not restricted to non-blacks. Rather, they are based upon the principles of social organization rooted in the pragmatics of community life.

This analysis has shown that, in this case, social policy in mental health institutionalization served not only to construct local sentiments and values, but also to strengthen the class position of middle-class black residents of South Shore and to encourage them to articulate their feelings in ways that had not been necessary before.

The lack of communication between Thresholds and the local middle-class black residents of South Shore reduced the chances that the social policy of deinstitutionalization would be successful. But, more importantly, local community sentiments and values were constructed by a network of urban channels--from a state bureaucracy, to a local municipal government, to a local urban community--which conveyed to local residents a collective responsibility to maintain their class interests and to control their corner of the world. The process of constructing local sentiments and values in a local middle-class black urban community preserves only the cyclical approach of social policy in mental health institutionalization.

NOTES

[1]Collection of data presented in this analysis was supported in part by the American Sociological Association's Minority Fellowship Program and a dissertation grant from the Cornerhouse Fund of New York.

[2]This paper was presented at the poster session for the Minority Fellowship Program Conference on Ethnic Minority Mental Health Research, Washington, D.C., April 24-26, 1986.

[3]Letter obtained from O'Keefe neighborhood area council meeting on August 24, 1984.

[4]Information obtained from an O'Keefe neighborhood area council meeting held August 24, 1984.

[5]Information from the August 24, 1984, O'Keefe Neighborhood council meeting.

REFERENCES

Bachrach, L. 1978. "A Conceptual Approach to Deinstitutionalization." Hospital and Community Psychiatry 29:573-578.

Blau M. Peter. 1967. Exchange and Power in Social Life. New York: John Wiley and Sons.

Clark, Terry N. 1975. "The Irish Ethnic and the Spirit of Patronage." Ethnicity 2:305-359.

Davidson, Jean. 1985. "On Their Own, Mentally Ill Left Out In the Cold." Chicago Tribune March 3:1

Duncan, Otis D., and Beverly Duncan. 1957. The Negro Population of Chicago: A Study of Residential Succession. Chicago: University of Chicago Press.

Franklin, John H. 1980. From Slavery to Freedom: A History of Negro Americans. New York: Alfred A. Knopf Publishers. Fifth Edition.

Frazier, E. Franklin. 1957. Black Bourgeoisie. New York: MacMillan Press.

Genovese, Eugene D. 1972. Roll Jordan Roll: The World the Slaves Made. New York: Random House.

Goodwin, Carole. 1979. The Oak Park Strategy: Community Control of Racial Change. Chicago: University of Chicago Press.

Hannerz, Ulf. 1969. Soulsside: Inquiries into Ghetto Culture and Community. New York: University of Columbia Press.

Hunter, Albert. 1983. "Persistents of Local Sentiments in Mass Society." pp. 178-194 in R.L. Warren and L. Lyons (eds.) New Perspectives on the American Community. Illinois: Dorsey Press. Fourth Edition.

Janowitz, Morris. 1967. The Community Press in a Urban Setting: The Social Elements of Urbanism. Chicago: University of Chicago Press.

Kilson, Martin. 1981. "Black Social Classes and Intergenerational Poverty." The Public Interest. 64:58-78.

Koehler, Bob. 1984. "Room to Live: Debate rages over housing for the Mentally Ill." Lerner Newpaper. September 4:1-3.

McAdam, Doug. 1982. Political Process and the Development of Black Insurgency, 1930-1970. Chicago: University of Chicago Press.

Manley, Jr. Theodoric. 1986. "By the Color of Their Skins: Socio-Political Transformations in a Chicago Neighborhood." Unpublished dissertation. Department of Sociology, University of Chicago.

Mechanic, D. 1969. Mental Health and Social Policy. Englewood Cliffs, N.J.: Prentice-Hall.

Molotch, Harvey. 1972. Managed Integration: Dilemmas of Doing Good in the City. Berkeley: University of California Press.

Morris, Aldon D. 1984. The Origins of the Civil Rights Movement: Black Communities Organizing for Change. New York: Free Press.

Morrissey, Joseph P. 1982. "Deinstitutionalizing the Mentally Ill: Process, Outcomes, and New Directions." pp. 147-176. in W. Gove (ed.), Deviance and Mental Illness. Beverley Hills: Sage Publications.

Odenwald, Karl. 1985. "Zoning for Group Homes." Missouri Municipal Review 50(9):4-5.

Paterson, Andrea and Rebecca Craig. 1985. "Special Needs Housing: In Whose Backyard?" State Legislatures 11(10): 24-28.

Rossi, Peter, and Robert A. Dentler. 1961. The Politics of Urban Renewal: The Chicago Findings. Glencoe, Ill.: Free Press.

Sowell, Thomas. 1975. Race and Economics. New York: David McKay Company, Inc.

Suttles, Gerald D. 1972. The Social Construction of Communities. Chicago: University of Chicago Press.

Taeuber, Karl, and Alma Taeuber. 1965. Negroes in Cities. Chicago: Aldine.

Wilson, William J. 1980. The Declining Significance of Race: Blacks and Changing American Institutions. Second Edition. Chicago: University of Chicago Press.

_____. 1981. "The Black Community in the 1980's: Questions of Race, Class, and Public Policy." American Academy of Political and Social Science Annals. 454:26-41.

Zunz, Olivier. 1982. The Changing Faces of Inequality: Urbanization, Industrial Development and Immigrants in Detroit. Chicago: University of Chicago Press.

PART FOUR

URBAN PLANNING AND MANAGEMENT

VII

CHANGING EMPHASES IN PLANNING THE PARIS REGION: THE CASE OF LA DÉFENSE

Mary Jo Huth

INTRODUCTION

Since 1946, the population of the Paris Region (known officially since 1976 as Ile-de-France) has grown by some 3.5 million, the 1982 census recording its population at 10,056,100 or 18.6 percent of the total population of France. This has occurred despite the fact that, since 1975, the Paris Region's annual rate of growth (0.3 percent) has actually fallen below the national average (0.4 percent), due mainly to the country's falling birth rate and restrictions on overseas migration. But there is a regional factor involved as well. For example, between 1954 and 1962, the Paris Region received each year an average of 43,000 more migrants from the provinces (other parts of France) than it sent back to them. By 1968, however, the net gain had fallen to little more than 11,000 and, during the succeeding intercensal period (1968-75), there was a net loss of around 20,000 a year in the number of internal migrants to the Paris Region, a deficit which increased to 42,000 a year between 1975 and 1982 (Scargill, 1983). Clearly, then, the Paris Region no longer dominates the growth of the French population as it did for over 150 years. Many explanations have been offered for this demographic change, including the high cost of rent and property and the tedium of long home-to-work journeys in the Paris Region, but the national government prefers to interpret it as a direct consequence of its decentralization policies.

Not only has there been considerable population migration from the Paris Region to other parts of France during the past ten to fifteen years, but there has been a marked redistribution of population within the Paris Region over the last thirty years. For example, whereas the core of the Region--the **département** of Paris which corresponds to the twenty **arrondissements** of the old Cité--contained 39 percent of the Region's total population in 1954, it accounted for only 21.6 percent

of it by 1982. Moreover, during this same period, while
the proportion of the Region's population living in the
inner suburbs--the three **départements** of Hauts-de-Seine,
Seine-Saint-Denis, and Val-de-Marne--rose very slightly
from 36.3 percent to 38.8 percent, the proportion
residing in the outer suburbs--the four départements of
Essonne, Seine-et-Marne, Val-d'Oise, and Yvelines--almost
doubled, from 22.4 percent to 39.6 percent. Additional
evidence of the spreading out of the Paris Region may be
found in the fact that the Parisian **agglomération**
(metropolitan area) suffered a small reduction in
population between 1975 and 1982 from 8,549,000 to
8,505,000, while the peripheral **villes moyennes**, such as
Melun and Mantes, experienced high growth rates. Thus,
at least part of the recent negative migratory balance
between the Paris Region and the provinces may be
attributed to the fact that the capital's dormitory ring
now extends well beyond the boundaries of the Region.
Parisian families have been increasingly moving out to
the **grands ensembles**, the new towns and estates of
pavillon housing built in recent years on the fringe of
the Paris Region and served by expressways and the RER
(Réseau Express Régional) rapid transit system (Lajugie,
1974).

**NEGATIVE EFFECTS OF RAPID SUBURBAN EXPANSION IN THE PARIS
REGION: 1920-1960**

Rapid expansion of suburbs in the Paris Region
began, however, after World War I, stimulated by the
speculative housing development associated with the
subdivision of farm holdings by **lotisseurs** and by the
expansion of the railroad network. These two factors led
to the creation of **lotissements**--tiny shanty-towns
located close to the mainline railways which featured a
variety of dwellings from converted buses and railway
wagons to do-it-yourself "villas" and which typically had
poor access to services such as schools and hospitals.
By 1936, the **lotissements** had spread out as far as
today's outer suburbs and their population exceeded that
of Paris itself. At the same time, because of the Great
Depression, housing construction in Paris and its inner
suburbs declined markedly, a trend which continued during
and after World War II. These years of neglect were
reflected in the census of 1954 which revealed that about
60 percent of all dwellings in the Paris **agglomération**
had been built before 1914 and that the average age of
housing in the City of Paris itself was 75 years.

Moreover, half to two-thirds of all dwellings in the City
of Paris and in its older industrial suburbs had only one
or two rooms, resulting in considerable overcrowding
(Rapoport, 1968).

Construction of the **grands ensembles** cited above was
the principal response to the housing crisis of the Paris
agglomération in 1954, initiating the second major stage
in the evolution of suburban Paris. These **ensembles**,
which, architecturally speaking, represented an
"urbanisme de volumes," grouped several thousand
dwellings in geometrically-arranged buildings with
barrack-like facades which were generally four to fifteen
stories high. For the young families who occupied them,
these dwellings were little better than "machines à
habiter." Moreover, the sites chosen for the **grands
ensembles** were frequently those left vacant by the
developers of the post-World War I **lotissements** because
they were considered unsuitable for housing due to their
steep slopes, proximity to unattractive features such as
quarries, or inaccessibility to the railways which tended
to follow the river valleys. Government-owned land was
also favored for the construction of the **grands ensembles**
because its use obviated lengthy negotiations with
private individuals and groups. Between 1954 and 1962,
over 500,000 dwellings were completed in the Paris
Region, but because its population grew by more than a
million during the same period, the census of 1962
revealed housing conditions that were little better than
those recorded eight years earlier (Rapoport, 1968).

Thus, congestion at the center and confusion in the
suburbs characterized the Paris Region during the early
1960's. In the City of Paris, housing was old and
overcrowded; there was little open space aside from the
Bois de Boulogne and the Bois de Vincennes on the
periphery of the city, which together constituted 1,840
of the total 2,200 hectares of public open space; and
commercial buildings were ill-equipped to accommodate the
expanding office-based industries of the new post-
industrial society. Beyond the city, suburbs had grown
in a random, unplanned manner and frequently lacked even
the most basic services--notably, public transit, which
had become urgently needed in view of increasingly long
journeys to and from work. According to the census of
1962, an average home-to-work journey took one hour and
twenty minutes--a trip which typically involved the use
of a car or bus to reach the nearest railway station, a
twenty-minute or half-hour ride on a crowded train, a

short trip by metro, and a walk to the office.   In
addition to travel between the suburbs and Paris, the
prevailing pattern of commuting involved a large number
of reverse movements, from Paris to the suburbs,
especially by managers and executives, as well as
journeys between one suburb and another.   Considerable
congestion resulted from the cross movements of all the
people involved in different kinds of home-to-work
journeys, not to mention those involved in trips for
schooling and shopping.   However, perception of the above
problems tended to be obscured by the prosperity of Paris
relative to the rest of France and by the fragmented
nature of local government outside the city which acted
as a deterrent to a search for solutions which would
involve the entire Paris **agglomération** (Tuppen, 1980).

PLANNING FOR THE PARIS REGION FROM THE LATE 1920's TO THE PRESENT

One of the first to recognize the need to plan for
the entire Paris Region was Henri Sellier, who served as
a minister in the Poincaré government of the late 1920's.
A major weakness of the planning which ensued over the
next thirty years, however, was preoccupation with
present problems and failure to make proposals for
anticipated future developments.   Finally, in 1955, the
Office of Commissaire à la Construction et à l'Urbanisme
pour la Région Parisienne was established, but the
commissioner's duties were not fully defined until 1958,
when he was given responsibility for developing another
plan for the Paris Region.   Two years later, in 1960, the
commissioner published the Plan d'Aménagement et
d'Organisation Générale de la Région Parisienne (PADOG).
Underlying this plan was the assumption that the growth
of Paris could be controlled so that its population would
not exceed 9 million.   Moreover, the limits of the Paris
metropolitan area were defined by means of a firm
boundary beyond which was to be a "country zone," similar
to London's Green Belt, where development was to be
severely restricted, except in satellite towns such as
Mantes, Melun, and Fontainebleau.   But with the Paris
Region's population growing by more than 150,000 a year,
as many as 20,000 dwellings were constructed outside the
restricted zone within four years of PADOG's publication
(Pinchemel, 1979).

When PADOG's policy of physical containment was seen
to be unrealistic, it was abandoned in favor of a policy

which sought to accommodate growth, and it became
necessary to prepare a new plan for the Paris Region.
The District de la Région de Paris, established in 1961
as an établissement public with access to funds for
carrying out studies on the planning needs of the Region
and for devising programs to meet them, delegated
responsibility for developing a new plan to the Institut
d'Aménagement et d'Urbanisme de la Région Parisienne
(IAURP) which had been organized in 1960. Work on the
new plan, called the Schéma Directeur, was carried out
in relative secrecy during 1963 and 1964 in order to
prevent land speculation at sites where proposals for
development were being made. Revealed to the public in
June, 1965, the Schéma Directeur was based on several
fundamental assumptions, the first being that the urban
populations of the Paris region and of France as a whole
would reach 11.6 million and 44 million, respectively,
by the year 1985. However, this proportional
relationship--26 percent--would be somewhat lower than
that revealed by the 1962 census--29 percent. A second
major assumption underlying the 1965 Schéma was that the
4 million employed persons in the Paris Region enumerated
by the 1962 census would increase to 6.2 million by 1985.
More than two-thirds of this increase was attributed to
growth in the service sector of the economy; expansion
of the industrial labor force was not expected to exceed
30 percent of the 1962 total. The Schéma's proposals
were based on a third assumption that there would be a
doubling of the amount of land devoted to industry, a
tripling of that allocated to offices, and a quadrupling
of that used for residential purposes in the Paris Region
by the year 2000, because the authors of the Schéma
stressed the importance of providing more space for all
functions. Fourthly, the Schéma anticipated that
purchasing power in the Region would increase three to
four times by the end of the century and that there would
be a similar increase in the number of trips undertaken
daily by all modes of transport, because the former trend
would probably result in more leisure-time activity,
shopping, and private vehicle ownership (Pinchemel,
1979).

To accommodate the changes cited above, the Schéma
Directeur of 1965 recommended the establishment of two
preferential growth axes to reduce traffic congestion on
the Region's radial thoroughfares, and the construction
of eight new towns large enough to provide a magnitude
of employment and a range of services sufficient to
offset some of the dominance of central Paris. The two

growth axes would follow the general direction of the Seine River valley--from southeast to northwest, one of them tangential to the Paris **agglomération** (metropolitan area) in the north and the other similarly so in the south. Along these axes, it was proposed to develop the eight new urban communities--three in the north and five in the south--for populations of 500,000 to one million each. These new towns, together with the seven suburban communities proposed for redevelopment at other nodes along the preferential axes (**pôles restructurateurs**), were expected to absorb at least two-thirds of the Paris Region's anticipated population growth by the year 1985. However, special attention was given to the preservation of open spaces between the proposed new towns and throughout the Seine River valley. Moreover, extensions of the RER rapid transit system were planned to expedite travel to central Paris, as well as along the two new growth axes (Kain, 1982).

While the 1965 **Schéma Directeur** was formally adopted by the Council of the Paris District in 1966, publication of the 1968 census data led to reassessment of its proposals. Not only was a decelerating rate of national population growth observed, but the migrational pull of Paris relative to the remainder of the country was shown to be on the decline, reducing the need for new towns within the Paris Region. Moreover, 75 percent of the new jobs created during the 1960's were located west of central Paris, so that 62 percent of the region's employment was found to be concentrated in this area. Thus, a problem of internal economic disequilibrium had developed during the intercensal period (1962-68). Also, because a large number of new office jobs were created in central Paris while the resident population declined, longer journeys to work were being incurred and the public transit system was facing the problem of mounting operational costs and deficits. Administrative changes which became effective on January 1, 1968, including the establishment of an executive position called **Préfet de Région**, which strengthened the planning powers of the Paris Region, also made it appropriate to re-examine the **Schéma Directeur** of 1965. Thus, to take account of the changed circumstances cited above, a revision of the **Schéma** was undertaken in 1969 (Evenson, 1979).

In recognition of the declining rate of population growth in France as a whole, as well as in the Paris Region, the revised **Schéma** reduced the number of proposed new towns from eight to five and lowered their projected populations from the 500,000-1 million range to the 300,000-500,000 range. Reflecting the need to strengthen employment opportunities in Paris' eastern suburbs, all three new towns originally proposed for this area--Cergy-Pontoise, Marne-la-Vallée, and Evry--were retained. However, of the five originally proposed for the western suburbs, only two remained. Plans for the proposed new town of Beauchamp northwest of Paris were scrapped because further consideration led to two conclusions-- that the town would be too close to Cergy-Pontoise and that the wooded countryside in that area should be preserved; a new town proposed for the area south of Mantes was likewise never developed to avoid jeopardizing plans for another new town at Le Vaudreuil in the lower Seine Valley; the two new towns planned near Trappes were combined into one, named Saint-Quentin-en-Yvelines, which was constructed sufficiently far from Versailles so as not to adversely affect this historic site; and the proposed new town of Tigéry-Lieusaint, renamed Melun-Sénart, was relocated southwards to avoid thwarting the success of Evry and duplicating the facilities at Melun. The original **Schéma's** plan to restore and reinvigorate seven centers in the older, inner suburbs was retained, as was support for extension of the RER rapid transit system (Tuppen, 1979).

While the Council of the Paris District did not approve the 1969 revised **Schéma** until July, 1976, this did not prevent immediate implementation of many of the plan's proposals. However, the door was thereby left open for further revisions which were, in fact, undertaken in 1975, partly in response to that year's census findings. As indicated above, the 1968 census had revealed a decline in the migrational pull of the Paris Region, a trend confirmed by the 1975 census, so that the population of 11.6 million predicted for 1985 by the 1965 **Schéma** was now being projected for the year 2000. Consequently, the target populations for the five new towns planned as foci of employment and higher-order services in the outer suburbs were cut back to 200,000. Moreover, the oil crisis which had begun in 1973 strengthened the case of ecologists who were advocating greater investment in public transit and the omission of several radial roads which would converge on the already congested Boulevard Périphérique. Indeed, concern for the environment in general was much more evident in the 1975 **Schéma** than in earlier editions of the document.

Thus, there were proposals for better hospitals, higher education facilities, and shopping provisions in the suburbs, and lengthening home-to-work journeys, as well as inner-city decay, were deplored. In particular, the plan designated five **zones naturelles d'équilibre** (ZNE) where it would be policy to preserve the landscape and protect farmers' interests and, at the same time, provide for the growing recreational demands of the population. These five zones combined occupied 20 percent of the total area of the Paris Region, constituting something akin to a green belt. Greater tertiary-economic-sector investments were recommended for the seven **pôles restructurateurs** of the densely-populated older, inner suburbs of the Paris Region in order to improve the "quality of life" there as well. The 1975 **Schéma** received formal approval from the Council of the Paris District on July 1, 1976, the date when the official name of the Paris Region became Ile-de-France and the Region acquired planning powers similar to those of the twenty-one other French planning regions. During the past ten years, the direction of planning in Ile-de-France has become increasingly oriented toward improvements in the physical and social environments. For example, in the interest of reducing residential densities, efforts have been made to satisfy the growing desire for single-family dwellings and the target populations of the Region's five new towns in the outer suburbs have been lowered to between 100,000 and 200,000. At the same time, Ile-de-France has completed redevelopment of the seven inner-suburban **pôles restructurateurs** cited in the 1975 **Schéma**--Saint-Denis, Bobigny, Rosny, Créteil, Rungis, Vélizy-Villacoublay, and, the largest, La Défense, which the remainder of this paper will discuss in detail (Katan, 1981).

LA DEFENSE: PARIS' LARGEST AND MOST SPECTACULAR RESTRUCTURED SUBURB

In the late 1950's, La Défense was a typical untidy suburb in the western inner ring of the Paris Region with narrow streets, small factories, and poor housing. The decision to restructure La Défense was made in 1955 when the Office of Commissaire à la Construction et à l'Urbanisme pour la Région Parisienne, cited earlier in this paper, was established. Principal reasons for the decision were to relieve pressure on central Paris where office accommodation had reached the saturation point, to improve the flow of road traffic through the Paris

Region, and to modernize La Défense itself in the best French tradition.   In 1958, a special board--the Etablissement Public d'Aménagement de la Défense (EPAD)- was set up to oversee the planning and development of La Défense, the most grandiose project carried out in the Paris Region since the Second Empire over 120 years ago. Built on an extension of Paris' east-west axis leading from the Louvre to the palace at Saint-Germain-en-Laye, La Défense derives its name from its location at the exact point where the defenders of Paris put up their last resistance to the Germans in 1871 during the Franco-Prussian War.   A sculpture by Barrias in the center of La Défense commemorates the episode.   Covering an area of 760 hectares in the districts of Courbevoie, Puteaux, and Nanterre, and set in a bend of the River Seine, La Défense stands on a natural rise (the low hill of Chantecoq) nine kilometers from Notre Dame Cathedral and four kilometers from the Arc de Triomphe (EPAD, 1985).

Three generations of architectural style are present in the business quarter of La Défense with its 40 tower-blocks.   Originally, the plan was to build tower-blocks with a maximum height of 100 meters, but to cover the financial objectives of the project and to satisfy the increasing demands from business, an amended plan was drawn up in 1972 allowing office buildings 180 meters high, thereby expanding the usable ground area by 50 percent.   In 1980, a further generation of tower-blocks was added as architectural ideas evolved to take account of the demand from business for energy-saving features. Representative of the first generation of tower-blocks is the Crédit Lyonnais Building with its 25 floors, while the Fiat Building with its 45 floors and 22 elevators, which are the fastest in La Défense (7 meters per second), is representative of the second generation of tower-blocks, and the Elf Building--the highest one in La Défense at 180 meters and just completed in 1985--is representative of the third generation of tower-blocks, being so designed that all its offices have direct sunlight.   Contrary to what certain views from the periphery might lead one to believe, the ground level density of the business area at La Défense is moderate; the plot ratio is below 2.5, which is comparable to those districts in Paris laid out by Haussman (EPAD, 1985). In another sense, however, La Défense has the densest concentration of business activity in Europe, with 330 national and international businesses, ranging from banks to petrochemical companies and from computer to engineering firms, located in the center's 40 tower-

blocks.   The most famous are Elf-Aquitaine, Esso, Mobil
Oil, and British Petroleum in the oil industry; Rhone-
Poulenc and Péchiney in chemicals; IBM in computers; and
UAP, GAN, and Winterthur in insurance.   However, EPAD has
also allocated 55 hectares of La Défense for the
establishment of small industrial and craft businesses
similar to those it expropriated when it began the
center's development.   Hence, 29 percent of the
approximately 50,000 employees in La Défense are managers
and executives, 16 percent are middle-ranking staff
persons, and 55 percent are clerical workers (EPAD,
1985).

But La Défense is also a place to live.   Its 15,500
dwelling units, ranging from subsidized housing for 4,200
families to the most luxurious apartments, house 20,000
people in the business quarter (160 hectares) and 30,000
persons in the much larger André malraux Park quarter
(600 hectares) (EPAD, 1985).   Designed by the landscape
architect, Sgard, Malraux Park has been modelled with
earth secured from excavations required for the
construction of the RER rapid transit system and the
motorway tunnels running through the business quarter.
Over 4,000 trees, 50,000 shrubs, and 100,000 plants
decorate the park, which is the largest created in France
since the days of Emperor Napoleon III over a century
ago.   Before EPAD took over the area, however, it was
literally a wasteland occupied by derelict factory
buildings, abandoned warehouses, and shanty-type
residences.   Today, Malraux Park contains Emile Aillaud's
cylindrical apartment towers decorated with clouds and
Kalisz's varicolored pyramid-shaped apartment blocks, old
people's homes, schools, sports centers, playgounds, the
1,000-seat Théâtre des Amandiers and its ancillary
exhibition halls and recording studios, the Maison des
Jeunes Musiciens, the Maison de la Culture de Nanterre,
the Paris School of Architecture, the Paris Opera's
Ballet School, and the main administrative buildings of
the Nanterre Préfecture whose boundaries encompass the
park.   A four-kilometers-long "green path" links Malraux
park to La Défense's business quarter and is a favorite
haunt of joggers (EPAD, 1982 and 1985).

From a distance, La Défense, with its spectacular
office towers, may look like an impenetrable fortress,
but, in reality, it is remarkably accessible.   The 3.5
kilometers-long ring road which encircles La Défense is
linked via side-roads to the twelve sections comprising
the business quarter, but these side-roads run beneath

the 40-hectare, pedestrian-only Esplanade where there are
also 25,000 underground parking places.   However,
priority has been given to public transport in planning
access to La Défense.   Since 1970, the fastest means of
access to La Défense has been the RER rapid transit
system.   On a route going from Saint-Germain-en-Laye to
Boissy-Saint-Léger, trains pass through La Défense every
three minutes, arriving five minutes later at the Etoile
de l'Arc de Triomphe, seven minutes later at the Opera,
and ten minutes later at the Les Halles station.   The
Saint-German-en-Laye to Boissy-Saint-Léger route also
makes connection with the line going out to the Paris
airport at Roissy and, beginning in 1986, will link up
with trains to Poissy and Cergy-Pontoise.   But the
station at La Défense, which is second in importance only
to that of Le Châtelet in central Paris, in addition to
serving the RER rapid transit system, accommodates 18
different bus routes and is a stopping point on the long-
established French National Railroad lines from Paris-
Saint-Lazare to Versailles and Saint-Nom-la-Bretèche.
Elevators and escalators provide easy movement between
the Esplanade and the underground car-parks and RER rapid
transit-bus-train station.   Thus, there are no streets
in the usual sense in La Défense, although there are
internal access roads open exclusively to buses (there
are 25 bus stops within the perimeter of La Défense),
taxis, and delivery vehicles, but these are covered with
footbridges for the safety of pedestrians who must cross
them.   The final phase of the La Défense traffic system
will involve the completion of the 14 Motorway which will
split into two tunnels under the pedestrian Esplanade--
one heading for the RN13 main road to Rueil and Saint-
Germain-en-Laye and, the other, for the RN192 main road
to La Garenne-Colombes and Pont-de-Bezons.   This new
motorway will enable 30,000 drivers to cross La Défense
in only a few minutes when heading out of Paris (EPAD,
1985).

     Like the ancient Roman Forum, the 40-hectare-area
Esplanade at La Défense, which is the largest pedestrian
precinct in the world, is a focal point for meeting and
community.   Here, the Exhibit Center (Centre National des
Industries et des Techniques or CNIT), planned to
accommodate shows that are too large for Paris' Grand
Palais, draws 4 million visitors a year.   Les Quatre
Temps, the Esplanade's shopping and leisure center, with
its 180 boutiques, Samaritaine Department Store, Auchan
Supermarket, 20 restaurants, ten cinemas, discotheques,
and art galleries, bustles with activity.   Youths roller

skate and wind surf on the Esplanade or splash about in its colorful ornamental pool, which forms a waterfall on one side, while men play France's most popular sport-- boules, and others sit on benches to eat a "brown bag" lunch, "people watch," and enjoy the natural landscaping, the sculptures, and live entertainment. During May and June, for example, folk singers, military bands, and classical ensembles play everyday from noon to 2 PM, providing the inhabitants of La Défense and the tower- block office workers with free cultural interludes to their day's work. Every weekend during September, close to Alexandre Calder's monumental spider stabile (a sculpture piece), a barter fair with over 250 stands draws thousands of visitors from all over the Paris Region, as do the summer night-time shows at Agam's mosaic pool, with its 66 mobile water jets rising 15 meters into the air. From 1972 onward, EPAD, La Défense's development agency, has involved a great many artists of international repute in bringing the suburb to life. In addition to Calder's spider stabile and Agam's mosaic pool mentioned above, sculptures such as Derbré's "The Earth," Silva's "Dame Lune," Moretti's "Monstre", Delfino's "Place of the Body," and De Miller's "Sleepwalker" are especially noteworthy artistic pieces at La Défense (EPAD, 1985).

In 1958, EPAD, under state control, was given 30 years to complete the task of clearing and rebuilding La Défense--a 760-hectare, densely-populated suburb directly linked to the historic heart of Paris: to equip it with road and rail infrastructure, to supervise its architectural development, to provide for the beautification of its open spaces, to ensure the project's economic viability, and to resolve any problems which might arise in connection with achieving these goals. Today, all of these objectives are well on the way to completion. There remains only the construction of the Tête Défense, which is planned to provide an apotheosis (a glorified ideal) of the project matching in splendor the Arc de Triomphe built by Napoleon I in 1806. In 1982, Francois Mitterand, President of the French Republic, decided to add "Tête Défense" to his list of grand architectural and town planning projects in order to create a new focal point on Paris' historic westward axis and to complete the development of La Défense. As the result of an international competition conducted between October 31, 1982 and March 1, 1983, EPAD received 424 entries. The Danish architect, Johan O. Von Spreckelsen, was declared the winner with his

entry, "Arc de Triomphe de l'Humanité," on May 25, 1983.
Cubical in form, this International Carrefour of
Communication, which is planned for completion in 1988,
will be situated between the CNIT Exhibition Hall and the
Quatre Temps Shopping Center at the junction of the
principal circulation routes serving La Défense. It will
provide exhibit, consultation, and debate facilities for
events and groups from all over the world, affording an
opportunity for residents and employees of La Défense,
as well as for visitors, to interact with one another and
with a variety of specialists, who will also have studios
and laboratories at their disposal. Not only will the
Carrefour be equipped with the latest communication
technology, but it will foster research in the
development of new communication methods and training in
their use. When announcing the winner of the Tête
Défense competition, Robert Lion, chairman of the
selection jury, remarked: "Just as cathedrals symbolized
Christian civilizations and, palaces, the power of
monarchies, so Von Spreckelsen's Carrefour of
Communication will symbolize the future of modern
civilizations" (EPAD, 1985).

REFERENCES

Ardagh, John. 1980. France in the 1980's. Harmondsworth, England: Penguin Books.

Chaline, Claude. 1980. La Dynamique Urbaine. Paris: Presses Universitaires de France.

Clifford-Vaughan, Michaline, Martin Kolinsky, and Peta Sheriff. 1980. Social Change in France. New York: St. Martin's Press.

Etablissement Public d'Aménagement de la région de la Défense (EPAD). 1982. La Défense. Paris: Montmorency Impressions. 1984. Tête Défense. Paris: Electa France. 1985. La Défense. Paris: Montmorency Impressions.

Evenson, Norma. 1979. Paris: A Century of Change, 1878-1978. New Haven: Yale University Press.

Kain, Roger J. 1982. "Europe's Model and Exemplar Still? The French Approach to Urban Conservation, 1962-1982." Town Planning Review 53: 403-422.

Katan, Yvette. 1981. Paris et la Région Ile-de-France. Paris: Librairie Hatier.

Lajugie, Joseph. 1974. Les Villes Moyennes. Paris: Editions Cujas.

Metton, Alain. 1982. "L'Expansion du Commerce Périphérique en France." Annales de Géographie 506" 463-479.

Pinchemel, Philippe. 1979. La Région Parisienne. Paris: Presses Universitaires de France.

Rapoport, Amos. 1968. "Housing and Housing Densities in France." Town Planning Review 39: 341-354.

Rubenstein, Jilbert M. 1978. The French New Towns. Baltimore: The Johns Hopkins University Press.

Scargill, Ian. 1983. Urban France. New York: St. Martin's Press.

Tuppen, John. 1979. "New Towns in the Paris Region: An
    Appraisal." Town Planning Review 50: 55-70. 1980.
    "Public Transport in France: The Development and
    Extension of the Metro." Geography 65: 127-130.

VIII

INNOVATIONS IN URBAN ECONOMY
AND FISCAL MANAGEMENT:
CANADIAN PERSPECTIVES

Dan A. Chekki

INTRODUCTION

During times of fiscal restraint, urban governments are under pressure to think of innovative ways of minimizing public expenditure and maximizing revenue sources. In the context of urban fiscal strain (Clark and Ferguson 1983) and variations in political cultures in Canada and in the United States, it would be useful to examine the following hypotheses.[1]

1. Municipal political leaders in Canada are more conservative and less innovative in their response to fiscal pressures than Americans.

2. Given the variations in political culture among the Canadian regions, it is likely that some regions are more innovative than others.

3. The magnitude and severity of fiscal pressures tends to create the institutional response that transcends differences in political culture which might otherwise limit innovative action.

4. Municipalities experiencing the greatest economic strain seem to be more likely to adopt more drastic cost-cutting strategies than their more fortunate counterparts.

Also, we can raise questions such as: Whether or not some service delivery sectors are more susceptible to innovative activity than others; or more specifically, are 'soft' services more vulnerable than 'hard' or 'protective' services such as police and fire? Although these hypotheses and questions are of great theoretical interest and of practical importance, additional data are necessary to test these hypotheses. Hence, this paper has limited objectives. Its purpose is to delineate some of the major innovations in service delivery and fiscal management adopted, in recent years, by urban governments in Canada. This exploratory study, hopefully, will serve as a basis for generating and testing relevant hypotheses.

This study forms a part of an international research project on "Fiscal Austerity and Urban Innovation." Using similar questionnaires data were collected (Chekki 1983) from mayors, councilors, and chief administrative officers of 42 cities in the provinces of British Columbia, Alberta, Saskatchewan, and Manitoba. The sample included cities with a population of 10,000 and over according to the 1981 Census. Furthermore, additional data related to cities in different regions of Canada were culled from a series of bulletins issued by the Federation of Canadian Municipalities.

Innovations may refer to any concept, strategy, method, technology or program which has not been widely adopted by local governments and which produces a cost saving without a corresponding reduction in the level of service. To be innovative, an idea or program does not have to be brand new. There may be things in a community that have been done in recent years that work very well, but which because they are not widely used in other communities -- would be novel to others. Accordingly, an item classified as an innovation might be intrinsically new or it might only be new to the setting in which we find. What is crucial is the perceived newness of the idea for the community. If the idea seems new to the community it is an innovation (Rogers 1983; Brown 1981).

To know whether an innovation is resulting in cost savings and/or increased efficiency, productivity or quality of service, it is helpful to have monitored its implementation carefully. For instance, some communities may think that they were saving money for contracting out services. But in fact they may neglect in accounting for the administrative costs of letting and supervising the contract, or of redeploying staff. This is not to say that contracting out services may not result in savings. It may or may not. But to know, one must be aware not only of the cost of the contract, but of all the hidden costs it entails.

Of course, some innovations do not result in readily measured cost savings. Most of those involving an immediate administrative or technological change do, but the savings that result from long-term programs, ongoing

projects or major policy decisions, the ones that
represent investments in the future of a community,
rarely   lend   themselves   to   precise   cost   saving
measurement. Parks and cultural or recreational programs
are frequently criticized as being mere frills. Such
programs, or the facilities associated with them, may be
poorly   or   wastefully   managed   of   course   --   and
improvements on that score can be measured -- but the
real pay offs are in improved health or a greater sense
of well-being, and you cannot measure the cost of medical
bills that were not incurred or of public services that
did not have to be deployed as a result of the presence
of such programs or facilities. They are nonetheless,
cost savings. As well, since a high quality of life,
which is dependent on cultural, recreational and physical
amenities, is known to be a major factor in business
location decisions and in attracting tourism, its
cultivation can pay off, albeit immeasurably.

Downtown revitalization schemes are another example
of long-term investments for which immediate cost savings
are   either   non-existent   or,   at   best,   difficult   to
measure. Still, it is readily apparent that a thriving
Main Street is good for the municipal economy. What can
be assessed with respect to such long-term investments
is not their own cost savings of their immediate
financial returns but the quality and efficiency of the
way in which a municipal government undertakes and
manages them.

Municipalities are increasingly employing computer
technology.   As   a   consequence,   future   staffing
requirements are going to change, as are the types of
service that can be offered. If as may be the case,
municipalities are saving money by cutting back on their
maintenance function, then it is possible that somewhere
down the road a rather large expense will be incurred.
To anticipate future needs and problems, and to identify
new opportunities, it is necessary to get as full a
picture of the municipal scene as possible.

In   our   study   (Chekki   1983)   of   urban   fiscal
management   strategies,   the   responses   of   chief
administrative officers of forty-two Western Canadian
cities   revealed   the   following   seven   innovative
expenditure strategies in rank order: reduce capital
expenditures, keep expenditure below inflation rate,
improve productivity through better management, impose
across-the-board   cuts   in   all   departments,   improve

productivity by adopting labor saving techniques, reduce work force through attrition, impose a hiring freeze. Among the innovative revenue strategies frequently used by urban government administrators are in rank order: increase taxes, increase user fees, obtain additional intergovernment revenues, drawdown surpluses, seek new local revenue, and increase long-term borrowing. Let us examine some of the specific innovative strategies adopted by municipalities in their effort to cut costs and maintain or increase the quality of services.

SERVICE DELIVERY

Having achieved high levels of service, it has become evident that quality, efficiency and equitability are no longer necessarily dependent on actual delivery of the service by the municipality itself. Municipalities have provided concessions, subsidies and incentives to stimulate or encourage the provision of public services by the private sector. Volunteers and self help neighborhood groups have been encouraged to undertake or participate in activities that benefit their own community. While contracting out such services as garbage collection, fire or police protection or parks maintenance has received the greatest attention, it is not the only cutback management technique in use. In combination with contracting out and other alternative service delivery methods, charging for the use of public services through user fees are also being employed.

Burnaby, British Columbia was faced with a choice between buying new garbage trucks or seeking a private firm to take over collection services. The most economical method of continuing to provide the service municipally entailed a switch to a two-man truck system from the old three-man trucks. Although this was not going to require the loss of jobs -- attrition combined with the need to service an expanded population made lay offs unnecessary. The resulting service is reported to be of an extremely high quality as well as being cost effective; the innovation is as much one of increasing productivity as of employing a new device.

In Etobicoke, Ontario, community's use of a private garbage collection service for 10% of the borough has given it the best of both worlds by introducing just enough of an element of competition to keep the 90% c? the system that is publicly-operated highly efficient.

In addition, this combined arrangement has paved the way for other municipal innovations. In-house options provide a novel way of municipally delivering services that may be more cost effective than a complete shift to a private operation. A few questions have been raised related to service. To what extent financial restraint is resulting in reduced levels of service and/or in reduced capital and maintenance budget allocations? The answer, with few exceptions, depends upon the circumstances in which the communities find themselves. The majority of communities indicated that a number of capital projects were either postponed or modified to reduce costs; and they are, contracting out at least one service to either the private sector or to community-based and volunteer organizations, but perhaps the most innovative technique employed is that of purchasing services inter-municipally.

Until a few years ago, Sudbury had what its mayor described as "perhaps the most deluxe service in all of Canada": five man crews, with two picking up garbage from the backs of houses, twice a week. Although long recognized as an extravagance, the political will to change the situation was a long time coming. Now, however, the city has made its service more efficient. Pickups have been reduced to once a week, backyard pickups have been cut out and the crews are down to three.

By contrast, Metro Toronto continues to have twice a week pickups with crews of from three to five, resulting in per capita costs ranging from $17 to $23 in its constituent municipalities -- an average that is almost 40% higher than Sudbury's per capita cost. Regina, too, has found that the task system offers a great incentive to increased efficiency. They estimate that since its inception, their crews are doing one-third more in half the time.

INTERMUNICIPAL ARRANGEMENTS

One of the primary rationales for establishing two tier or regional municipal governments has been that economies of the scale could be realized. Rather than having several separate police forces, planning departments, parks departments, and so on, a single department could serve several communities of varying size thereby avoiding duplication of services and

additional costs.   The region of Hamilton-Westworth has
been working to overcome these problems by entering into
a number of purchase of service arrangements with
municipalities in the region.   Engineering, real estate
and computer time are among the other functions being
provided to individual municipalities on a fee for-
service-basis.   In addition, a cooperative purchasing
program that allows for savings by buying in large
quantities has been established.   On the whole, these
arrangements are permitting duplication to be avoided and
efficiency maximized.   A second level of government is
not, however, a necessary feature of such arrangements.
Sherbrooke, Quebec, for instance, is providing police,
fire and transit services to several neighboring
communities on which might be called a "contracting-in"
basis.   Here a balance has had to be struck between
providing service of a quality to warrant its use and
offering one of such a high quality that people might be
induced to move out of Sherbrooke.

ENERGY MANAGEMENT

Cutting down on energy is without a doubt one of the
easiest, most straight forward ways a municipality can
save money on its operating expenses.   With this in mind,
almost all of Canada's municipalities have taken steps
to conserve energy.   Turning out unneeded lights,
switching from gasoline to propane powered vehicles,
changing from mercury vapor to sodium street lights,
cutting idling engines, sealing doors and windows and
insulating municipally owned buildings are all becoming
standard practice.   A sizeable number of communities is
now moving beyond this first step to undertake
sophisticated energy audits that will enable them to
realize the maximum savings possible on their fuel and
electrical bills.

Some municipalities are finding ways to make money
while they save energy.   Montreal, for example, is
turning refuse into a marketable commodity, steam.
Refuse burned at Montreal's Des Carrieres incinerator is
now generating steam which the city is using for some of
its own buildings and distributing to seventeen
industrial customers at a cost of 20 cents below that of
steam produced with natural gas.   Net revenue for the
first year is estimated at about $2 million.   At this
rate, investment costs should be recovered in about three
years.   The city of Winnipeg has plans to introduce a

similar plant to convert garbage into steam for heating
downtown buildings. Several Canadian cities are using
computers to monitor energy consumption in municipal
facilities. Energy management is not a new priority for
the council and staff of the Hamilton-Westworth region.
It undertook a comprehensive energy audit of 134
buildings owned or leased by the region which enabled it
to reduce its approximately $2.4 million annual energy
expenditures by between $200,000 and $300,000. Hamilton-
Westworth's commitment to encouraging energy conservation
activities that are economically justifiable has resulted
in one of the most comprehensive and innovative energy
management programs in Canada.

TRENDS IN MUNICIPAL BUDGETS

The Federal government fiscal austerity program
seems to have an effect on local government budgets.
This effect is being compounded by the caps placed on
increases in some provinces' grants to municipalities.
In Alberta, a five percent increase is in effect. In
Nova Scotia, $11 million was trimmed from the $38 million
in capital and operating grants to municipalities. What
are the effects of such cuts in grants to municipal
governments? Will it lead to higher property taxes
and/or reduction in services provided to citizens? What
trade-offs are being made to cover short falls? We do
not have adequate information as yet to answer these
questions.

The following, however, offers some interesting
insights on the problems faced by some urban communities.
In Vancouver, expenditures have risen by just slightly
more than 6% per annum in 1982 and 1983. The main change
to the city's budget has been the decline in Provincial
transfer payments from about $31 million in 1981 to $17
million in 1983 (from 13.8% of all revenues to 6.9%).
Edmonton's overall 1983 budget increase was kept to 6.5%,
and the mill rate[2] increase was held at 8%, a
considerable reduction from the 17% increase of 1982.
The provincial government under increasing pressure from
a rising operating deficit, put a 5% cap on 1983 grants
to municipalities. For Edmonton, even by eliminating
virtually all discretionary expenditures, it was evident
that the budget could not be balanced without some
adjustment for wages and salaries. With the exception
of police, who agreed to a reduction in certain fringe
benefits in return for foregone layoffs, civic unions

showed little interest in deferring 1983 increases or renegotiating the second year of their contracts. Attrition began dropping sharply in late 1982 and it is now a negligible factor in reducing civic expenditures. This left the city with no option but to institute a program of staff reductions.

Transfer payments affect the day-to-day operations of most municipal programs. Richmond (1981:170) noted, "Being creatures of the provinces, the municipal sector in each province has been molded by the style, philosophy and legislative characteristics of the respective provincial governments." He found it difficult to make interprovincial comparisons about the provincial-municipal transfer systems because of the size, composition and responsibility of the municipalities vis-a-vis the provincial sector vary from province to province.

As a percentage of the general revenue, the municipal property taxation in 1978 varied from province to province ranging from 31% in Alberta to 55% in British Columbia. A longitudinal study (Richmond 1981:200) showed that during the period of 1971 to 1978, property taxes as a proportion of total municipal revenue have (a) remained constant in Manitoba and Alberta (decreased in Alberta in 1979), (b) increased in Newfoundland and British Columbia, and (c) decreased in all other provinces.

In Halifax, the property tax share of total revenue has been declining (from 59.7% in 1979 to 53.8% in 1983). This is the result of the City's effort to protect tax payers from large tax increases by aggressively seeking revenue from other sources, i.e. investment income, fines, etc., and a marginally greater contribution from provincial transfers. On the expenditure side, most categories held a relatively constant share of the budget. The dramatic financial strategy has been in the capital budget. Responding to high interest rates, the city embarked on a program of funding the capital budget from general revenues rather than incurring debt.

MUNICIPAL REVENUES AND ECONOMIC DEVELOPMENT

The communities with the greatest dependency on the property tax maintain that it is an inappropriate vehicle for generating municipal revenues and that alternatives are needed. The majority of communities seem to be relying increasingly on user fees to offset some of the rising cost of services.

For the past several years, Surrey, British Columbia, has had an average annual population rate of about 4 to 6%. It recognized that this growth was going to put an enormous strain on its ability not only to provide basic infrastructure, but to construct the recreation facilities and other community buildings the new population was likely to demand. Its leaders were faced with two options: to hoist major tax increases on rate payers or to find an innovative means of financing all types of capital projects. By adopting a by-law to impose development cost charges, Surrey was able to insure that funds would be available from a source other than the property tax. To finance capital projects, Surrey adopted the policy of holding the development cost charge money it received until the following year and hired a money manager to invest the principal. Additional money for investment was obtained by making a practice of borrowing up to the total amount the municipality's borrowing authority whether the money was needed immediately or not. In the interim, the money manager had full use of the cash. The return on these investments has paid for all of Surrey's capital projects and allowed the municipality to keep the mill rate down.

In Ontario, like most of the other provinces, municipalities both administer welfare and social service programs and contribute 20% of the welfare costs and 50% of the administration costs. Unemployment in Ontario places a direct financial burden on local governments as well as reducing business and other tax revenues. This provides an added incentive for the province's municipalities to utilize government works programs to the fullest extent possible.

The city of Brantford, in which 4,000 jobs were lost when the Massey-Fergusson plant closed in 1980, adopted the policy of incurring that projects undertaken under job creation programs would be of lasting benefit to the community, rather than of merely a make-work nature, and low in long term maintenance costs.

Few communities have been left unscathed by the current economic situation. The desire to see new jobs created, to get closed plants back into operation, to get businesses back on their feet is universal. Even in times of prosperity, the vast majority of communities hope for at least enough expansion in the job market to hold young people, and enough new income to provide their residents with improved facilities and a higher quality of life.

Municipalities can do a great deal to foster economic development. They play a central role in generating economic growth by providing the infrastructure needed for economic activity. The quality of life, the quality of schools and the availability of cultural and recreational attractions, the local government's attitudes towards business and the existence of a market to be served are the primary considerations in business location decisions. In addition, municipalities traditionally have had very close ties to small businesses operating within their communities. These small businesses create as much as 80% of new private sector jobs.

Some Canadian cities have taken the lead in encouraging economic development. Vancouver, for instance, began work on an economic development strategy for the 1980's back in 1978. At that time, the city established an Economic Development Office to act as a catalyst in the creation of an industrial/commercial /public environment such that the business sector is strongly encouraged to undertake the projects that will provide a healthy balance both in employment opportunities and the city's tax base.

Since 1980, the city has used this agency to embark on the creation of such an environment. The Economic Development Office undertook surveys of business requirements for space and personnel, and of the business community's perceptions of the city's future, taxes, labor and other related matters and provided the necessary support and background information for the Vancouver Economic Advisory Commission, a body comprised of the upper echelons of Vancouver's academic, business, labor, government and consulting community.

Edmonton has also established an Economic Development Authority. This Agency is expected to take advantage of the expertise and knowledge that exist within the community to priorize the needs and abilities of that city. Other municipalities are also discussing the possibility of developing their own economic strategies. Though none of these can provide blueprints for the future, they do provide the municipality with a clear assessment of its strengths, and a means of utilizing them to their best advantage.

All of these efforts represent a marked change from the days when it was thought sufficient to merely advertise a community's existence and offer companies a few tax-free years and some cheap services. To avoid direct competition among cities for the same source of economic growth, Canadian cities have a Task Force to work together to plan and organize a comprehensive strategy for economic development. The task force has determined that a proactive rather than a reactive stance is vital to the orderly economic progress and financial stability of urban communities. The task force through exchange of information among communities and coordinating efforts works with other levels of government. It has established a variety of means to facilitate economic growth and create job opportunities in different communities.

ECONOMIC DEVELOPMENT: PUBLIC-PRIVATE VENTURES

The city and private sector joint urban development projects are not uncommon. The Charles Center-Inner Harbor Management, Inc., project established by the City of Baltimore and the city's Retail Merchants Association is a good example. In the U.K. businesses and government together established the Financial Institutions Group (FIG) for "urban regeneration."

Canada is not without its own examples of similar ventures. In Burnaby, British Columbia, for example, the city established the Loaned Executive Assistance Program (LEAP) which draws on the skills of corporate executives from such firms as Dairyland, Shellburn Refinery, B.C. Telephone and AEL Microtel for projects requiring specialized knowledge and a high degree of expertise. Those undertaken to date include development of a strategic long range plan for the municipal library system, analysis and development of food services at municipal recreation facilities, and establishment of a procedure for municipal vehicle maintenance and replacement.

The benefits of the program work both ways: the municipality gains from being able to draw on specialized skills, the private sector participants become more familiar with the way their community works and the problems it faces. Like other successful private and public joint ventures, LEAP is based on the assumption that municipalities and local companies have a common interest in improving their community, and that each has skills that can benefit the community if jointly deployed.

COST SAVINGS

Municipalities buy a lot. Their purchase in 1982 amounted to over $7.5 billion -- 25% more than federal government procurement -- or about 22% of all municipal expenditures. Since savings realized in this area can have a marked effect on a community's overall budget, it is little wonder that considerable attention is being devoted to formalizing and streamlining purchasing practices.

Regina, for example, estimates that by consolidating its parks and central stores, the city saved at least $25,000. In addition, by reducing overall inventory levels by approximately $500,000 in 1981, some $82,000 in carrying costs were avoided. Edmonton, too, is using its Common Inventory System (COINS) to keep stock levels down. The system uses a computer program which, incidentally, Edmonton has sold to the city of Montreal for $168,000.

COOPERATIVE PURCHASING

The municipal associations of British Columbia, Alberta, and the Northwest Territories are offering their members group insurance packages that reduce costs significantly. In Alberta cooperative buying scheme obtains savings for its members guaranteeing good service, high quality and a good price. The cooperative's sales for 1982 totalled $20.6 million with net earnings of $642,000. The city of Ottawa serves as a 'broker' for a 30-member purchasing cooperative in the National Capital region. Its members do not pay a fee, however, nor do they receive dividends. Rather they gain by purchasing selected items in bulk. Regionally based cooperative purchasing programs are operating on a smaller scale in Kitchener-Waterloo, Peterborough and Sarnia. Others are being established in Sudbury and

Hamilton-Westworth.   Similar,   often   less-structured
cooperatives exist across the country.

MANAGEMENT AND PRODUCTIVITY

The emphasis is now switched from the traditional
concentration on new ideas and methods to a focus on
total management strategies that will achieve the best
service for the least total cost. In the United States,
the current focus on improving public works maintenance
and management has been brought about by the extremely
critical condition of roads, bridges, sewers and other
infrastructure. Past neglect now demands a total, and
extremely costly, management approach. Canada is more
fortunate in being somewhat behind the United States.
The crunch here is still a bit in the future. There is
time   to   learn   how   to   prevent   such   extensive
deterioration. It is unlikely that any Canadian city
will encounter the 1975 fiscal crisis of New York. Yet
despite the differences in scale, the problems faced by
New York and a few other American cities do not vary
greatly in kind from those faced by Canada's cities.

In recent years, Edmonton has been facing unique
constraints   on   expenditure   reductions   because   of
extremely rapid growth and inordinately high arbitrated
wage settlements. The city of Edmonton has adopted
several measures to economize. New methods of reducing
tax-supported debt, better utilization of the city's
limited   reserves,   streamlining   tax   collecting   and
administrative procedures, increasing the cash flow
situation   and   productivity,   developing   alternative
revenue sources and seeking alternative private delivery
mechanisms for municipal services have contributed to
urban fiscal austerity program.

INTERNAL MANAGEMENT

Staffing, as well as being a resource, is a cost and
that cost has to be managed. In St. Albert, Ontario, a
lot of emphasis has been placed on the care and feeding
of staff resource. The care begins through labor
relations. Poor relations with unions will always cost
money, whether in pay out or loss of productivity. It
is felt necessary, particularly in times of restraint,
that the approach towards unions be one of problem
solving rather than the traditional one of "us-them"

confrontation. Over the past three years, St. Albert has adopted a no lay-off policy. Nonetheless, staff costs have been reduced by eliminating overtime except where essential and by better controlling sick leave and other unproductive time. At the same time, staff size has been reduced through attrition and staff are being encouraged to take additional unpaid time off.

In Oshawa, city's staff reduction from a high of 710 in 1978 to 648 in 1983 produced a cost avoidance for 1984 alone of about $1.8 million. This was done by forcing the administration to justify every replacement of any vacancy created, whether through quitting, retirement or transfer. The replacement of all vacancies must be approved by two separate committees of council.

Sherbrooke, Quebec has realized major savings, approximately 41 million in 1984, from staff reductions that are intended ultimately to cut the city work force by 20%. In addition to relying on attrition, the city has been buying out contracts. To date this has been done only for non-union workers, but an agreement is being negotiated to offer union employees compensation and accelerated pensions. The offer would be tagged to positions that are not to be replaced; should they ever be replaced, they would again be made union positions. Quebec City, meanwhile, has used departmental reorganization as a means of reducing its auxiliary employees from as many as 125 per year to 10 or 15.

ENHANCING MANAGERIAL EFFECTIVENESS

Among the major factors providing the impetus to improve municipal management skills in recent years is the growth in size and complexity of local government, wider acceptance of the notion that governments should be run along the same lines as private business and the growing pressure to cut costs and to give tax payers a good accounting of how their money is spent.

At the same time, there have been enormous strides made in developing the tools needed to achieve these aims. Computers and new management techniques are simultaneously a cause as well as a result of the push for greater efficiency and effectiveness. Ontario's Ministry of Municipal Affairs offers matching grants of up to $50,000 for improved management systems. In Ottawa, a $33,850 grant is being used to help the fire department develop an advanced computer aided dispatch (CAD) system that will simultaneously provide the dispatcher and crew with information on the structure and contents of a fire site and daily-monthly fire incident reports, etc. Mississauga has introduced an automated information retrieval system for its by-laws and council recommendations and resolutions. One of the particularly useful advantages of this retrieval system is that it allows "blind" searches; you don't have to know whether the material sought is contained in a by-law, a resolution or a recommendation, each of them is searched concurrently by topic.

Rarely do municipal financial audits in Canada have uncovered cases of graft, corruption or misappropriation of funds. That Canada's communities are squeaky clean is justifiably cause for pride. Unfortunately, a dollar spent legally is not necessarily a dollar spent wisely. It is not uncommon to find wasted dollars in existing programs due to inefficiencies, insufficient cost recovery and ineffectiveness.

Preparing and approving the annual budget has always entailed selecting priorities, weighing short-term benefits against long-term needs, picking projects and programs that give the greatest value and asking pertinent questions about revenue sources and unnecessary expenditures. But until recently, budgetary exercises were relatively straightforward. The technique employed could be called "applied common sense." Common sense is still needed. But the premise that the previous year's budget provides an adequate yardstick for allocating new funds no longer seems valid. Instead, councils and administrators are seeking new and more intricate ways of assessing programs and projects, of projecting long-term costs, of keeping track of expenditures and of forecasting revenues.

As part of its effort to balance demands for increasing, or at least maintaining, levels of service despite recessionary constraints on revenues, Regina embarked on a strategy of cohesive, rational corporate financial planning. The city of Regina determined that any new financial planning process would have to include development of multi-year expenditure budgets, development of three-to-five year plans by department managers and development of budgets by programs. As well, it was considered essential that the programmatic budgets incorporate the central feature of zero-base budgeting in that alternative levels of service were to be delineated.

The city's new budgeting system integrates the capital, operating and utility budgets and includes program reviews in a coordinated dynamic budget cycle. An aggressive revenue strategy has been established, as has a computerized budget control system. The role of the internal auditing division has also been expanded to include operational as well as financial reviews. The comprehensive approach to budgeting and fiscal control is allowing Regina to keep its mill rate increases to acceptable levels. The Zero-Base Budget (ZBB) and Financial Trend Monitoring System (FTMS) are being used in numerous Canadian cities.

The Quality of Working Life (QWL) program in Ontario is concerned with improving the workplace, making the work situation more humane, creating a working environment which is personally satisfying. The plea behind the QWL program is to involve employees in creating a setting in which the solutions to work-related problems can be resolved thereby increasing productivity. The program aims at reducing absenteeism, overtime, grievances and stress.

Quality circles have become one of the management phenomena of the 1980's. They are simply a group of five to ten employees who come together, usually from the same work area, to identify work-related problems, investigating causes and suggesting solutions. In effect they serve as internal consultants. Depending on their structure and tasks, operating costs for quality circles can be minimal while benefits can be substantial in terms of increased productivity, renewed effectiveness and enhanced communications.

In Regina the Participation Management Group is composed of people drawn horizontally from similar managerial levels throughout the organization to address such corporate side concerns as workload equitability, internal communications and paper flow. Using quality circle techniques the group was involved in clarifying administrative directives to department heads and eliminating redundant copies of Council meetings -- saving $8,000 to $10,000 annually. By improving meeting habits and increasing their effectiveness, i.e., a five percent reduction in the length of meetings, savings were estimated to be $50,000 per year. A few other proposals were intended to enhance corporate communication and increase productivity. Cambridge, Ontario, is in the process of setting up a participatory management program with some of the features utilized in the quality circle approach in order to increase productivity in the Department of Engineering and Public Works.

How much is a good idea worth? Edmonton and Fort McMurray have instituted employee awards programs for innovative ideas that lead to measurable cost savings valued at ten percent of the first year's net savings to a maximum of $10,000. In Fort McMurray, employees can gain five percent of the City's first year net savings.

Both communities are among those keen on rewarding staff for suggestions that save money, time or material. The awards programs they have developed also encourage ideas aimed at improving equipment, forms procedures or services to the public and eliminating or avoiding safety hazards, duplication, breakage or spoilage. Ideas that result in savings that cannot be measured in dollars are also acknowledged, by between $24 and $100 in Edmonton, and by a minimum of $50 in Fort McMurray. The aim of the program is to recognize employee involvement and initiative in improving municipal efficiency, productivity and service to the public. The programs provide a convenient method for eliciting ideas and a systematic, organized procedure for evaluating their worth.

British Columbia, Saskatchewan, and Nova Scotia have used several "Save-A-Buck" ideas such as reduction of staff hours from 40 to 32 in slow months, sharing seasonally used equipment with other municipalities, rather than having envelopes printed, a plate made for the postage meter, cutting the number of permits needed to construct a house from eight to three (cutting costs by 50% and staff time), staff parking plug-ins operating on 30 minute on/off intervals, using automatic sprinkler in parks (allowing less frequent grass cutting), etc.

NEW TECHNOLOGY

The introduction of new technologies, materials or equipment that increase the accuracy, quality and efficiency of municipal operations holds wide appeal for Canadian municipalities. In larger communities, computerized systems for information storage, job scheduling, purchasing, preparing financial statements, tracking bill collection, keeping tabs on permit applications, mapping and, of course, word-processing are being rapidly installed. Specialized programs, such as Public Technology Inc., Fire Station Location Package have been used in Ottawa, Regina, Oshawa, Red Deer, Sault Ste. Marie, Brampton and Kitchner.

Computers are far from being the only area in which technology is lowering costs. Energy conservation has sparked numerous examples of cost effective innovations. In Edmonton, for example, the Parks and Recreation Department undertook an energy management program in 1980 with notable results. Using a three-phase program of "quick-fix" items, "retro-fits" (such as changing from mercury vapor lighting to metal halide lights) and detailed analysis, the city was able to decrease kilowatt hour consumption in the first year by 42%, for an energy cost saving of 40%.

The borrowing powers of municipalities vary and are limited by provincial legislation. In general, long-term borrowing by municipalities is generally restricted for capital budget purposes and is also subject to provincial approval. The municipal government relies heavily on federal and provincial government grants to help defray the cost of its operations. In 1976, 70.8 percent of the provincial government conditional grants received by municipalities was for education, 9.0 percent for transportation and communications and 14.2 percent for health and social welfare.

With respect to the provinces, total unmatured debt increased by 70 percent between 1950 and 1960 and by 480 percent between 1960 and 1975. Similarly, municipal debt increased dramatically by tripling during the 1950 to 1960 period and then increasing 170 percent from 1960 to 1975. These trends reflect the growing public demand for goods and services under provincial and municipal jurisdiction, the limited tax capacities of these two levels of government, and their reluctance to increase taxes to the level that would be necessary to meet the rapidly growing expenditures (Strick 1978).

The most obvious thrust of the Federal government's fiscal austerity program introduced in 1982 was its emphasis on wage restraints and public sector spending. The majority of Canadian municipalities have endeavored to apply this Federal fiscal austerity policy not only to wages, but to property tax increases, to increases in gross expenditures and to all other areas within their jurisdiction. Saskatchewan, for example, adopted inflation minus 1% as its target for wage settlements. Both Calgary and Edmonton, Alberta's two largest municipalities, however, were locked into a settlement of 13.5% negotiated in 1981, still highly prosperous times for that province.

The aims of increasing efficiency, improving productivity and ensuring overall effectiveness in municipal government are now made imperative by these times of economic difficulty. Several management techniques have been used to elicit greater productivity, increase operational efficiency and, in general, ensure that the municipality gives good value for the money it collects.

DOING MORE WITH LESS

Although municipalities can justifiably claim to have been practicing restraint for longer than other governments, their search for innovative ways of doing more with less on a systematic basis is of fairly recent origin. While municipalities experiencing the greatest economic stress are more likely to have adopted more drastic cost-cutting strategies than their more fortunate counterparts, the diverse programs and policies illustrate that there are few areas of municipal responsibility being overlooked in the drive to utilize public funds more effectively and efficiently regardless of economic circumstances.

Despite the seeming diversity of the specific restraint measures introduced there is a readily identifiable set of factors underlying the adoptions of these various programs and policies. In the area of internal management, municipalities are focusing on productivity improvement. To achieve this aim, greater emphasis is being placed on more highly-skilled and creative managers and on employee participation. This is leading to a greater willingness to invest in good training and development programs and to various employee suggestion and award programs. Although efforts are being made in this direction, it is clear that there is much to be done to develop appropriate incentives to motivate municipal staff and management. Change must be made to seem desirable rather than threatening.

In the area of service delivery, municipalities are endeavoring to determine exactly what the public desires and needs. To do this, no one is trying to reduce the number and range of services available to citizens. Instead, local governments are learning to distinguish between what they must provide and what can be provided by other sectors within the community. They are also starting to set standards for delivery that will meet safety requirements and the stated aims of residents, rather than relying solely on past practice as a basis for determining effectiveness. Again, while efforts are being made in these directions, few municipalities have developed systematic techniques to implement these practices across the board, for the full range of services they provide.

The findings of a recent survey (Chekki 1985) of citizen attitudes toward city services and taxes in Winnipeg show an overwhelming majority of citizens favor a policy of increasing property taxes only when necessary to maintain existing services. It seems that citizens want existing services to continue even if it involves necessary tax hikes. However, citizens seem to resist significant tax increases to maintain existing services.

For the time being, municipalities seem more willing to rely on traditional resources of revenue other than the property tax and other levels of government. Furthermore, they are laying greater stress on ensuring that government funds are better targeted to meet their needs and on developing more enterpreneurial attitude toward the conduct of their own affairs. To act on this basis, municipalities must have a clear understanding of their needs and objectives. Inroads are being made in the areas of economic forecasting and financial planning, but many of the tools needed to undertake these activities are in their infancy. There seems to be widespread agreement that if municipalities are to set and achieve objectives appropriate to today's economic situation, public participation and good public relations are essential.

One of the major problems facing the municipal government is the lack of correlation between expenditure needs and revenue sources. The financial burden experienced by urban governments has become increasingly acute during the past decade. The growth of urban communities, the deterioration of the city core, of suburbs, the growing public demand for goods and services, inflation, recession, the growing municipal debt, limited tax capacities, and reluctance to increase taxes have increased the strain on municipal finances. In the years to come these trends are unlikely to change. Moreover, the huge budget deficits of the Federal and Provincial governments and the recent efforts at reducing these deficits will lead to increased fiscal strain forcing municipal governments to innovate in the near future.

NOTES

[1]The author wishes to thank Terry N. Clark, University of Chicago and two of the anonymous reviewers for their helpful comments on an earlier version of this paper.

[2]"The first step in the imposition of the property tax is to place a value on, or assess, the property. The tax rate is then applied, determined by revenue need, and expressed as mills per dollar of assessed value. A mill is equal to one-tenth of one cent. For example, if property is assessed at $10,000 and a tax rate of fifty mills is levied, the tax will amount to 5 cents per dollar of assessed value or $500." (Strick 1978:91).

REFERENCES

Brown, Lawrence A. 1981. Innovation Diffusion: A New
    Perspective. London New York: Methuen.

Chekki, Dan A. 1983. Urban Innovation in Fiscal
    Management. (Unpublished Mss.)

_____. 1985. Citizen Attitudes Toward City Services
    and Taxes. Research and Working Paper 13.
    Winnipeg: Institute of Urban Studies. University
    of Winnipeg.

Clark, Terry N. and Lorna C. Ferguson. 1983. City
    Money: Political Processes, Fiscal Strain, and
    Retrenchment. New York: Columbia University Press.

Richmond, Dale E. 1981. "Provincial-Municipal Tax and
    Revenue Sharing Reforms Accomplished, 1978 compared
    with 1971". pp. 162-201 in Lionel D. Feldman (ed.),
    Politics and Government of Urban Canada: Selected
    Readings, Fourth Edition. Toronto: Methuen.

Rogers, Everett M. 1983. Diffusion of Innovations.
    Third Edition. New York: The Free Press.

Strick, J.C. 1973. Canadian Public Finance. Second
    Edition. Toronto: Holt, Rinehart and Winston of
    Canada.

PART FIVE

PROBLEMS, POLICY AND DEVELOPMENT

IX

RECONSTRUCTING PATTERNS OF CRIME IN
HALIFAX AND SAINT JOHN:
A PRELIMINARY HISTORICAL ANALYSIS

Peter McGahan

A continuing need in the study of urban crime is
analysis of comparative and historical data.
Identification of criminogenic patterns requires
consideration of an array of community settings over time
(Robinson, 1982; Woods, 1983; Brantingham and
Brantingham, 1984). Recent years, indeed, have seen what
some scholars have characterized as an "explosion of
interest in the history of crime" (Jones, 1981:1), as "a
scholarly coming of age" (Lane, 1980:2)--especially in
Britain and the United States (e.g., Schneider, 1978;
Monkkonen, 1975; Lane, 1979; Field, 1981; Tobias, 1967,
1979; Philips, 1977; Sindall, 1983). Although less
extensive in Canada, valuable research in this country
has been conducted on the types of offenses in a variety
of nineteenth-century communities. These include, for
example, studies of the nature of crime in Southern
Alberta between 1878 and the turn of the century
(Thorner, 1979), of the "criminal class" in
industrializing Hamilton (Katz, etc., 1982), and of the
sources of violence in the Ottawa Valley of the 1830's
(Cross, 1973). Consideration has been given to how
social control has been exercised in an industrializing-
capitalist society, how legislative changes defining the
nature of crime stemmed from the need to expand that
control (e.g., Murray, 1986; Reitsma-Street, 1986). As
agents of control the urban police force's role,
composition, and relation to the elite have been explored
(Marquis, 1982, 1986; Acheson, 1985; Rogers, 1984;
Keeley, 1984). Nor have the more subjective dimensions
of criminogenic patterns been ignored. How crime was
perceived by the "respectable classes", how it was
interpreted within their "world-view", have been usefully
examined (Beattie, 1977; Craven, 1983).

The long-term trends in crime have also been
identified. Unlike in England and the United States,
Canada did not experience a decline in the crime rate in
the late nineteenth century (Brantingham and Brantingham,

1984:192). As Figure 1 illustrates, the rate of persons indictable under the Canadian criminal code per 100,000 population increased between 1880 and 1970.   Some fluctuations did occur, such as the sharp rise around 1914. Charges for all indictable criminal-code offenses showed more than a fourfold increase through this 100-year period.

Changes have also occurred with respect to the types of crime. Table 1 indicates a decline in crimes against the person. In contrast, burglary and robbery showed an increase between 1886 and 1970. Such offenses as theft and fraud fluctuated, but property crime--consistent with modernization theory (Shelley, 1981)--remained the most prevalent type of indictable offense. In each year New Brunswick and Nova Scotia contained a small proportion, as did the entire Atlantic region, of the total convictions in Canada (Table 2).

There is need for further study of these patterns in the Atlantic region. As a rather basic focus of inquiry, it is necessary to examine more thoroughly the characteristics of crime and of offenders at different periods of time in the past among the largest urban communities in these Provinces. We are seeking to address this need by reconstructing the patterns in Halifax and Saint John from the late 1800's to the mid-1900's.[1] Selected sources for these data include an assorted array of extent material in the police department archives for both cities. In particular we have examined Police Court Books, Police Charge Books or Arrest Ledgers, Detectives' Department Records of Reports Investigated supplemented by other sources--newspapers, journals, oral histories--that provide qualitative material. Analysis of these data focus on the changing nature of offenses in these cities, selected characteristics of offenders, and, to a limited extent the nature of police activity and the ecology of crime during this period. Comparisons between Halifax and Saint John with respect to the nature of criminality are possible with these data.

Figure 1.   Rate.of Persons Indictable under Canadian
            Criminal Code, 1880-1970 (per 100,000
            population). (Source: Brantingham and
            Brantingham, 1984:193)

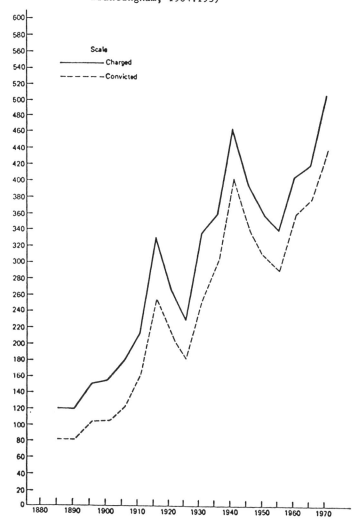

Table 1. Convictions for Indictable Offences, by Type of Offence,
Canada 1886-1970 (%).

Year	Crime vs. Person[1]	Violent Crime vs Property[2]	Crime vs. Property Without Violence[3]	Other Indictable Offences[4]	(N)
1886	20.9	7.6	58.6	12.9	(3,509)
1890	22.3	7.3	61.4	9.0	(3,934)
1895	20.2	8.8	63.0	7.9	(5,474)
1900	21.4	7.5	62.8	8.3	(5,768)
1905	21.1	8.8	55.4	14.7	(7,624)
1910	22.5	8.1	57.9	11.5	(11,700)
1915	19.3	10.9	61.2	8.6	(20,625)
1920	15.7	12.5	54.3	17.4	(18,443)
1925	16.9	11.2	51.1	20.8	(17,219)
1930	15.2	13.0	51.9	20.0	(28,457)
1935	11.9	12.4	48.2	27.6	(33,531)
1940	11.3	11.6	40.9	36.2	(46,723)
1945	14.8	12.6	37.1	35.6	(41,965)
1950	13.5	14.0	46.8	25.7	(10,772)
1955	12.4	18.3	43.5	25.8	(46,239)
1960	9.5	22.8	54.2	13.5	(64,707)
1965	10.5	21.1	51.9	16.5	(75,300)
1970	9.5	17.7	55.1	17.7	(75,334)

[1] Crimes vs. person = murder, manslaughter, all other forms of
homicide except suicide, kidnapping, all forms of assault and
battery, and all forms of sexual offences.
[2] Crimes vs. property with violence = breaking-and-entering
offences, robbery, and extortion.
[3] Crimes vs. property without violence = theft, receiving stolen
goods, fraud, embezzlement, and obtaining property through
false pretences.
[4] Includes malicious offences against property, forgery and
offences against currency, arson, vice-related offences, and
beginning in 1923 narcotics offences.

Source: Extracted from: M.C. Urquhart and K.A.H. Buckley
         (eds.), Historical Statistics of Canada. Second
         Edition. (Ottawa: Stats. Canada, 1883).

Table 2.   Proportion of Total Convictions in Canada for Indictable
Offences for Persons Aged 16 Years and Over, Atlantic
Region, New Brunswick and Nova Scotia, 1886-1970 (%).

Year	Atlantic Region	New Brunswick	Nova Scotia	(Total Convictions in Canada)
1886	5.9	1.9	2.7	(3,123)
1890	5.8	2.0	3.3	(3,340)
1895	7.6	2.2	4.9	(4,648)
1900	8.0	2.2	5.3	(4,853)
1905	7.1	1.6	5.0	(6,824)
1910	8.5	1.6	6.6	(10,327)
1915	6.1	1.2	4.8	(17,575)
1920	6.4	2.5	3.8	(15,088)
1925	5.1	1.4	3.6	(17,219)
1930	4.5	1.2	3.1	(28,457)
1935	4.9	1.7	3.0	(33,531)
1940	6.3	2.4	3.4	(46,723)
1945	8.6	3.0	5.0	(41,965)
1950	5.9	2.6	3.1	(10,772)
1955	7.9	2.0	3.9	(46,239)
1960	6.3	2.1	3.0	(64,707)
1965	6.9	1.9	3.1	(75,300)
1970	11.0	4.1	4.2	(75,334)

Source: Extracted from: M.C. Urquhart and K.A.H. Buckley
(eds.), Historical Statistics of Canada, Second Edition
(Ottawa: Stats Canada, 1983)

As with any archival material, the years covered and the specific types of data available reflect what is extant in the relevant depositories. Similarly, as with any such records of crime there are limitations in these sources. They only capture partially the level and types of crime--the "dark figure of criminality"--in the two cities during these years (Brantingham and Brantingham, 1984). They are restricted to the offenses brought to the attention of the police. The Halifax police Court records also may not include cases for which an arrest or charge was never made and therefore never listed (an example of "case filtration"). In addition, the characteristics of the offenses and offenders listed in these records are quite limited. For the offense, only a general category is identified. For example, "disturbance" may refer to a number of different types of incidents; yet this variety is lost with such categorization. For the offender, age, place of birth, place of residence, religion are all that are provided. In general, the extent to which these records accurately reflect crime and disorder in these cities is unknown (Hagan, 1984). The distinction between "official crime" (which we are examining) and "total crime" is a truism worth keeping in mind (Phillips, 1977). As Lane points out, there are rather intractable problems in the historical study of crime and policing that have yet to be resolved:

> No one has as yet even attempted to solve some of the most fundamental problems involved in the continued effort to distinguish between 'real' and merely 'labeled' offenses, ... What proportion of assault arrests were by policemen on their own initiative, what proportion as the result of complaints by aggrieved losers? How many 'order' arrests, even, represent felt needs, responses to community demands, and how many represent attempts to impose alien values, to suppress a neighborhood's enjoyment of its regular Saturday night fights? The statistics in themselves offer few clues. (Lane, 1980:33-34).

Despite these limitations, such sources are quite useful in that they provide at least some data on patterns of crime over an extended period of time, and are sources that have not heretofore been extensively tapped for these cities. They do not possess the limitations inherent in conviction statistics (as presented in Tables 1 and 2). By including both minor and serious offenses, regardless of the subsequent outcome (viz.: dismissal, fine, imprisonment) these records suggest the types of crime and disorder with which the police dealt during these years.[2] They will permit us, in time, to document more thoroughly the threats to social order that marked Maritime cities over past decades, the agents of these threats, and the strategies adopted by these communities in response.

HALIFAX, LATE 1800's

The earliest period for which we have data for either Maritime city is that of the late 1800's and turn-of-the-century Halifax. The most prevalent offense during these years was drunkenness (Table 3). Also a problem was disorderly conduct and disturbances -- frequently associated with drunkenness. There were relatively few incidents of crime against the person, apart from those linked to drunkenness. Nor were crimes against property proportionately very common.[3]

As Philips (1977) found in the English Black Country in the mid-nineteenth century, we see in Halifax a "prosaic and undramatic profile of crime occurring". Katz (1982) too presents a similar profile for Hamilton between 1851 and 1871. This prosaic character is captured in the entries of the 1891 **Report of the Halifax Day Police**, for example:

* (Woman) found drunk and in company with a colored man in a barn on Maynard Street after midnight, also for being a common prostitute.

* Drunk, disorderly, breaking glass in a shop door on Albemarle Street and making use of profane language on the street.

* Drunk and continued standing around street corners to the annoyance of the public.

*   Given in charge by the Manager of the 'Sailors
      Home' for being drunk and refusing to go aboard
      his ship. The Manager will appear against him.

Table 3. Distribution of Type of Offences, Halifax, 1883-1901 (%)

Year	General Type of Offence				
	Crime vs. Person	Crime vs. Property	Drunken- ness	Vagrancy	Distur- bance
1883	3.8	11.3	61.9	1.9	15.0
1891-1892	2.7	10.0	74.9	1.3	5.5
1900:					
May	3.1	1.0	83.3	0.0	10.4
October	3.9	9.2	77.6	1.3	6.6
1901	0.0	12.9	71.8	2.4	12.9

Sources: Reports of Day Police, Halifax: February 1, 1883 - March
          31, 1883; August 22, 1891 - June 29, 1892.
          Halifax Police Charge Books: May 1, 1900 - May 31, 1900;
          October 1, 1900 - October 31, 1900; February 1, 1901-
          March 31, 1901.

In the late nineteenth century Halifax was not
marked by serious crime. Public disorder caused by
drunkenness was the major problem with which the police
had to contend. Violations of the liquor law also were
prevalent. During the 1890's the police became more
involved in enforcement of the liquor act. Violations
of the law which they encountered included, for example,
hotel bars staying open after hours; licensed
establishments selling liquor to minors; selling liquor
without a license (the most common offense); having no
sign on the liquor shop; refusing police admission to a
licensed saloon. Securing sufficient evidence to ensure
successful prosecution was not always possible:

          Mrs. Francis McDonald, keeper of a
          boarding house on Upper Water Street,
          was charged in the police court with
          selling intoxicated beverages without

license. Two bottles of Lindberg's
beer had been found at Mrs.
McDonald's by the chief of police on
a recent visit he made there. The
accused acknowledged selling the
beer, but said she had purchased it
as a temperate drink.... Lindberg's
delivery express driver was called
and said the bottled beer found at
the accused's boarding house was sold
to her by him in good faith as a
temperate beverage. It is a new
drink known as Pilsner beer. The
witness did not know the constituents
of the liquid or how it was made....
His Honor continued the hearing to
give the prosecution time to have
the beer analyzed and its nature
determined by expert testimony....
The chief of police stated he had
applied at Lindberg's brewery for a
bottle of Pilsner beer to have it
analyzed, but could not obtain it at
the time. At retail shops elsewhere
in the city he failed to get a sample
also.   Judge Motton thereupon
dismissed the defendant for lack of
proof ·ɜ to the Pilsner beer being
a proscribed beverage. He advised
Mrs. McDonald's counsel to warn his
client against selling the beer any
longer.   (**The   Halifax   Herald**,
September 1, 1893).

As the above suggests, this was one type of offense in
which women may have been involved almost as frequently
as men. The locations of offenders, of course, became
patterned over time. The police and liquor act
inspectors identified St. Margaret's Bay Road and Upper
Water Street as areas in which special vigilance was
needed.

Repeated problems with liquor violations and with
public drunkenness led to concern for whether legislative
reform was appropriate. In March and April of 1901, for
example, city council and the legislature debated the
merits of a revised liquor license act. The bill
proposed would allow for the selling of liquor in hotel
rooms at any hour on Sunday, doubled the fee for a liquor

license, extended the hours for sale of liquor on
Saturdays, and vested the rights of city council, with
respect to liquor licenses, in the police commission.
The need to hold a plebiscite on these issues were also
promoted. The intensity of the debate reflected the
sharply opposing views of the merits of prohibition.

The illegal sale of liquor, nonetheless, continued.
Raids by the police were repeatedly mounted:

> Several members of the police force
> made a tour of inspection Sunday.
> They visited a number of dives on
> Albemarle and Grafton streets,
> extending their visits to the big
> hotels, but everything was locked up
> at those places. They visited Lower
> Water street and found evidence of
> illegal liquor selling on Mrs.
> Gulickson's premises. The officers
> then visited Upper Water street, and
> made a capture on the premises of
> Mrs. Coleman, opposite Pickford and
> Black's wharf. They made it warm
> for a few of the licensed liquor
> dealers who sell on Sunday. The
> offenders had continued out as usual,
> but officers took up positions in the
> vicinity of suspected places, and the
> business for the day was suspended.
> (**The Halifax Herald**, May 28, 1901).

In their search for alleged violations, the police and
inspectors were at times aided by observant citizens:

> Saturday evening a girl about
> eighteen years old, well dressed, and
> fairly good looking, called at a
> store on Cornwallis street, where
> temperance drinks are dispensed. She
> was sadly under the influence of
> liquor, and called out to the
> proprietor of the store "to fill them
> up again". A man who happened to be
> in the store at the time, judged from
> the girl's remarks that she had been
> in the shop before, and that she had
> previously drank liquor there. He

> left the premises, and after waiting
> near the door saw the girl open a
> door in the rear of the shop and
> enter a room to obtain, as he
> thought, another drink. The facts
> of the case have been reported to
> License Inspector Banks, who will
> endeavour to ascertain whether liquor
> is sold on the premises or not. The
> place has been suspected by the
> Inspector. (**The Halifax Herald,**
> September 3, 1901).

The failure to control adequately the sale and
distribution of liquor was evident daily; public
drunkenness was a common occurrence on the streets of
Halifax. Each day's report of the cases appearing in the
police court repeatedly reflected the prominence of this
problem. Arrests for drunkenness on a Saturday night
could number thirteen or more. The court's occasional
concern for moral reform was perhaps revealed in the
discharge of some offenders on their promise "to sign the
pledge". The latter was ordinarily effected in the
presence of a clergyman.

Drunkenness was linked to disturbances, damage to
property, assaults, and the fights that created periodic
condemnations by those concerned with the moral standards
of the community:

> A disgraceful scene took place in
> front of Warner's office, Dartmouth
> just as the half past twelve boat was
> in yesterday. It was a fight between
> a colored chap named John Mansfield
> and William Fanning. Both were under
> the influence of liquor. The negro
> got the worst of the fight. He was
> knocked down and then kicked under
> the chin by Fanning, inflicting a
> long gash. Fanning had his ear
> considerably lacerated. The
> disgusting part of the fight was that
> part of the time Fanning was stark
> naked, save for a singlet that did
> not come much below his waist. (**The
> Halifax Herald,** August 2, 1901).

Such incidents serve to remind us of the need "to give more critical attention to what was described in the nineteenth century as minor or petty crimes.... So-called minor offenders, who frequented the summary courts and municipal jails, were often a serious threat to themselves and to others, especially the people with whom they were most familiar" (Fingard, 1984: 99-100).

As in other seaports of Eastern Canada, prostitution was not uncommon (Fingard, 1982). Incidents of theft from the waterfront occurred. A common event was that of truckmen driving their horses recklessly through city streets. At times the police themselves were either threatened or directly assaulted frequently in the context of making an arrest. Cases of domestic problems (disputes, assaults) occurred, in which one member of the family was prepared to appear in Court against the individual causing the trouble. All these comprised the routine pattern of social problems and occasional disorder. The system of justice that prevailed in Halifax (and in Saint John) at the time was one in which the Court and police were used to mediate family disputes (Fingard, 1984; Marquis, 1986). This role contributed to the legitimacy which the "police establishment" obtained to a degree in Maritime cities in the latter part of the nineteenth century.

HALIFAX AND SAINT JOHN, 1916-1917

As noted earlier, one objective of this research is to compare characteristics of offenders and patterns of crime in Halifax and Saint John for selected years. This comparison is derived from sources which are not identical--police court data for Halifax, police arrest data for Saint John. Nor are the types of data identical. In later years we are not given in Saint John the religion of the offender, his place of residence, or whether he was born in the city. These limitations will affect the quality of the inter-community comparisons. In the period surveyed here, 1916-1942, each city experienced several dramatic events that we would expect to have exerted some impact on social order. War, the quest for prohibition, and the Depression influenced the social and economic structures of these communities. We wish to examine, in a preliminary way, whether these changes were linked to the patterns of crime.

Table 4 compares the two cities during the war years, 1916 and 1917. In both communities the highest proportion of offenders were in their twenties. More than half were between the ages of 20 and 39. The Halifax offenders were less apt to be natives to the province, in comparison to those in Saint John. The former were slightly more likely to have been born outside Canada. As a major embarkation point for servicemen going overseas, Halifax attracted a greater density of transients, some of whom came in touch with the "long arm of the law".

That Halifax served as a major route for young men from a diversity of communities on their way to the front gave added impetus to the quest for prohibition. The city, it was argued, must protect the moral welfare of these youths while they were its wards. Groups sought to address the recreational needs of servicemen. In December, 1915, for example, the Khaki club opened, provided entertainment, a billiard-room, cafe, and even a reading room for those in the military. Its services also included currency exchange for non-Canadian sailors in port.

The presence of the military was expressed in a less congenial manner. Damage to property, theft, robbery, disturbing the peace, were offenses involving servicemen- at times with themselves as victims. Occasionally the level of violence intensified, as occurred in February, 1916 when one Private Charles Fielder of the 63rd Halifax Rifles shot and killed his sergeant. Fielder was the son of a British rear-admiral. Later described as a neurotic and alcoholic, the private told Detective Hanrahan that "something came over him", giving no further explanation. Such acts were rare. Rather, the military contributed to the routine patterns of disorder with which the police had to contend.

Despite these imprints of war on the city, the patterns of crime remained similar to those identified at the turn of the century. Assaults frequently arose out of disputes in the home or tavern. Petty theft continued to be the pre-eminent type of property crime. The most common offense remained public drunkenness. As in Halifax, incidents involving soldiers appeared repeatedly on Saint John streets:

> Five soldiers were charged with
> drunkenness. They were strongly
> reprimanded by the Magistrate who
> read a paragraph from a European
> paper as to what Lord Kitchener said
> concerning soldiers subject to
> intoxication. They were handed over
> to military authorities. One of
> these soldiers had the distinction
> of being before the Court nineteen
> times over the past two and a half
> months. (**The Saint John Globe**,
> January 19, 1916).

> Private Harold Simpson was fined $8
> in answer to a charge of drunkenness
> and interfering with the police in
> the execution of their duty.
> Commissioner of Public Safety
> interposed to say that a certain
> class of men who were in khaki seemed
> to think, on this account, that they
> could run the city, but he would like
> to inform them that they would not.
> (**The Saint John Globe**, February 2,
> 1916).

Of continued concern to the Saint John police was where
the "men in khaki" obtained their liquor. Saloons which
they frequented while in uniform were raided. Local
residents were arrested for selling liquor illegally to
soldiers in back-alleys of City streets or in public
toilets. This was part of a broader effort by police to
curb the smuggling and distribution of illegal liquor
throughout the City. Problems of public drunkenness,
both of civilians and of soldiers, clustered in certain
parts of the City. The district from Brussel's Street
to Charlotte Street was called "run avenue". Women, it
was said, could not pass along without being insulted.
In protest, one Magistrate observed, "This is the sort
of thing we despise the Germans for; let us not act like
them" (**The Saint John Globe**, January 22, 1916).

It was during this period that prohibition came to
each city (Halifax, on July 1, 1916; Saint John, May 1,
1917). The crusade for prohibition derived from a strong
temperance tradition dating back to the mid-1880's
(Forbes, 1971). The emergence of a vibrant social gospel
movement sharpened and legitimated the attack on

intemperance, which was increasingly perceived as the paramount source of poverty, disease and social disruption. The call for prohibition became a central part of the programme for social reform.

In Halifax those favoring total abstinence were appalled at the "dives" and "blind pigs" where the illegal selling of intoxicating liquor was a routine matter. Neither police raids nor the efforts of the License Inspector were successful in curbing these activities. One man charged with selling liquor without a license on Water Street had been fined seven times between March and December, 1915. With the more than 50 saloons legally dispensing liquor in the city, the opportunities for drunkenness and dissipation were, to the eyes of the prohibitionists, excessive. The Liquor Licence Act, they argued, was not being enforced. This was especially troubling, given the large number of young men in military service present in Halifax. Rev. F.E. Barrett echoed the views of reformers who clothed prohibition with the finery of patriotism:

> The CRISIS has come in the great struggle that has been waged for years against the liquor traffic in this province. The trade for some years has been clinging tenaciously to its last stronghold, and today the temperance forces are closing in on 'Germany's greatest ally' and the most deadly foe our province ever faced, determined to take its citadel and destroy it forever.
>
> For many years the temperance and Christian forces have been patiently and persistently pressing the war against this foe, so securely entrenched behind the law which licensed its existence. Today patriotism and economic influences have come up to reinforce the allied temperance forces, because it has been clearly demonstrated that the liquor business is the ally of our enemies, for it has put out of action thousands of men and utterly unfitted them for making their manhood count against our foe across the seas, and

it has been proved the most wanton
destroyer of the nation's wealth.
(**The Halifax Herald**, March 9, 1916).

The first day of prohibition in Halifax brought
optimism. Drunkenness and rowdyism seemed less evident
on the streets, as one Temperance Alliance official
observed after one week of prohibition:

Hats off to Water street! Think of
it! there she was, dry, orderly and
quiet. While walking down that
thorofare we fairly stared at each
other to be sure we were not in a
nightmare. Spectres of the past
loomed up before us, for never had
we passed thru that street, day or
night, without policemen leading
along a 'drunk' or a patrol wagon
rambling along with a senseless human
sot, or a lot of intoxicated men who
wanted all the sidewalk. Frequently
the program would be varied by a
fight or two with frightened women
and a dozen wild-eyed youngsters as
spectators.

This night the dazed policemen
looked as if they were lost or had
been sent on the wrong beat.
Restaurants and lunch-rooms were
filled with sober and jolly sailors,
soldiers and civilians. Children
were playing in the street and women
were chatting cheerfully on the
doorsteps. (**The Halifax Herald**, July
8, 1916).

Such optimism was short-lived.

In both Halifax and Saint John prohibition did not
appear to have had a significant effect on the patterns
of crime (Grant, 1984). Drunkenness, bootlegging, and
the illegal selling of liquor continued. These offenses
insofar as they constituted "conflict crimes" (Hagan,
1984) persisted because of the lack of a strong social
consensus in each community to eradicate them. Table 4
shows that in 1916-1917 more than half of the offenses
listed involved drunkenness. More particularly, for

example, in July of 1916, the first month of prohibition in Halifax arrests for drunkenness as recorded in the Halifax Police Court Book did show a decline from previous months (Figure 2). But they rose substantially thereafter; the number of arrests for drunkenness more than tripled in August. Increasingly flagrant violations of the prohibition act became more noticeable. "Blind pigs" continued to plague the police. Repeating, as we saw earlier, their efforts of the late 1880's, raids were conducted on Water Street, on Hollis and other streets, various hotels, and in the county along St. Margaret's Bay Road. The confident expectations that had been expressed in each city with the enactment of prohibition were soon recognized as aspirations that would not be fulfilled, and for many **should** not be fulfilled, as revealed in how one Magistrate reacted in Saint John:

> A defendant admitted selling liquor for fifty cents a flask. Eighteen flasks of brandy were found in a suitcase under his bed in a Main Street boarding house. He was from Shippegan, and worked on the West Side docks. The Magistrate, in imposing sentence, felt the necessary penalties under the Act were too severe. He had taken it up with the Government, but with no result: "It is doing away with all our ideas of individual liberty". (**The Saint John Globe**, May 4, 1917).

To return to Table 4, we do find some differences between the two cities in 1916 and 1917. Halifax showed a higher proportion of crimes against the person and disturbances in comparison to Saint John, but a slightly smaller proportion of vagrants. Finally, arrests for assault during this period were more common in Halifax.

Figure 2. Arrests for Drunkenness as Proportion of
Total Arrests for Each Month, May –
December, 1916. (Halifax Police Court
Book)

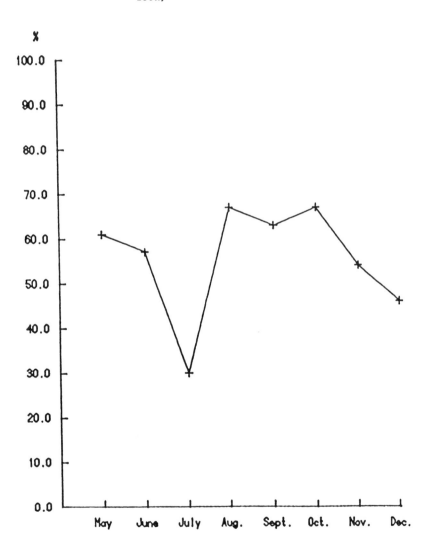

Table 4.   Characteristics of Offenders and Offences, Halifax and
Saint John, 1916-1917 (%).

	Halifax 1916-1917[a]	Saint John 1916[b]	1917[c]
Age of Offender			
Under 20	9.7	9.1	13.9
20-29	34.9	35.3	28.5
30-39	26.8	25.3	25.9
40-49	18.1	16.9	17.7
50-59	7.8	8.4	10.9
60+	2.3	3.2	3.0
Origin of Offender			
Native to the Province	47.2	57.9	60.4
New Brunswick	3.5	-	-
Nova Scotia	-	2.9	5.8
Prince Edward Island	2.1	0.4	2.0
Newfoundland	5.7	0.8	2.0
Quebec	1.7	6.8	0.8
Ontario	1.5	0.2	1.5
Other Canada	0.4	-	-
U.S.A.	2.4	4.6	4.8
England	12.3	6.7	8.5
Ireland	3.2	4.4	3.3
Scotland	4.3	3.4	3.3
Other	11.4	10.4	7.2
Religion of Offender			
Proportion Catholic	47.3	48.9	52.4
Proportion Non-Catholic	52.0	32.4	32.4
General Type of Offence			
Crime vs. Person	14.8	8.8	7.3
Crime vs. Property	9.0	7.7	13.9
Drunkenness	57.2	52.1	53.8
Vagrancy	0.4	4.0	4.0
Disturbance	13.4	4.0	4.2

Table 4. (Cont'd.)

Specifc Type of Offence	Halifax 1916-1917[a]	Saint John 1916[b]	1917[c]
Homicide	0.3	0.0	0.0
Sexual Offence	0.9	2.1	3.0
Assault	13.6	6.4	4.2
Robbery	0.1	0.0	0.2
Break and Enter	0.6	1.9	1.5
Theft	6.8	4.6	9.0
Fraud	1.0	0.5	1.0
Arson	0.1	0.1	0.0
Trespassing	0.3	0.0	1.5
Damage to Property	0.4	0.7	1.0
Drunkenness	57.2	52.1	53.6
Possession of Liquor	0.0	2.3	1.0
Vagrancy	0.4	4.0	4.0
Held for Extradition	0.0	11.0	6.0
Desertion	3.8	5.1	2.2
Non-support	0.8	0.1	1.0
General Disturbance	13.4	4.4	4.2

[a] April 15, 1916 - April 14, 1917.

[b] January 1, 1916 - June 30, 1916.

[c] January 1, 1917 - April 10, 1917.

Source: Halifax Police Court Book, 1916 - 1917; Saint John City Police Charge Books, 1916,, 1917.

HALIFAX AND SAINT JOHN, 1929-1943

We can examine whether these differences continue by comparing the two cities for selected years, where the data are available, in the period 1929-1943 (though we are constrained to compare 1942 Saint John with 1943 Halifax). In the following we will focus on the origin, age, and religion of offenders in each community, and how these characteristics relate to types of offense.

ORIGIN (Table 5)

1. In most years Halifax offenders were more likely to be native Nova Scotians than their Saint John counterparts were native New Brunswickers (the reverse of the pattern evident in 1916-1917).

2. Reflecting the above difference in migration, from 1933 on Saint John appeared to attract more offenders from other parts of the Atlantic region than did Halifax. This is an intriguing pattern, in part because it is not consistent with the economic primacy of Halifax in the region. As the dominant "node" one might have expected the flow of such migrants to have been greater to that city. We know little about the migration patterns of offenders, in past decades. Because of their relative anonymity it is difficult to trace their movements before they arrived. Whether their mobility responded to the same social and economic forces influencing the wider population is, in addition, unknown.

3. Similarly, Saint John contained a higher proportion of foreign-born offenders, with the exception of 1929 and 1942 when Halifax police court dockets included many non-Canadians.

4. In neither city were many of those arrested by the police from outside the region. That many did not originate from other parts of Canada is consistent with the failure of the region to experience significant in-migration during these years. Again, however, perhaps reflecting the presence of many servicemen, there was a modest rise in this category of offender in 1942 Halifax.

Table 5.   Place of Birth of Offenders, Halifax and Saint John, 1929-1943 (%).

Year	Halifax				Saint John			
	Native to Province	Other Atlantic Region	Other Canada	Foreign-Born	Native to Province	Other Atlantic Region	Other Canada	Foreign-Born
1929	55.4	12.8	5.1	23.9	86.8	6.1	1.0	5.8
1931	59.7	11.4	6.4	21.0	60.4	8.3	8.5	22.4
1933	88.8	3.1	0.9	7.3	74.4	9.4	3.1	13.2
1934	90.5	2.7	1.9	4.6	79.2	8.6	1.8	10.2
1935	91.3	2.6	1.6	4.6	78.2	10.9	2.5	8.4
1938	94.4	1.9	1.4	1.0	80.0	12.7	1.7	5.6
1939	94.4	2.6	0.9	2.2	80.9	11.5	1.5	6.1
1940	84.3	4.0	2.7	8.7	72.6	12.6	2.7	11.8
1941	67.3	3.0	3.7	26.1	48.5	14.7	2.3	34.5
1942	53.5	3.2	7.2	36.1	Not Given			
1943	Not Given				63.3	12.7	2.8	20.8

Source: Selected years of Halifax Police Court Books and Saint John City Police Charge Books.

AGE (Table 6)

1. In most years Saint John **Arrest Records** included a slightly higher proportion of young (under 20) offenders, in comparison to Halifax.

2. Conversely, Halifax showed a higher proportion of offenders in their twenties and in the 20-39 category.

3. Although there were some variations in age composition from year-to-year--such as the especially high proportion, in relative terms, of older (age 40+) offenders in Saint John in 1929--generally through this period in each city the proportion in each age group remained relatively constant. Offenders clustered in the 20-39 age range, as they did earlier in 1916 and 1917.

RELIGION (Table 7)

1. The breadth of years compared here is quite narrow because of limitations in the data for Saint John, as noted earlier. Consistent differences in the religion of offenders did not appear in Saint John during these years. This may partly reflect the crudity of the categories used ("Protestant" does not allow us to differentiate denominations).

2. In contrast to Saint John, the proportion of Catholic offenders in Halifax declined through this circumscribed period. With the exception of 1942, those appearing in Halifax police court still were more likely to be Catholic than Protestant. (Anglicans were consistently the most prevalent denomination of Protestants).

TYPE OF OFFENCE (Table 8)

1. Drunkenness, as we have repeatedly seen, was the most prevalent offence in both communities. That prevalence, however, was less evident for Halifax in 1938 and for Saint John in the years 1932-1935. The explanations for these fluctuations may have been different for each city. In 1938 drunkenness was only slightly more common than crimes against property in Halifax. Yet in that year one-fifth of the offenses involved possession of liquor or violation of the Nova Scotia Liquor Act. It is unclear whether this variation

in the rate of drunkenness may have been due to a change
in the type of charge levied against an offender.   In the
early 1930's, in Saint John, from one-fourth to a third
of those listed in the Saint John arrest ledgers were
"brought in for their own protection".   Reflecting
economic conditions, the police offered these men
accommodation for the night.   Such occurred in each city
and illustrates the impact of the Depression.   One
important public service of the police was the provision
of shelter for transients (Marcus, 1986):

> Eleven homeless men occupied the
> women's ward in the police station
> last night. All had come to Halifax
> in search for work. Unable to find
> any work, they were returning to
> their homes throughout the province
> today. This was the largest number
> sheltered over night at the police
> station for years.   (**The Halifax
> Herald**, November 15, 1929).

> Seeking shelter from the cold and a
> place to sleep, a forty-eight year
> old man, native of Bridgewater, came
> to the police station last evening
> and remained for the night. He had
> left Lancaster Hospital, West Saint
> John, a short time ago. This man had
> served with the Royal Army Service
> Corps in the late war. He had been
> a passenger on the steamer Anglia,
> the first hospital ship to be sunk
> during the war.   The vessel was
> torpedoed in the English Channel
> November 17, 1915. The injuries the
> man had received that time aggravated
> his war wounds, and he was on pension
> ever since.   (**The Halifax Herald**,
> January 17, 1929).

> Protectionists who slept in police
> cells last night were ages 19, 21,
> and 23. At dawn they started out on
> the King's highway (**Saint John
> Evening Times-Globe**, May 10, 1935).

> A 17-year-old boy obtained free
> lodging and a 25-cent breakfast from

> police. He was given protection at
> 11:50 last night. Two others,
> "pros", were ages 21 and 23, the
> latter getting his free board at 2:30
> a.m. (**Saint John Evening Times-
> Globe**, June 13, 1935).

The inadequacies of the relief system operating in each
community heightened this role. The sheltering of these
groups may have aided the police in their efforts to
secure public order. Providing lodging was not simply
a humanitarian service, but rather a means of controlling
a potentially threatening stream of disaffected and
disadvantaged itinerants. The movement of the unemployed
from city to city was a source of considerable concern:

> When these 'drifters' first appeared
> in Saint John, the city had attempted
> to keep them moving by actively
> enforcing laws of vagrancy and
> begging. These measures had proven
> costly. Rarely able to pay the
> fines, arrested men had ended up in
> jail with long-term bed and board at
> the city's expense. Giving up the
> attempt to keep 'drifters' out of the
> city, Saint John instead tried to
> keep them off the streets. Appealing
> to the public 'not to feed the
> unemployed', police requested
> citizens to send them to the police
> station where they would be provided
> with a night's lodging and a meal
> which was paid for by the city.
> Having benefitted from the city's
> hospitality, they were then
> encouraged to move along. (Ferguson,
> 1984: 98).

Table 8 also indicates that from 1938 on a higher
proportion of offenses in Saint John involved drunkenness
compared to Halifax. This was a substantial difference.
Whether this reflected dissimilarities in police
enforcement or in actual occurrence of this offence is
unknown.

2. In each year crimes against the person (chiefly
assault) were more prevalent in Halifax than in Saint

John--again continuing a pattern we observed in the 1916-1917 comparison.

   3.   Halifax and Saint John were, however, similar in that crimes against property were generally more frequent than crimes against the person.

   We noted earlier some of the limitations in the Police Court records. They may not reflect all of the types of calls, investigations, problems, etc. to which the police responded during these years. It is necessary, therefore, to examine other sources, especially the records of more specialized policing units, such as those of the Detective Department. Several of these are extant, and provide useful quantitative and qualitative data on crime and policing in Halifax for selected years. We have not been able to locate a similar source for Saint John.

Table 6.   Age Composition of Offenders, Halifax and Saint John, 1929-1943 (%).

Year	Halifax				Saint John			
	Under 20	20-29	20-39	40+	Under 20	20-29	20-39	40+
1929	10.3	39.6	57.9	30.8	7.4	21.4	39.0	45.1
1931	15.3	43.4	63.2	21.2	15.4	34.8	56.0	28.2
1933	8.9	35.2	59.5	30.4	18.1	31.6	49.6	31.9
1934	6.3	33.5	57.9	34.9	21.1	29.4	49.1	28.8
1935	3.7	34.1	65.3	31.5	23.4	26.5	47.4	28.5
1938	10.3	36.0	63.4	25.8	12.8	22.9	48.1	39.0
1939	7.4	28.3	57.7	34.3	14.8	22.5	48.5	36.7
1940	8.3	29.2	56.8	34.8	16.1	24.8	48.4	35.1
1941	9.8	34.6	62.5	27.5	11.2	31.2	60.4	28.5
1942	9.0	36.9	60.5	24.0	Not Given			
1943	Not Given				11.2	27.9	52.6	35.4

Source: Selected Years of Halifax Police Court Books and Saint John City Police Charge Books.

Table 7.   Religious Composition of Offenders, Halifax and Saint
John, 1938-1943 (%).

Year	Halifax		Saint John	
	Catholic	Protestant	Catholic	Protestant
1938	55.6	42.0	46.3	46.4
1939	56.4	42.1	49.9	46.4
1940	55.0	43.6	48.2	41.8
1941	44.5	39.9	43.2	48.5
1942	42.7	49.6	Not Given	
1943	Not Given		45.5	45.9

Source: Selected years of Halifax Police Court Books and Saint
John City Police Charge Books.

Table 8.   Types of Offences, Halifax and Saint John, 1929-1943 (%).

Year	Halifax			Saint John		
	Crime vs. Person	Crime vs. Property	Drunk-enness	Crime vs. Person	Crime vs. Property	Drunk-enness
1929	9.7	8.0	66.5	4.1	7.1	62.0
1931	20.6	24.9	31.4	9.1	12.1	23.8
1933	14.7	20.1	51.7	5.4	14.5	35.6
1934	13.8	15.4	37.5	5.0	17.3	35.9
1935	12.9	16.4	42.6	4.2	21.4	33.4
1938	10.6	21.8	28.3	4.1	15.5	64.6
1939	10.4	14.4	43.3	5.0	17.6	60.1
1940	9.0	13.9	47.5	4.0	15.6	63.7
1941	13.8	18.8	46.6	4.3	7.6	75.9
1942	21.5	9.4	53.9	Not Given		
1943	Not Given			5.8	11.9	68.4

Source: Selected years of Halifax Police Court Books and Saint John City Police Charge Books.

The Halifax Detectives' Department Records of Reports Investigated provide examples of the types of incidents and offenses that occupied the attention of the detectives. For the period August 1932 - June 1933, we find such incidents cited as these:

245 Oxford St.--reports bicycle stolen between 4 and 6 p.m.

1 Duke St.--shirt, tie, cuff links, stolen from room this evening--Suspect another roomer there.

Mrs._____ of YMCA, Barrington. Reports premises entered by some person who climbed up the fire escape to dining room window. Cash register found open with some sharp instrument and $10 in silver stolen. Nothing else missing.

Stolen from a truck parked at Shed 20, South Terminals-pump and jack.

Man reports his brother missing since yesterday--age 12.

75 Buckingham St.--house entered and large amount of cash stolen.

Store at Queen and Fenwick St. entered sometime this evening. Large quantity of groceries stolen and later recovered.

YMCA, Barrington--Reports premises entered sometime through the night in the same manner as entry made above.

43 Falkland St. reports $16 cash missing from house after fire this evening. May have been burned.

Room 214 Roy Building. Reports the theft of one cedar box containing handkerchiefs stolen from his office.

Armdale Service Station--Broken into $1 in cash also half dozen tail light bulbs stolen.

Brown checked rug stolen from car this evening on Argyle St. near Sackville St. between 7 - 9 p.m.

Acadia Store 166 Spring Garden Road--broken into through rear window. $138 stolen.

North Park St. Caretaker reports the following stolen from there last night--4 sweaters, also 9 pairs of rubber gym shoes.

Stolen from 76 South St. tools stolen.
Auburn Motors--Market St. Report gasoline being stolen from trucks and cars in their garage. Suspect lives on 778 Barrington and who stores his car there.

980 Robie St. Reports the theft of three hens from there.

These data suggest that property crime, especially theft, may have been a greater problem than was indicated in the Police Court records. In each year the highest proportion of reports investigated involved thefts, followed by break and enter incidents. Overall, property crime in general occupied the attention of city detectives far more than did crimes against the person.

The prevalence of petty thefts (theft from clotheslines, theft of foodstuffs and clothes) is evident. We see some evidence of how stolen goods were disposed (not infrequently with the assistance of junk dealers and second-hand dealers). The different types of occasions or opportunities for theft are also described--shoplifting, theft from an employer, theft from a drunk, purse-snatching on the streets. While property crime, including vandalism and auto theft, was the most prevalent type of offense, the detectives were also called on occasion to investigate cases of assault, suicide, and domestic disputes. Juvenile involvement in property crime is underscored in these records as well. Finally, the links that were developed between police forces of different cities are illustrated repeatedly. Improvements in communication enabled the Halifax detectives to exchange information and requests for assistance with their counterparts in the surrounding region.

OFFENDERS AND OFFENSES

1. Because of the difference in origin data between the two cities (the Halifax records indicate whether an offender was born in the city, whereas those in Saint John only identify whether he was a native New Brunswicker or not), we cannot provide precise comparisons. Nonetheless, it is of interest to note in

Table 9 that in most years examined Haligonians were more apt to be charged with crimes against the person than were non-natives. This may reflect the tendency for these offenses, such as assaults, to have occurred among persons linked within the same social networks. Natives resident in the city were more prone to have such locally based networks. Yet in Saint John we see no consistent difference between native New Brunswickers and non-natives in this regard. This may be a function of the crudity of the categories used, or may indeed reveal an actual difference between the cities' patterns of crime or policing.

2.   In both cities by the 1940's, in contrast to earlier years, non-natives were more apt than natives to be arrested for drunkenness (Table 9).

3.   A striking similarity in the patterns of crime is evident in that in each community throughout this period those under 20 were more likely than other age groups to be charged with property crime (chiefly theft) (Table 10). It would appear that this was not a problem confined to one Maritime urban centre at the time.

4.   Yet it was more pronounced in Saint John. A much higher proportion of the youthful offenders in that city in most years compared were arrested for crimes against property in comparison to their Halifax counterparts. Police Court reports in the newspapers contain poignant illustrations of such youthful misadventures:

> A 14-year-old boy admitted stealing a dollars' worth of coal from the C.N.R. and after being warned Saturday by the magistrate he was freed. His only police record was for breaking glass--back in 1932. But a next offense may mean the Boys' Industrial Home. (**The Saint John Evening Times Globe,** June 10, 1935)

> An 18-year-old youth admitted theft of one dollars' worth of coal from a C.N.R. box car, and after being warned in the police court yesterday afternoon was freed. Nervous and picking at his cap, he said he would never return again. Court said that

he would have been sentenced to jail
except that Constable Young of the
C.N.R. interceded, saying that he
felt the youth would go straight in
future. He has a job. (**The Saint
John Evening Times-Globe**, June 14,
1935)

A 13-year-old boy wanted money. So
he smashed up three cup-vending
machines in C.P.R. coaches at
Gilbert's Lane coach shed. From two
of the machines his profit was 15
cents. Each machine is valued at
$20. They're probably ruined. He
hung his head before the magistrate.
Last time he promised to attend
school. "Your parents can't do
anything with you. Nothing left but
the Boys' Industrial HOme, so you'll
be sent there for not longer than
five years." At noon he bade goodbye
to city streets. (**The Saint John
Evening Times-Globe**, May 22, 1935)

5. Conversely, in many of the years within this
circumscribed period Halifax youths were more frequently
charged, in relative terms, with drunkenness and vagrancy
than were those of the same age group in Saint John
(Table 11). The fascinating question again raised is
whether this represented a substantive difference in the
patterns of crime, an artifact of the types of data
collected in the two communities, or the result of
variations in enforcement and policing. The possible
relevance of the latter is underscored in conflict
theory. Hagan (1984:29), for example, observes: "Some
attacks on persons and property are held criminal in most
societies ... beyond this basic consensus there is much
variation in what is considered problematic, and
therefore deviant or disruptable." Policing practices
may have been influential here.

6.   Finally, although we have no comparable data
for Saint John, in Halifax through this period there was
a consistent link between religious affiliation and type
of offense (as illustrated in Figure 3). Baptists were
more commonly charged with crimes against the person
(chiefly assault) than were other religious groups.
Conversely, Baptists were less apt to be charged with

drunkenness. Catholics mirrored the reverse patterns--
i.e., in each year, Catholics were under-represented
among those appearing in court for crimes against the
person and were over-represented among those charged with
drunkenness.   Whether this was indeed a subcultural
difference is unclear.[4] One must be careful here in
using such data: the listing of religious affiliation
in these records is only a crude measure of religious
identification.   Nonetheless, the consistency of these
contrasts throughout these years suggests that religious
affiliation, as a social and cultural factor, may have
exercised some influence on deviance and criminality.
The data at best pose this as an intriguing question.

Table 9. General Type of Offence by Place of Birth, Halifax and Saint John, 1929-1943 (%).

Year	Halifax		Saint John	
	Proportion Native Haligonians Charged With:		Proportion Native New Brunswickers Charged With:	
	Crimes vs. Person	Drunkenness	Crimes vs. Person	Drunkenness
1929	10.5	66.7	4.2	70.3
1931	28.6	24.8	Not Given	
1933	14.6	53.2	5.5	40.1
1934	13.9	39.5	4.9	38.6
1935	13.9	43.2	4.8	35.8
1938	11.5	29.6	3.8	64.1
1939	11.4	44.2	5.3	59.1
1940	10.9	46.4	4.7	61.9
1941	17.3	39.0	6.3	67.5
1942	27.5	43.5	Not Given	
1943	Not Given		5.9	67.8
	Proportion Non-Native Haligonians Charged With:		Proportion Non-Native New Brunswickers Charged With:	
	Crimes vs. Person	Drunkenness	Crimes vs. Person	Drunkenness
1929	9.5	66.4	5.9	41.2
1931	15.2	35.8	Not Given	
1933	15.2	46.8	5.5	24.0
1934	13.1	29.4	5.1	25.8
1935	8.9	40.0	2.8	25.0
1938	3.9	18.2	5.3	66.3
1939	4.4	38.0	3.8	64.2
1940	2.5	51.5	2.2	68.7
1941	9.0	57.0	2.5	83.7
1942	16.6	62.6	Not Given	
1943	Not Given		5.7	69.9

Source: Selected years of Halifax Police Court Books and Saint John City Police Charge Books.

Table 10. Proportion of Selected Age Groups Charged with Property Crime, Halifax and Saint John, 1929-1943 (%).

Year	Halifax			Saint John		
	Under 20	20-29	30-39	Under 20	20-29	30-39
1929	18.9	11.2	3.0	70.6	10.6	0.0
1931	50.0	26.4	16.1	63.2	27.8	13.7
1933	67.7	17.8	19.0	65.6	16.4	15.3
1934	40.4	20.1	16.3	67.9	23.5	8.5
1935	37.0	23.6	12.6	77.5	31.9	12.7
1938	54.3	23.0	15.1	69.4	16.1	6.7
1939	35.4	22.4	9.5	58.9	21.7	7.3
1940	39.4	17.6	12.3	64.0	11.4	4.5
1941	27.1	23.3	19.0	47.7	4.9	2.6
1942	28.4	8.9	7.7	Not Given		
1943	Not Given			61.6	8.2	5.8

Source: Selected years of Halifax Police Court Books and Saint John City Police Charge Books.

Table 11. Proportion of Youthful Offenders (under age 20) Arrested for Drunkenness and Vagrancy, Halifax and Saint John, 1929-1943. (%).

Year	Halifax		Saint John	
	Drunkenness	Vagrancy	Drunkenness	Vagrancy
1929	29.7	35.1	11.8	11.8
1931	10.7	20.8	4.6	13.8
1933	15.1	4.3	9.0	7.4
1934	13.5	25.0	8.2	6.7
1935	7.4	18.5	6.2	2.3
1938	5.7	5.7	9.9	5.0
1939	10.4	18.8	8.9	6.5
1940	11.3	19.7	14.0	5.2
1941	28.2	14.1	30.0	4.6
1942	29.7	6.8	Not Given	
1943	Not Given		16.9	8.7

Source: Selected years of Halifax Police Court Books and Saint John City Police Charge Books.

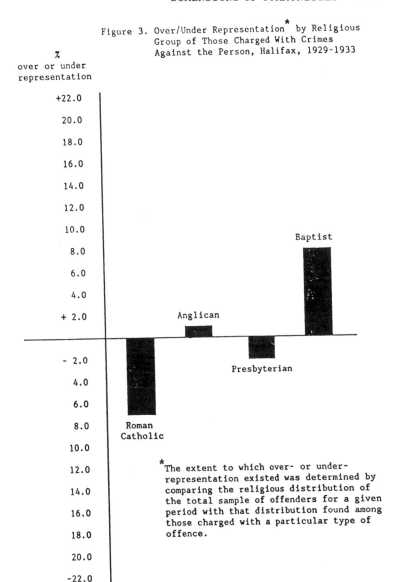

Figure 3. Over/Under Representation* by Religious Group of Those Charged With Crimes Against the Person, Halifax, 1929-1933

%
over or under
representation

*The extent to which over- or under-representation existed was determined by comparing the religious distribution of the total sample of offenders for a given period with that distribution found among those charged with a particular type of offence.

THE ECOLOGY OF CRIME: DRUNKENNESS IN SAINT JOHN

In the investigation of how patterns of urban crime have evolved historically the ecological dimensions need also to be examined (Morris, 1957; Pyle, 1974; Harries, 1980). Although we do not have comparable data for Halifax, we have examined the spatial distribution of crime in Saint John, in a restricted manner. Given the continued prominence of drunkenness through past decades, we have charted, as illustrated in Figures 4 - 6, the locations of arrests for this offense among the different police beats of the city. The beat was selected as the unit of spatial analysis rather than the census tract because the latter was not delineated in Canadian cities over the time span covered by this study. We are extrapolating these beats to the past when, for example, 15 and 16 beats were part of Lancaster and separate from Saint John's municipal jurisdiction. We have, thus, in a sense "imposed" the beats as standardized spatial units to provide comparisons over a number of decades.

The data reveal relative stability and continuity in the distribution of arrests for public drunkenness between 1915 and 1967. Consistently, beat 3 represented that area of the city where these arrests were more likely to occur. This section of Saint John encompassed King Square and at least part of the community's central business district. In addition, the old police station was located adjacent to this area. The clustering of this type of arrest in beat 3 may have reflected the greater visibility of such offenders to the police or some concentration of this kind of disorder in the area. Nonetheless, that this continuity in the city core marked the fifty-year period is striking. The continued prominence of drunkenness in Saint John was matched by the persistent mode of its spatial distribution in the city--a city that did not experience the same changes in land use and spatial differentiation found in other Canadian urban centres. Other sections of the city where arrests for drunkenness occurred through this period included the Prince Edward Street area (beat 4), the South End (beat 5), Main Street Central (beat 9), and the waterfront (beat 1). In the oral histories we have collected from retired police officers in Saint John the first three especially were identified as "trouble areas", within which public drunkenness was only one of several types of offence or disorder that preoccupied the police.[5] For example, this is one such portrait of Beat

9 from these oral histories as this area existed 30 years ago:

Figure 4.

Figure 5.

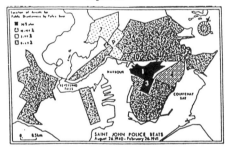

Figure 6.

There was a slum down behind present-day Keddy's. That was quite an area when I was on the beat. We always had problems there. Some didn't even hit the log books because of the fact they didn't really warrant that severity. They were things you could almost handle by yourself alone. They were pretty well all domestic disputes. The only things we had primarily were the three classes--intoxication, domestic disputes, and assaults. Those were primarily the three major matters that we had to concern ourselves with. And, of course, resisting arrest.... As a matter of fact we had huge ledgers just for one name alone of the people that we arrested. John Smith is picked up again last night. John Smith is picked up again two days ago. John Smith is picked up last week. John Smith is picked up a month ago. This sort of thing. Just repetitious....

We also had every drunk and every troublemaker in town used to hang right in front of that restaurant on Main Street on Saturday night. This is why they had the two men doubled up in that area. Now we'd wait until 2 o'clock until everything had calmed down. Then the man on the other beat he would carry on. He would go back to his beat, and this man here he would carry on and start doing his....

We used to have a lot of problems checking the doors down here, a lot of bootlegging going on. Used to be a street here called Sheriff Street which a lot of bootlegging was going on.... As a matter of fact I found a couple of bodies on Sheriff Street--people who were drunk and fell down the stairs and killed themselves. This was

quite an area. Well, let's put it
this way, you made sure you had your
rest before you hit this beat! If
you go this particular beat, you
psyched yourself into sort of combat
readiness sort of thing. There used
to be a dance hall down here--on
Hilyard Street and Simonds. When it
broke up around 12 o'clock on a
Saturday night rest assured there
would be problems between here and
up the other part of Main Street.
Assault. This was a bootlegging
area-along Simonds. It wasn't unique
in the sense that for the whole city
this wasn't just the isolated
bootlegging area. But it sure made
up for a lot of other places in the
area....

We have some limited sets of data on the spatial
distribution of offenses other than drunkenness for
contemporary Saint John. Break-and-enters, for example,
appeared to be more dispersed in the city than were
arrests for drunkenness. There is a need to extend this
analysis back over several decades as we have done with
drunkenness. In addition, it would be of considerable
interest to compare these patterns with what might be
found for Halifax.[6]

CONCLUSION

In the above we have presented a preliminary sketch
of the patterns of crime in these two communities. There
are gaps both in the data and in their interpretation.
This "reconstruction" is as yet incomplete. It is
evident that minor offenses such as public drunkenness
must be given greater prominence in understanding the
types of disorder in such cities, in past decades. The
general persistence of drunkenness as the most
predominant problem is itself noteworthy. We have noted
the failure of the temperance crusade, culminating in the
establishment of prohibition, to eradicate such a
"conflict crime". The economic interests served by the
illegal sale of liquor linked with the absence of a
strong moral consensus undermined reformers' efforts to
eliminate this "ill".

The lack of dramatic change in the patterns of crime evident in these two cities, at least as documented in the records reviewed here, partly reflected the absence of that level of industrialization, of population growth, and of economic development found elsewhere in Canada. Both the War and the Depression certainly did have some impact on those with whom the police had to contend (disorderly and drunken servicemen, the transient poor, respectively). But the continuity in the patterns overall is what stands out.

Some interesting questions are also raised. For example, why from 1933 on did Saint John attract more offenders from other parts of the Atlantic region than did Halifax? The persistent problem of juvenile property crime in each city and the consistent link between religious affiliation and type of offense in Halifax merit further exploration. Why was assault more prevalent in Halifax than in Saint John, with the reverse in the case of drunkenness--a difference in actual incidence, or rather a reflection of the impact of policing on the type of charged levied? This raises a rather central and persistent issue in the study of the history of urban crime: to what extent are differences in the patterns of crime between cities influenced by variations in their respective types of enforcement and policing activities (Wilson, 1968; Hagan, 1984; Manning, 1980)? Would that spatial continuity evident in Saint John with respect to the location of arrests for drunkenness also be found in a larger city with more pronounced changes in land use and population types? Finally, and most importantly, how do these patterns relate to community structure and change? The persistence of drunkenness despite prohibition, for example, suggests that change in one part of that structure--in this case, the formal, legislative sector-- will not necessarily redirect other segments--especially strongly rooted patterns of behavior (contrary to what a social system model of community might have predicted). An historical and comparative study of urban crime also requires that we explore further whether unique demographic or economic characteristics of each community accounted for these patterns.

NOTES

[1]The findings presented in this paper are extracted from **Reconstructing Patterns of Crime in Halifax and Saint John**, report submitted to Solicitor General, 1987.

[2]The official statistics on convictions for indictable offenses presented in Tables 1 and 2 do not take account of such minor offenses as public drunkenness. Examination of Police Court Books and Police Charge Books is, therefore, of particular value because these records do include these offenses. These sources tell us more about the day-to-day social problems and types of disorder the police encountered. That minor offenses were generally more prevalent than "serious" crime (Hagan, 1984) underscores the need to explore these sources.

[3]In this study, "crime against the person" includes homicide, sexual offense, assault, and robbery. "Crime against property" includes break-and-enter, theft, fraud, arson, trespassing, and damage to property.

[4]We cannot attribute these differences to contrasting characteristics of each--at least in terms of the data extracted from the sources used in this study. Baptist and Catholic offenders were not significantly different in terms of place of birth, place of residence, or age composition. It is of interest to note that Katz, et al. (1982) too found in 19th-century Hamilton that Irish Catholics were under-represented among those arrested for crimes against the person.

[5]With respect to the clustering of drunkenness in beat 3, one retired police officer observed, in his oral history:

> An inherited habit of 'meeting up town' is a contributing factor in terms of cluster of arrests in the uptown area (three beat). Persons from all parts of the city would congregate in the central core. It was due to the availability of liquor outlets; both legal and illegal.... The vicinity of the police station was also an added factor in view of the fact that the police station was located in the uptown area, provided

a form of protection. In some cases, particularly in the winter seasons, the drunks would feel they would not have far to go in order to get protection by means of being arrested for being in an intoxicated condition. This automatically meant a ten-day jail term. This law eventually changed.... Taverns and bootleggers were plentiful in the uptown core during the time span. Both prospered....

[6]An exploration of the ecology of crime in contemporary St. John's, Newfoundland is contained in McGahan (1982). That study does not provide historical data, however, with which we might compare the spatial continuity evident in Saint John.

[7]Schneider (1978), for example, traces through the impact on the ecology of crime in Detroit as the population grew with immigration and as spatial differentiation and suburbanization became more pronounced. Similar dynamic changes did not occur to the same degree in Saint John.

REFERENCES

Acheson, T.W.   1985.   Saint John: The Making of a
    Colonial Urban Community.   Toronto: University of
    Toronto Press, 1985.

Beattie, J.M.   1977.   Attitudes Towards Crime and
    Punishment in Upper Canada, 1830-1850: A Documentary
    Study.   University   of   Toronto: Centre   of
    Criminology.

Brantingham, Paul and Patricia.   1984.   Patterns of
    Crime. New York: Macmillan.

Craven, Paul. 1983.   "Law and Ideology: The Toronto
    Police Court. 1850-1880."   IN David H. Flaherty
    (ed.), Essays in the History of Canadian Law. pp.
    248-307. Toronto: University of Toronto Press.

Cross, Michael. 1973.   "The Shiners' War: Social
    Violence in the Ottawa Valley in the 1830's." The
    Canadian Historical Review, LIV, 1 (March):1-26.

Field, John. 1981.   "Police, Power and Community in a
    Provincial English Town: Portsmouth. 1815-1875."
    IN Victor Bailey (ed.), Policing and Punishment in
    Nineteenth-Century Britain.   pp. 42-64.   New
    Brunswick, New Jersey: Rutgers University Press.

Ferguson, Carol Ann.   1984.   Responses to the
    Unemployment Problem in Saint John, New Brunswick,
    1929-1933.   M.A. Thesis, University of New
    Brunswick.

Fingard, Judith. 1982. Jack in Port: Sailortowns of
    Eastern Canada. Toronto: University of Toronto
    Press.

Fingard, Judith.   1984.   "Jailbirds in Mid-Victorian
    Halifax." In Peter Waite, Sandra Oxner and Thomas
    Barnes (eds.), Law in a Colonial Society: The Nova
    Scotia Experience. pp. 81-102. Toronto: The
    Carswell Company Limited.

Forbes, E.R. 1971.   "Prohibition and the Social Gospel
    in Nova Scotia." Acadiensis, 1, 1 Autumn):11-36.

Grant, B.J. 1984. When Rum Was King. Fredericton: Gooselane.

Hagan, John. 1984. The Disreputable Pleasures. Second Edition. Toronto: McGraw-Hill Ryerson.

Harries, Keith D. 1980. Crime and the Environment. Springfield, Illinois: Charles C. Thomas.

Jones, David. 1982. Crime, Protest, Community and Police in Nineteenth-Century Britain. London: Routledge & Kegan Paul.

Katz, Michael B., Michael J. Doucet, and Mark J. Stern. 1982. The Social Organization of Early Industrial Capitalism. Cambridge, Mass.: Harvard University Press.

Kealey, Gregory S. 1984. "Orangemen and the Corporation." IN Victor L. Russell (ed.), Forging a Consensus: Historical Essays in Toronto. pp. 41-86. Toronto: University of Toronto Press.

Lane, Roger. 1979. Violent Death in the City: Suicide, Accident, and Murder in Nineteenth-Century Philadelphia. Cambridge, Mass.: Harvard University Press.

Lane, Roger. 1980. "Urban Police and Crime in Nineteenth-Century America." IN Norval Morris and Michael Tonry (eds.), Crime and Justice: An Annual Review of Research, Vol. 2, pp. 1-43. Chicago: University of Chicago Press.

Manning, Peter. 1980. "Organization and Environment: Influences on Police Work." IN R.V.G. Clark and J.M. Hough (eds.), The Effectiveness of Policing. pp. 98-123. Westmead, Eng.: Gower.

Marquis, Michael G. 1982. The Police Force in Saint John, New Brunswick. 1860-1890. M.A. Thesis. University of New Brunswick.

Marquis, Michael G. 1986. "'A Machine of Oppression Under the Guise of the Law': The Saint John Police Establishment, 1860-1890." Acadiensis, 16, 1 (Autumn):58-77.

McGahan, Peter. 1982. "Criminogenesis and the Urban Environment: A Case Study." Canadian Police College Journal, 6:209-225.

Monkkonen, Eric H. 1975. The Dangerous Class. Crime and Poverty in Columbus, Ohio, 1860-1885. Cambridge, Mass.: Harvard University Press.

Morris, Terrence. 1957. The Criminal Area: A Study of Social Ecology. London: Routledge & Kegan Paul.

Murray, Glenn F. 1986. "Cocaine Use in the Era of Social Reform: The Natural History of a Social Problem in Canada, 1880-1911." Paper presented at the 1986 annual meetings of the Canadian Sociology and Anthropology Association, University of Manitoba.

Philips, David. 1977. Crime and Authority in Victorian England: The Black Country. 1835-1860. London: Croom Helm.

Pyle, Gerald F., et al. 1974. The Spatial Dynamics of Crime. Chicago: University of Chicago, Department of Geography. Research Paper No. 159.

Reitsma-Street, Marge. 1986. "More Control Than Care: A Critique of Historical and Contemporary Laws for Delinquency and Neglect in Ontario." Paper presented at the 1986 annual meetings of the Canadian Sociology and Anthropology Association. University of Manitoba.

Robinson, Cyril D. 1982. "Criminal Justice History Research in Progress in the United States." Criminal Justice History, 3:97-124.

Rogers, Nicholas. 1984. "Serving Toronto the Good." IN Victor L. Russell (ed.), Forging a Consensus: Historical Essays on Toronto. pp. 116-140. Toronto: University of Toronto Press.

Schneider, John C. 1978. "Public Order and the Geography of the City: Crime, Violence, and the Police in Detroit, 1845-1875." Journal of Urban History, 4, 2 (February):183-208.

Shelley, Louise I. 1981. Crime and Modernization: The Impact of Industrialization and Urbanization on

Crime.   Carbondale   and   Edwardsville: Southern
Illinois University Press.

Sindall, Rob. 1983. "Middle-Class Crime in Nineteenth-
Century England." Criminal Justice History, 4:23-
40.

Thorner, Thomas. 1979. "The Incidence of Crime in
Southern Alberta, 1878-1905." IN D.J. Bercuson and
L.A. Knafla (eds.), Law and Society in Canada in
Historical Perspective. University of Calgary.
Studies in History, 2:53-88.

Tobias, J.J. 1967. Crime and Industrial Society in the
19th Century. London: B.T. Batsford.

Tobias, J.J. 1979. Crime and Police in England 1700-
1900. Dublin: Gill and Macmillan.

Wilson, James Q. 1968. Varieties of Police Behavior:
The   Management   of   Law   and   Order   in   Eight
Communities. Cambridge: Harvard University Press.

Woods, J.G. 1983. "Criminal Justice History in Canada:
A Brief Survey of Work in Progress." Criminal
Justice History, 4:119-30.

X

COMPARATIVE NATIONAL URBAN POLICIES

Bernd Hamm

INTRODUCTION

Discussions about urban development have considerably changed during the past 15 years, from euphoric approaches towards "integrated urban development planning" in the late 1960's and early 1970's to piece-meal engineering after the advent of the economic crisis in 1974. Before this background it may appear strange to dedicate a paper to National Urban Policies -- what might nation states have to do in cities? What kinds of policy might they pursue?

A number of catchwords can serve to recall that the nation state intervenes in urban development in manifold ways:

- city election campaigns are more than ever before influenced by federal policies and federal political parties, and federal politicians run for office in local governments in the biggest cities;

- city budgets depend more than ever before on federal and state transfers, and no bigger investment on the local level is possible without grants from other levels of government;

- federal economic policies very obviously affect the cities, if only to remind to heavy industry, coal, and steel;

- this is also true for social policy; e.g., the cutbacks in unemployment aid severely burden local expenditures.

A large number of other examples could be cited to illustrate the dense interrelationships in the whole policy network. A very simple argument makes clear that there can be no way to avoid state intervention. In all highly developed, post-industrial societies some 80 percent of the total population live in cities and under urban conditions. If so, any policy measure necessarily must affect the cities and their population, their economy, their budgets, even if this might happen indirectly. Any policy is urban even if those making decisions, or those affected, may not be aware of this situation. The question cannot be whether national urban policies exist or not, but whether they are consciously conceived and made explicit, and how they work.

Let me, first, define some of the terms I will use in this paper: the term "urban development" refers to changes in land use, of the residential structure, of the organizational and administrative system, of the economic network, and of the infrastructural equipment of an urban area. "Urban Policy", then, is that part of the activities of public authorities directed towards urban development. Urban policies are said to be "explicit" when urban development is their sole or dominant target, and said to be "implicit" when this is not the case.

Having defined these terms, the purpose of this paper can be more precisely described, and its scope limited:

1. Urban policies are made at all levels of government, including municipalities, regions, states, the federal government, or even the European Community, or other supranational bodies. This paper refers only to the national level, i.e., the federal or central government.

2. I will only consider explicit forms of urban policy, even if they may appear under different rubrics, such as housing, infrastructure, urban renewal, or administrative reform. I will not deal with policies implicitly relevant for urban development as, e.g., employment, social welfare, public health, energy, education, finance, or economic policy.

It is easy to understand that such a tentative attempt to give some structure to a complex range of objects can not be without problems: It is, very often, difficult to decide which policy is explicitly urban and which is not -- regional policies intended to advance peripheral areas may lead to changes in migration which indirectly affect the cities; the development of peripheral infrastructure may result in net gains of urban areas when the goods and services necessary have been produced in cities; and there are numerous policy fields the effect of which on cities can only be maintained by following long causal chains, as is the case, e.g., with tax policy. Thus, it becomes clear that there are no plain contours of what urban policies are.

The following section will describe some trends in urban development in post-industrial societies, as far as they can be generalized for the past fifteen years. Then I will turn to focus on national urban policies in the U.S., Canada, Great Britain, France, and the Federal Republic of Germany. The last section will try to find a broad synthesis and address some of the possible consequences.

TRENDS IN URBAN DEVELOPMENT

In capitalist societies, a need for public policies arises when market regulations do not provide the goods and services considered necessary, or not in the appropriate quality or quantity; when negative effects of market regulation (externalities, spill-overs) need to be corrected; or market regulations should be stimulated and directed toward specific goals. Public policy is considered subsidiary to compensate for deficits in the self-regulating mechanisms. Thus, deficits in urban development have to be demonstrated to justify urban policy.

In all post-industrial societies, economic development may be characterized by pointing to the change from production-oriented to service-oriented systems; by ongoing rationalization and automatization of production; by decreasing growth rates; high structural unemployment; increasing integration in, and dependence on, the development of the world economy and the international division of labor. This macro-scale change brings about a number of consequences for cities and agglomerations:

1. functional specialization and hierarchical polarization of the urban network (in the U.S. the rise of the sunbelt and the decline of the snowbelt; in Canada the rapid growth of Alberta and the relative decline of Quebec; in the Federal Republic of Germany the prospering areas in the south, Stuttgart and Munich, versus the old industrial areas in the Ruhr and Saar regions; in the U.K. the

southeast versus the industrial belt). In general, the pattern reveals the decline of the traditional heavy industries versus the rise of tertiary services and the conforming fate of industry-based or service-based urban agglomerations.

2. This change is most deeply felt in the modification in quality and quantity of available work-places and chances for employment.

3. Employment becomes territorially redistributed.

4. The average amount of space per work-place increases.

Demographic development in post-industrial societies is marked by decreasing birth rates and the diminution of natural population growth. Changes in family structure and household composition result in a growing proportion of small households. Immigration, together with higher birth rates in the immigrant population, partly correct for the decay in the domestic population.

From the early 1970's on, central cities experienced net losses in population, with an increasing proportion of smaller and lower-income households. This turn-over in population is especially due to suburban migration of expanding middle-class families. Gentrification, although widely addressed in the media, seems to rest relatively unimportant in quatitative terms, and depends on specific local conditions. The growth of medium-sized cities has received some attention and has been contrasted against the decline of big cities; but it seems to take place, first of all, in the wider catchment areas of such cities. Decentralization seems to be the more appropriate description than deurbanization. Only the prosperous service-based agglomerations experience migration gains.

Social development is closely interconnected with economic and demographic change. Declining economic growth rates and high state indebtedness result in cutbacks in social welfare expenditures. Differences in the standard of living between the social classes tend to polarize. The foreign population stock will become an increasingly problematic category. The new conservative majorities governing many of the western societies since the early 1980's tend to reinforce the polarization process.

Conspicuous consumption on the part of some population groups, sharply decreasing means on the part of others, together with cutbacks in social welfare and increasing ethnic or national heterogeneity will work for a generally higher level of conflict and deviancy, including the rise of an increasingly important shadow-economy. Residential segregation according to ethnic-cultural background or socio-economic status will tend to become more pronounced, with higher levels of discrimination and ignorance between different social groups being the probable consequence. Urban renewal policies tend to reinforce gentrification and will create new slums and distressed areas in other parts of the central cities.

As the public budgets become more restricted, from both the receipt and the expenditure sides, the margins for political action become narrower on all levels of government.

In short, a number of factors resulting from supra-local changes will deeply affect the cities and create severe urban problems for many of them, first of all those which are industry-based. These cities lack means and influence to correct for such deficiencies. The resulting difficulties are mutually interrelated, cumulative, and mutually reinforcing. It remains unclear whether this process signifies a new quality of urban development or, via negative feedbacks, the rise of a permanent crisis, as we could assume from some American (Detroit, Newark, Cleveland) or British (Liverpool, Manchester) examples. What seems clear, however, is that such tendencies create the need for political action not only on the local level, but on the state and federal levels as well, in all post-industrial nations.

NATIONAL URBAN POLICIES

THE UNITED STATES

The U.S. has a highly complex administrative structure with some 80,000 different administrative units - 50 states, 3,000 counties, 19,000 municipalities, 17,000 townships, 15,000 school districts, and 26,000 special purpose districts, each with its own sources of revenue. This system has resisted against all attempts for reform, and up to now administrative reform seems to be a non-issue. Traditionally, American federalism served as a major link between the central government and the states which were responsible for executing federal laws. Up to the New Deal, the cities were not considered partners in American federalism. The most significant change arrived with the New Deal, when cash grants-in-aid to the cities became possible especially with the Industrial Recovery Act of 1933 and its Low Rent Housing Program, and with the Housing Act of 1934 providing funds for urban renewal -- its supplement in 1954 marking the beginning of large scale bull-dozing. The states were free to participate in such programs, provided they enacted their own accompanying legislation and contributed their own additional funds.

But it was not before the ghetto revolts of the late 1960's that the federal government became conscious of the urban problems. President Nixon, as one of his first acts in office, introduced the Urban Affairs Council expected to lay grounds for a National Urban Policy. It became law in 1970 with the Community Development Act. By this, the president became obliged to deliver to the Congress a state of the cities report every two years. This was, as a matter of fact, the only result: The reports regularly pointed to the increasingly severe problems of the central cities, without implementing political policy. By the end of the Nixon administration, some formal reforms were enacted: numerous special purpose programs became substituted by the Community Development Block Grant Program, administrative regulations became simplified, and cities and states were granted greater margins for own action. In March 1978, the Carter administration passed its Comprehensive National Urban Policy Program which had, however, only minor practical effects and lost its significance with the end of Carter's presidency.

The Carter administration bequeathed a National Agenda for the Eighties, published in 1981, to the new administration. Its authors maintained that there were no general urban problems, but only locally specific difficulties. They recommended a change in political perspectives from places to people.

This was the Reagan administration's occasion to cut back the urban aid programs by almost 55 percent. But at the same time it refused to strengthen social welfare as recommended by the National Agenda for the Eighties commission, reducing instead already existing aid programs. The municipalities and states were said responsible for social welfare, and not the federal government. Instead, supply oriented economic policy was introduced, the heart of which became the Urban Jobs and Enterprise Zone Act of 1982. This act allowed free enterprise zones to be defined in some of the most distressed urban areas where investors received tax exemptions and were relieved from most of the construction and environmental protection regulations.

After two presidencies with some insight in the necessity of a National Urban Policy, this policy was discontinued under the conservative government of the Reagan administration. Even the Urban Impact Assessments of national policies prescribed by the Carter program were brought to an end.

CANADA

Canada has a federal system with three levels of government: municipalities, provinces, and the federal government, although the relative power of the provinces is greater than with the states in the U.S. or the Lander in the FRG. In general, the federal government has no legal competence to act on the local level directly, although it indirectly does so via the provinces (National Housing Act 1944, Central Mortgage and Housing Corporation 1945).

In 1968, the Minister of Transport, responsible at that time also for housing, was commissioned to submit a Report on Housing and Urban Development in Canada to the federal government. To a large extent, this was in reaction to the ghetto riots in the U.S., and the report therefore especially emphasized the urban slums and deteriorated areas in Canadian cities. Among its numerous recommendations was one to establish a Ministry of State for Urban Affairs, which became effective in 1971. This ministry, however, had neither a budget on its own nor any program competence. Its task was to coordinate sectoral policies on the federal level for the benefit of the cities, and to stimulate and mandate urban research.

Important, and successful, efforts were taken towards slum clearance and urban renewal, and today there are hardly any such areas comparable to what can be found in U.S. cities. The 1976 census revealed that many Canadian central cities had experienced population losses. Under the impression of this changing situation, but also for reasons of public austerity following the oil shock and, probably most important, the provinces opposing federal intervention, the ministry was liquidated in 1979. Its tasks were taken over by Canada Mortage and Housing Corporation which used to be responsible for housing and urban renewal programs before. The corporation was successively withdrawn to its indigenous duties since. In Canada, as in the U.S., an attempt to enact a national urban policy has failed.

GREAT BRITAIN

Public administration in the U.K. differs from the federal systems of the U.S. and Canada in at least two important aspects (and continues to do so after its reform in 1974): there is, first, no third level of government between the central government and the municipalities; and, second, there is no coordinating top position with general competence in local government like, e.g., the mayor. Every local head of department thus is in direct communication with the respective ministry in the central government. The municipalities are regarded executive organs of the central government, without local autonomy.

Essentially, what existed as national urban policy was based on the Town and Country Planning Act of 1947 and especially focused on growth control of Greater London and the construction of new towns.

Since the beginning of the 1970's, some basic conditions for urban policy, in the U.K. too, changed: economic growth rates decreased, unemployment became more pressing, the problems of central cities came to the foreground, foreign immigration started to be seen as a severe social problem, and organized pressure groups increasingly interfered in urban policy and politicized urban planning through the means provided for citizen participation.

There is, in Great Britain, no coherent program for urban policy. Political priorities in the central government are rapidly changing, according to the majority party. In general, the Conservatives tend to support private enterprise and rural areas where most of their votes traditionally come from, whereas Labor stresses social welfare and urbanized regions. The implementation of public policies tends to be effective and successful when the same party is in office at the central and local levels, but tends to be counteracted where central and local majorities do not coincide.

The Urban Aid Program of 1968 was, with total endowments of 1.7 million pounds, relatively modest and was primarily effective in social work. In 1977, the Labour government passed the Inner Urban Areas Act with 125 million pounds of total funds, 75 million of which were dedicated for the inner areas of the seven most deeply distressed cities. The funds were intended to promote and realize local development plans. But in fact they mostly served to finance already existing shopping lists instead of consequent urban policy. The Conservative government, in 1980, considerably reduced the program, and cut its urban policy down to free enterprise zones. Emphasis changed, again, towards rural areas and peripheral regions, and to private enterprise.

FRANCE

The administrative organization of France very closely resembles a military command structure: extremely hierarchical, strongly formalized, and directed towards efficient execution of central regulations from top to bottom and regular reporting from bottom to top. In fact, there was not much change since Napoleon introduced this system. On each level (ministry of domestic affairs, regions, départements, arrondissements, cantons, and, finally, some 36.000 municipalities) there is a person of general competence responsible for anything that happens to the next higher level. Very often, such persons hold offices on different levels of government as, e.g., mayor of a big city and member of the central cabinet. Besides this formal system of general administrative organization, there are numerous departments of the central government with field offices on other levels, which rest outside of the control and supervision of the respective generalist but are directly responsible to their Paris agency. Administrative conflict is the unavoidable consequence, enforced by strong competition between the central government departments.

This rigid formal structure is, however, mediated and counteracted by a highly personalized system of exerting power and making decisions: improvising, good connections with other decision-makers, complaisants, neglecting formal regulations, and ineffectiveness are the often lamented consequences.

During the 5th Plan (1966-1970), national urban policy was dominated by the conception of metropoles d'equlibres: The special advancement of, and support for, eight urban agglomerations intended to promote their attractivity and therefore slow down the growth rates of Paris. During the 6th Plan (1971-1975) this general policy became extended and central funds available for medium-sized cities, too. The 7th and 8th Plans continued along this line of extension and thus, in fact, changed their orientation from locally defined goals to sectoral policies. Funds from housing, traffic, energy, or preservation of historic monuments programs became available for smaller communities, too.

The first steps towards local government reform enacted in 1982 are to be seen in the context of the socialist governments' efforts for decentralization. Municipalities received some competences of their own (zoning, rights of pre-emption in certain zones, strengthening of municipal councils). Comprehensive administrative reform, including territorial, functional organizational, and financial reforms, is still lacking.

FEDERAL REPUBLIC OF GERMANY

The FRG follows the principles of federal system's organization, with three levels of government: municipalities, Lander, and federal government. In the late 1960's and early 1970's, administrative reform was conducted but only partially accomplished. Territorial reform changed the number of municipalities from approximately 24,000 to some 8,000; financial reform, in 1969, changed the revenue base of municipalities from commercial taxes to commercial and income taxes and there were minor changes in functional and administrative reforms. The federal government has no formal competence to act directly on the local level the Länder have jurisdiction over the municipalities. Thus there is no national urban policy in the FRG.

There are, however, several programs providing federal funds for municipalities, the most important of which is the Städtebauförderungsgesetz of 1971. Although it was not exclusively directed towards urban renewal, it turned out to be mainly perceived and used for this purpose. Here, too, the competence for granting funds is with the Lander which prepare their respective urban renewal programs according to the demands of the municipalities, and very often contribute additional means from their own sources. In 1976, some of the laws and regulations (concerning construction, citizen participation, and compensation for special hardships) were transferred into the Federal Construction Law. Federal funds for urban policies are provided from a number of other special-purpose programs, e.g. G e m e i n d e v e r k e h r s - f i n a n z i e r u n g s g e s e t z , Wohnungsmodernisierungsgesetz,   Programm   für Zukunftsinvestitionen, etc., but they regularly follow the same pattern for execution with the Länder being responsible for implementation.

CONCLUSIONS

     Attempts towards national urban policies seem to be rooted in the reform movements of the late 1960's and early 1970's, with continuing economic affluence presumed. With the economic crisis starting in 1974, there was an obvious shift in political priorities towards economic growth, unemployment, state indebtedness, the problems of heavy industries, and, although at a slower pace, environmental issues. The administration of scarcity lead urban governments to give up integrated urban development and to focus on casual bottle-necks. The "places-or-people"-debate has received answers in practice (neither one nor the other), although they are ideologically justified by all kinds of New Federalisms, and the like.

     Political reactions to the new restrictions were, however, not unitary, as may be seen in administrative reform - while it seems impossible, in the U.S., to clear the administrative jungle, there have been more or less successful efforts in Great Britain, France and the FRG.

     The conservative governments want to successfully withdraw from some of the policy fields they inherited from their more liberal, or socialist, predecessors, among them the urban field. They rely on the market forces and supply side economics, and national urban policies have no importance in their frame of reference. Although it is obvious that local problems, in their most severe instances, do not emerge from local, but from

supralocal   factors,   the   new   federalism,   or
decentralization, formula are most often used to shift
problems to the local levels, the municipalities. The
reasons motivating early conceptions for national urban
policies have not disappeared, nor lost in significance.
But theory may also tend to overgeneralize as explicit
urban policies certainly are much less important than
implicit urban policies directed towards sectoral goals.

If the trends in urban development are, as was
assumed, mutually interdependent and cumulative, the
cities will probably run into very severe phases of their
existence as we can see especially in the U.S. The least
that ought to be done with respect to urban development
at the level of central government seems to be continuing
urban impact assessments and the appropriate coordination
of sectoral policies.   Where some 80 percent of a
nation's population reside under urban conditions, the
people-or-places-debate seems to ask the wrong question.
Any national policy inevitably affects the cities and
urban agglomerations, a fact that needs to be taken into
account by decision-makers. It is not less planning that
is necessary under conditions of scarcity and austerity,
but better planning.

NOTE

The research reported in this paper was made possible by a grant from Swiss National Science Foundation.   Angelo Ross Lausanne, and the author worked closely together in preparing the report.   Although I wrote this paper, and am responsible for its shortcomings, it would not have been possible without his extensive contribution.   The original report also includes chapters on National Urban Policies in The Netherlands, Denmark and Switzerland.

REFERENCES

Selective Literature

1. Comparative

Allen, B. (ed.). 1982. Making the City Work. Glasgow.

Berg, L. van den, et al. 1982. A Study of Growth and Decline (Urban Europe, vol. 1). Oxford.

Conseil d'Europe. 1979. Séminaire sur les effects des tendances démographiques actuelles sur les villes et les régions d'Europe. Strasbourg.

Gunlicks, A.B. (ed.). 1981. Local Government Reform and Reorganization. Port Washington.

Hall, P., and D. Day. 1980. Growth Centres in the European Urban System. London.

Hanson, R. (ed.). 1982. National Policy and the Post-Industrial City, An International Perspective. Washington.

Hellstern, G.-M., F. Spreer, and H. Wollmann (eds.). 1982. Applied Urban Research. Bonn.

Illeris, S. 1980. Research on Changes in the Structure of the Urban Network. Copenhagen.

Klaasen, L.H., W.T.M. Molle, and J.H. Paelinck (eds.). 1981. Dynamics of Urban Development. Aldershot.

Lagroye, J. and V. Wright. 1979. Local Government in Britain and France. London.

OECD, Ad Hoc Group on Urban Problems: Décentralisation et coordination des politiques urbaines. Paris. 1982.

OECD, Ad Hoc Group on Urban Problems: Cities and Regions, Conflicts and Policy Coordination. Paris. 1982.

OECD: Urban Growth Policies in the Eighties. Paris. 1982.

OECD: Urban Capital Finance. Paris. 1983.

OECD: Managing Urban Change, vol.1.   Paris.   1983.
Fossi,   A.   and   B.   Hamm.   1984.   Nationale
    Stadtentwicklungspolitiken   ein   internationaler
    Vergleich.   Bern.

2. National

United States of America

Clark, T.N. (ed.).   1981.   Urban Policy Analysis:
    Directions for Future Research.   Beverly Hills.

Committee on National Urban Policy, NRC: Critical Issues
    for National Urban Policy.   Washington.   1982.

Glickman, H.J. (ed.).   1980.   The Urban Impacts of
    Federal Policies.   Baltimore.

The President's National Urban Policy Report, Washington.
    1980, 1982.

The President's Commission for a National Agenda for the
    Eighties: Urban   America   in   the   Eighties.
    Washington.   1980.

Canada

Ray, M. (ed.).   1976.   Canadian Urban Trends.   Toronto.

Streich, P.   1981.   Policies to Guide National Urban
    Growth in the 1980's in Canada.   Ottawa.

Streich, P.   1981.   Policies to Address Urban Decline in
    Canada.   Ottawa.

Federal Republic of Germany

Bundesminister für Raumordnung, Bauwesen und Städtebau:
    Rechtsvorschriften zur Städtebauförderung.   Bonn.
    1981.

Einem, E.V.   1982.   National Urban Policy -- The Case of
    West Germany.   APA Journal.

Prognos, A.G.   1978.   Erfahrungen der Gemeinden mit dem
    Städtebauforderungsgesetz.   Bonn.

Prognos,   A.G.   1980.   Wohnungspolitik   und
    Stadtentwicklung, vol. 1. Bonn.

Bundesregierung: Raumordnungsberichte 1972, 1974, 1978,
    1982. Bonn.

Bundesregierung: Städtebauberichte 1970, 1975. Bonn.

Great Britain

Cox, A. 1980.   Continuity and Discontinuity in
    Conservative Urban Policy, Urban Law and Policy.

Dearlove, I. 1979. The Reorganization of British Local
    Government. Cambridge.

Short, J.R. 1982. Urban Policy and British Cities. APA
    Journal.

France

Goze, M. 1982. De la politique urbaine centralisée à
    la démocratie de l'urbanisme, Revue d'économie
    régionale et urbaine.

Loinger, G. 1981. Esquisse d'analyse de l'évolution de
    la politique urbaine en France depuis la liberation.
    Espaces et sociétés.

Pages, T. 1980.   La maî rise de la croissance urbaine.
    Paris.

XI

COMMUNITY DEVELOPMENT AND NATIONAL DEVELOPMENT:
TOWARDS A SYNTHESIS

James Midgley

Of the many changes which have taken place in the global social system during the years since the Second World War, the collapse of the European world imperial order has probably been the most dramatic and profound. After centuries of foreign domination, repression and struggle, the nations of Africa, Asia and Central and South America have secured sovereignty and national independence. And a once rigidly structured international order has been transformed into a more fluid and heterogeneous world system.

The struggle for political self-determination has been accompanied by a determined effort to secure economic and social development for the previously colonized societies. Disadvantaged by imperialism, a dependence on primary commodity production, poverty and other impediments to progress, the pursuit of economic growth and social prosperity has become an international preoccupation. The concept of development has been widely used to characterize this activity and, in addition to comprising a technical term, it has gained currency in the popular vocabulary. Denoting progress, change and the application of knowledge to the promotion of economic and social growth, the concept of development is now widely used and generally understood.

However, popular usage fails to recognize that development is a multi-faceted and complex idea. Its shared connotations of growth, progress and improvements in social conditions conceal a plethora of disparate ideas, theories and ideologies which conceive of the end state of development in different ways and offer different policy prescriptions for its realization. These different conceptions are given formal expression in a variety of development models which, in turn, reflect, wider political views about the social universe and the best way of ordering society.

One example of the different ways in which development is defined is the dichotomous focus in the literature on national and local forms of activity. Transcending specific social science theories, this antinomy alludes to two major perspectives that place emphasis on large scale societal interventions on the one hand and small scale, local programs on the other. While the idea of **national development** implies a centrally directed and statist style of policy making, **community development** evokes the image of ordinary people acting cooperatively and utilizing communitarian institutions to promote progress through their own efforts.

This dichotomy is pervasive and generally social scientists writing on development issues approach their subject matter from one or the other perspective. And while there are exceptions, most ignore the other approach. This is true of development administrators whose programs tend to focus either on national or local activities. Although it would appear that these different levels of intervention complement each other, they have in fact become antagonistic. The emphasis which is placed on large scale infrastructural and industrial investments and the problem of urban bias are some symptons of the tendency among the proponents of national development to neglect local needs. At the same time, the proponents of community development are disdainful if not hostile of national development. Indeed, in recent years, criticisms of large scale, state sponsored programs have increased and there have been more frequent calls for 'popular' and 'community' participation in development effort.

An analysis of these different orientations is not only of academic interest but of policy relevance. In view of the persistence and pervasiveness of underdevelopment and its associated problems of poverty, inequality, hunger, ill-health, illiteracy, homelessness and landlessness in the Third World, the need to harmonize apparently antithetical development strategies that facilitate overall economic and social progress is paramount.

COMMUNITY AND NATIONAL APPROACHES TO DEVELOPMENT

Although only popularized in recent times, the idea of development is not a new one. Indeed, the philosophical notions which it encapsulates may be traced back to antiquity. The belief that societies move through time along a linear path towards higher levels of civilization is closely associated with the idea of progress which, as Nisbet (1970) revealed, has been a recurrent intellectual theme since classical times. Although classical historicism is usually associated with conceptions of a retrogressive decline of humankind from a Golden Age, the writings of Hesiod, Lucretius and others reveal an explicit optimism that predates the explosion of progressivist ideals in renaissance thought. Fused with powerful utopian elements and an emergent belief in the virtues of interventionism, this progressivism finds formal expression in evolutionary sociological theories that provided a conceptual climate within which the concept of development would be articulated. Although not defined formally until well into the 20th century, the concept of development drew on this philosophical tradition and coming at the height of European imperial power, gave intellectual substance to the formative efforts of colonial officials to promote trade, communications and economic growth in the imperial possessions.

The notion of development was implicit in much colonial administration. The construction of roads and railways, the introduction of plantations and processing industries, the exploitation of mineral and other natural resources and the introduction of missionary education, health and other social services laid the foundations for the subsequent emergence of development as a national and international ideal. The British **Colonial Development Act** of 1929 was one of the first attempts to implement the development idea on a generalized scale (United Kingdom, 1960) and although economic planning had been introduced in some of the colonies during the years following the First World War, the British legislation institutionalized the development idea by sanctioning state interventionism and the purposeful manipulation of economic processes. The adoption of national planning by the Soviets at about this time attracted widespread attention and inspired many nationalist leaders. Waterston (1965) reveals, for example, that the Congress Party in India had, by the mid-1930's, established a committee to examine the Soviet experiments and to advocate for the introduction of planning; it was hardly surprising, therefore, that India should have been one of the first newly independent states to adopt national planning.

The adoption of planning by the developing countries in the 1950's and 1960's gave expression to a conception of development that drew on collectivist ideas and placed emphasis on national level, state interventionism in economic and social affairs. Although relatively few developing countries officially declared an allegiance to socialism, the influence of these ideas was pervasive and throughout the Third World, regimes of diverse political characteristics have espoused the tenets of state directed national development. The expansion of the civil service, the creation of new parastatals, the growth of national planning, the introduction of centralized economic controls, nationalization and similar events sanctioned an emerging view of development as a state sponsored, centrally directed and bureaucratically administered activity.

Early development theory supported this conception by offering models and policy prescriptions for the economic transformation of the developing societies that focused primarily on national activities and advocated the adoption of industrial development strategies. Although many formative proponents of development economics espoused liberal ideals, most legitimated interventionism on the ground that the problems of underdevelopment demanded concerted state action and the centralized mobilization of development effort. Rosenstein-Rodan (1943), Lewis (1954) and the proponents of Keynesian economic management such as Harrod (1948) and Domar (1946) all adopted a macro focus and placed the task of development firmly within the purview of the state and its agencies. More recent conceptions of development that emphasize egalitarian and welfarist ideals are also essentially statist in their approach even though there is a greater recognition of the need for participatory activities that harmonize the nationally directed development effort. But here too, redistribution with growth (Chenery et al, 1974), basic needs (Streeten et al, 1981) and similar 'developmentalist' strategies (Hardiman and Midgley, 1982) are essentially dependent on state sponsored, macro focused interventions.

Although pervasive, these historical events were paralleled by the emergence of an alternative approach which became known as community development. In stark contrast to the tenets of national development, community development espouses the ideals of participation, self-reliance and cooperativism. Unlike national development which   focuses   on   state   sponsored,   macro-level intervention, community development emphasizes small scale, people centered activities that enhance social and economic conditions at the local level.

Like national development, community development also evolved during the colonial era. Its first proponents were missionaries and colonial officials who saw the potential of utilizing indigenous institutions such as the tribal authorities to promote Christian education, mobilize labor for public works and strengthen political institutions that were supportive of the **status quo**.

In India, these efforts fused with the communitarian experiments of Tagore and Gandhi to produce a program with strong indigenous roots (Brokensha and Hodge, 1969). In the British territories of Africa, community development was fostered by missionary efforts to mobilize government support for education. In addition to promoting conventional schooling, the authorities recognized the need for adult education or mass literacy as it was known. But in the early 1940's, when the first of these programs were established, literacy training was only one of several components of the mass educational campaigns; others included agricultural extension, sanitation, health and public works (United Kingdom, 1954). And, in most British colonies, these programs were sponsored not by educational agencies but by the welfare departments which stressed their social and developmental rather than educational function.

Although the British probably did more to formalize community development than the other imperial powers, similar ideas emerged elsewhere; in the French territories, **animation rural** (Goussalt, 1968) had much in common with British conceptions of community development and there were comparable although less extensive programs in the colonies of the other European powers. In the cold war years, as American influence spread rapidly, community development practice was infused with theoretical ideas drawn from American social work which transcended the pragmatism of the original British approach (Brokensha and Hodge, 1969). Concepts such as self-help, self-determination, democratic decision making and leadership were articulated and operationalized in many American sponsored community development programs. In some regions of the developing world, such as South East Asia where the threat of communist subversion was taken very seriously, community development was regarded as a useful mechanism for inculcating liberal democratic values among peasant communities and for preserving Western influence.

The use of community development as a counterinsurgency mechanism, ubiquitous problems of corruption and indifference and the bureaucratic ossification of many programs, fostered widespread disillusionment with community development and by the 1970's, many of its original ideas and methods of operation had been severely criticized. But instead of causing its demise, these criticisms resulted in a reformulation of community development principles which infused the movement with a new radicalism and vitality.

The impetus for this has come from the United Nations and its constituent agencies, particularly UNICEF and the World Health Organization, and from non-governmental organizations which have long been skeptical of the public sector and its ability to deal with the serious problems facing the developing countries. Arguing for less emphasis on public management and official procedures, they advocate the active involvement of ordinary people, and particularly the poorest groups, in the development process. Known as community or popular participation, this reformulation of community development ideas involves a vociferous critique of established structures of authority and calls for a radical re-distribution of power and the mobilization of resources on behalf of the poor. Concepts such as grass-roots participation, people's empowerment and 'bottom-up' development characterize the new approach and have become appealing slogans in its rhetoric (Midgley et al, 1986).

The new community participation approach has enjoyed considerable popularity in development circles in recent years and while it undoubtedly brings a new focus to established community development ideas, its central premises do not differ substantially from community development's formative concern with small scale, cooperative, localized activities. While community participation infuses community development with a new dynamism, its focus is essentially the same and, as such, it stands in sharp contrast to the ideals of national development. Indeed, in its new conceptualization, community development involves an aggressive critique of national development and its emphasis on large scale, industrially based and centrally directed development effort.

THE ANTITHESIS OF COMMUNITY AND NATIONAL DEVELOPMENT

It is fair to recognize, however, that community and national development have much in common. Both share a commitment to the ideals of progress, interventionism, growth and change all of which characterize the development idea. Both seek to mobilize human and material resources to promote improvements in economic and social conditions. Both reflect an underlying concern about the problem of mass poverty and both are committed to ameliorating the problems of underdevelopment. Indeed, community and national development may be regarded as little more than different strategic approaches for attaining the same objectives. While community development seeks to mobilize local resources, national development is concerned with those issues and problems that cannot be dealt with locally and which require intervention at the highest level. As such, community development and social development may appear to be complementary; provided that their different modes of functioning are understood and articulated within a comprehensive operational framework, community and national development can reinforce each other and enhance the efforts of the developing societies to transform their economic and social systems and eradicate mass poverty.

The creation of community development programs by many Third World governments during the 1950's and 1960's would suggest that political leaders, planners and civil servants recognized the value of a comprehensive approach to development which combined national and local effort. Indeed, the politicians made frequent use of the rhetoric of community development and its ideals of self-reliance, democratic participation and grass roots involvement. Many equated the principles of community development with traditional values arguing that they were not only compatible with the indigenous culture but represented an authentic response to the problem of underdevelopment by which the peoples of the developing societies would solve their problems through their own efforts. The politicians frequently promised that larger resource allocations for community development would be made and that expertise, materials and cash would be provided to enhance locally initiated development activities.

However, reality belied the idea that community and national effort could be readily combined to promote the overall development of the Third World societies. Generally, community development programs were badly funded and given little support. Often entrusted to low status Ministries of Social Welfare, these programs lacked political, economic and administrative backing and contrary to the political rhetoric, they were given low priority in comparison to large scale, national level projects. In addition, community development was cynically exploited by many political leaders. Onibokun (1976) revealed, for example, that Nigerian politicians often made extravagant promises to fund local projects in order to win political support. But these promises were seldom kept and local people soon became disillusioned. Disillusionment was exacerbated as it was realized that scarce community development resources were being used to finance projects in the politician's own communities or to bribe local chiefs or even to enhance the incomes of civil servants. These programs have also been harmed by the creation of large community development bureaucracies that consume more resources on administration than services. Karunaratne (1976) claimed that the bureaucratization of the Indian community development program seriously impeded its effectiveness. Excluding ordinary people from participating, it imposed national priorities on local people and became just another arm of national development policy.

The failure of political leaders and the administrative establishment in Third World countries to support community development and properly integrate national and local effort, reflects a widespread bias towards centralized, macro-focused and large scale strategies in development policy. This preference has been extensively documented and criticized in the literature. Conventional macro economic models that have sought to promote rapid growth through extensive investments in industry have been condemned for failing to deal directly with the problems of poverty and deprivation (Seers, 1969; Myrdal, 1970, et al, 1981). Lipton's (1977) characterization of this problem as 'urban bias' not only alludes to a proclivity for the comforts of city life among Third World elites but to a more generalized predisposition towards Western technologically dependent industrialization strategies that cause massive imbalances between urban and rural areas. Schumacher (1973), McRobie (1980) and others associated with the Intermediate Technology Development

Group in London have put forward a similar argument claiming that conventional national development policies are both inappropriate to the economic circumstances and needs of Third World countries. In addition, they claim that these strategies have harmed development effort; the importation of large scale, mass production technologies results in the displacement of traditional artisinal forms of production exacerbating the problem of labor underutilization and poverty.

Although these arguments may be criticized for overstating the case and romanticizing indigenous institutions, there can be little doubt that conventional national development strategies have been antithetical to the needs of ordinary people and antagonistic to the objectives of community development. There are, of course, exceptions such as China and Tanzania where political leaders have attempted to integrate national and community development ideals. But the preference for national development has been pervasive and it has not addressed the needs of impoverished communities particularly in rural areas. In spite of recording high rates of economic growth, the problem of poverty in many developing countries has not only persisted but proved to be intractable.

The neglect of community development by political and administrative elites of the Third World has engendered a strong antipathy to national development among the proponents of community development. Although they have long been suspicious of state sponsored, 'top down' programs, this antipathy has now blossomed into open hostility. As the failure of conventional community development has been recognized, they have become more severe in their judgments and have increasingly called for interventions that exclude the state and its commitment to centrally directed change.

As was noted earlier, these ideas are associated with the new community participation approach which offers a radical critique of the condition of underdevelopment and proposes a much more activist style of intervention than that of conventional community development. Also, unlike the old community development approach, many of the proponents of community participation are opposed to the state sponsorship of local programs claiming that they are inefficient, paternalistic and oppressive. They argue for example, that state sponsored development is costly, bureaucratic and wasteful and that in spite of spending vast resources on large scale projects, little is achieved. Often the only beneficiaries are corrupt politicians, bureaucrats, contractors and the foreign governments which provide credit to finance what are often empty symbols of national prestige. Community development advocates are also critical of the paternalism of national development which imposes services and programs on local people instead of facilitating local solutions to local problems. This type of development creates a complacent dependence on the state and stifles local initiative and authentic participation. Often, this paternalism is associated with a repressive style of government which seeks to use development projects conspiratorially to gain political support and maintain social control.

Although these arguments are not explicitly formulated within the context of particular ideologies, they are in fact highly ideological in character and reveal a strong commitment to political theories that embody an inherent dislike of the state. Many community development advocates use socialist or even Marxist rhetoric when arguing their case but as Midgley (1987) has shown, their views are not inspired by socialism but by a blend of individualism, anarchism and populism all of which are hostile to state sponsored, national development. The emphasis on local democracy reveals a debt to liberal political theories and particularly to the concept of neighborhood democracy which advocates the fact to face involvement of all citizens in the decision making process rather than representative democracy which is regarded as remote and removed from the citizen's daily concerns. Similar ideas are found in anarchist thought which favors small, localized communitarian forms of social organization and rejects centralized authority and state control over social and economic institutions. The populist elements in community development theory extol the virtues of the simple folk and their institutions, denigrating an allegedly uncaring establishment, an indifferent bureaucracy and a hostile economic system. These ideologies fuel community development's opposition to national development and impede efforts to reconcile the two.

In spite of the antipathy of community development advocates to national development, it is doubtful whether the massive social and economic problems facing Third World countries can be solved through local effort alone. Local people may have great reserves of enthusiasm and initiative but they are often too poor to solve the serious problems they face.   As Midgley and Hamilton (1978) showed in a study of community development in Sierra Leone, local people are anxious to improve their circumstances and will give their time, effort and even money to initiate community projects but without the support of government, the impact of these activities is marginal.   The state is not only able to mobilize resources on a massive scale but to redistribute these resources.   Community development proponents fail to recognize the need for mechanisms that transfer resources from wealthier to poorer groups.   Without institutions that transcend local level activities, redistributive flows of this kind are unlikely to occur.   There is also a need to coordinate community effort and integrate it with national priorities.   By focusing narrowly on the local situation, community development is unresponsive to needs that transcend the local level.   It is doubtful also whether local development effort based on agricultural pursuits can raise the levels of living of an impoverished rural population much beyond subsistence standards.   Although conventional industrial development models are no longer as popular as they were twenty years ago, a careful study by Kitching (1982) has shown that the capacity of agriculture to absorb labor and raise national income appreciably is limited; only strategies based on planned industrialization can attain this goal. And this requires national policies that foster growth and ensure, at the same time, that ordinary people benefit from its attainments.

HARMONIZING COMMUNITY AND NATIONAL DEVELOPMENT

The need to balance community and national development strategies and to harmonize the two is obvious.   National approaches that pursue large scale, macro strategies without considering the needs of ordinary people and directing the benefits of development to the poor, produce a lop-sided pattern of growth that fails to deal with the pressing human problems of underdevelopment. Conversely, parochial community-based strategies which assume that the massive problems facing the developing countries can be solved through local effort alone, are unlikely to bring about real social and economic improvements.   Clearly, ways must be found of integrating these disparate development conceptions to promote maximum, feasible well-being for the peoples of the Third World.

Although the task is formidable, the initial steps towards fostering the harmonization of community and national development have already been taken and there have been various proposals for promoting their integration. Although they have not been implemented on a significant scale in the developing world they reveal that national and local development programs can be linked within a comprehensive development framework. In some countries, where there have been efforts to implement these proposals, some progress has been made; although not fulfilling the expectations of utopian development thinkers, they reveal that there are prospects for achieving a balance between national and community development objectives.

Much depends on the attributes of national governments who must set the framework for the integration of these approaches. Without their support and commitment, community development is likely to remain little more than a marginal activity and a basis for political sloganeering. As a United Nations (1975, p. 29) report argued: "Underlying all discussion of popular participation is the assumption that national leaders actively desire such participation." If they do not, the exercise is pointless.

In addition to national sponsorship, community development ideals can operate effectively only if a climate favorable to genuine local involvement is created. And this demands more than political will on the part of national leaders. In addition to administrative and financial backing, the effective integration of community and national development strategies is dependent on an institutional framework of programs and procedures supported by law and public ideologies that facilitate community development ideals. This, as Stiefel and Pearce (1981) noted, is a long-term process in which the habits of self-reliance, participation and administrative responsibility are acquired and practiced. Specific proposals for promoting the integration of community and national development will be most successful if they emerge within an established institutional framework of this kind.

However, it is not at all certain that these prerequisites can be met. As has been shown already, established styles of national policy making in the Third World have been neglectful of local communities and particularly of the poor. In addition, institutionalized patterns of political authority in many developing countries are not conducive to the involvement of ordinary people in the development process. Both suggest that the required political will and institutional climate for harmonizing community and national development may not be readily available.

But in spite of the pervasive tendency towards centralization and even autocracy in Third World politics and the underdevelopment of participatory institutions, there is room for maneuver. Tyranny is not an ubiquitous form of government in the Third World, many of the most notorious Third World dictators (including Duvalier, Marcos, Pahlavi and Somoza) have been deposed and electoral processes have been used with positive effect. It should also be remembered that many developing countries do have indigenous capacities for fostering community development and, in others, new forms of local organization have been established. Even in one party systems such as China and Tanzania, local institutions of this kind have flourished. If properly supported these can reinforce institutional facilities for community involvement in the developmental process.

Two types of techniques which facilitate the harmonization of community and national development can be identified. The first derives from a consensus view of society in which the state is regarded as essentially benevolent in its intentions and modes of operation. Although this view recognizes that there are deficiencies in the way governments function, it suggests that political leaders and administrators are committed to development ideals and amenable to reasonable proposals for harmonizing community and national development goals. The second class of techniques are based on a less sanguine view of the state; drawing inspiration from conflict models of society, it believes that the bias towards national development can best be redirected towards the interests of local people through the use of confrontational tactics that bring political pressure to bear on policy makers and bureaucrats and compel them to take account of the needs of those who have been excluded from the development process. Although most writers on the subject favor one of these two approaches, it is likely that a combination of the two will be the most effective.

Consensual proposals for harmonizing community and national development are usually phrased within the wider theory of decentralization which grants authority to local and intermediate political institutions over their recognized jurisdictions. This requires legislative sanction, administrative support and authentic control over local affairs. And to the effective, decentralization involves more than the creation of local representative bodies; the rights and responsibilities of the different levels of government must be clearly defined, local decisions must be implemented without constant reference to higher authority and powers must be granted to permit local bodies to raise local revenues and control their expenditure.

There are, of course, major political, administrative and economic impediments to the attainment of the decentralization ideal. Poverty limits the capacity of many Third World local authorities to raise their own revenues, administrative elitism draws capable civil servants out of local areas towards the center and a general climate of political centralization is hardly conducive to an authentic devolution of authority. Nevertheless, under the prodding of the international development agencies, there has been a gradual acceptance of the need for decentralization and in some cases real progress has been made (United Nations, 1975). In addition, a variety of techniques have been proposed for the promotion of community involvement in development. These include policies for retaining capable civil servants at the local level, community leadership training, joint meetings between ordinary people, bureaucrats and politicians, regular reviews by local communities of public agencies and the wider dissemination of information about development and governmental activities (United Nations, 1981).

Conflict approaches, which are today widely advocated by non-governmental organizations, seek to inspire self-confidence in local people and to assure them of their rights as citizens. Through conscientization, community workers assist local people to understand the structural causes of poverty and deprivation and to formulate viable courses of action (Freire, 1972). They are trained in the tactics of protest, of campaigning, of building coalitions with other interest groups and of functioning with solidarity and singularity of purpose. And, as Hollnsteiner (1982) revealed, tactics of this kind have been very effective, especially in the urban context where squatter groups have been able to secure concessions from recalcitrant public agencies.   Similar tactics can be used with considerable effect in other fields as well.

While there is evidence to show that the use of these and other techniques have facilitated a greater awareness of the need to harmonize community and national development, much more needs to be done if an authentic integration of these approaches is to be achieved.   The case for harmonization is overwhelming but while various proposals for realizing this goal have been made, political force that gives effect to these ideals is still needed.   Ultimately this depends on the predispositions of political elites and on their capacity to embrace ideologies that are committed both to national development and the involvement of ordinary people in the development process.

REFERENCES

Brokensha, D. and P. Hodge. 1969. Community
Development: An Interpretation. San Francisco:
Chandler.

Chenery, H. et al. 1974. Redistribution with Growth.
London: Oxford University Press.

Domar, E. 1946. 'Capital Expansion, Rate of Growth and
Employment' Econometrica 15, 137-147.

Freire, P. 1972. Pedagogy of the Oppressed.
Harmondswroth: Penguin.

Hardiman, M. and J. Midgley. 1982. The Social
Dimensions of Development: Social Policy and
Planning in the Third World. New York: Wiley.

Harrold, R. 1948. Towards a Dynamic Economics. London:
MacMillan.

Hollnsteiner, M.R. 1982. 'Government Strategies for
Urban Areas and Community Participation' Assignment
Children 57/58, 43-64.

Goussalt, Y. 1968. 'Rural Animation and Popular
Participation in French Speaking Black Africa'
International Labour Review. 97, 525-550.

Karunaratne, G. 1976. 'The Future of Community
Development Programmes in India' Community
Development Journal 11, 95-118.

Kitching, G. 1982. Development and Underdevelopment in
Historical Perspective. London: Methuen.

Lipton, M. 1977. Why Poor People Stay Poor: Urban Bias
in World Development. London: Temple Smith.

Lewis, W.A. 1954. 'Economic Development with Unlimited
Supplies of Labour' The Manchester School 22, 139-
199.

McRobie, G. 1980. Small is Possible. New York: Harper
and Row.

Midgley, J. 1987. 'Popular Participation, Statism and Development' Journal of Social Development in Africa 2, 5-15.

Midgley, J. et al. 1986. Community Participation, Social Development and the State. New York: Methuen.

Midgley, J. and D. Hamilton. 1978. 'Local Initiative and the Role of Government in Community Development: Policy Implications of a Study in Sierra Leone' International Social Work 21, 2-11.

Myrdal, G. 1970. The Challenge of World Poverty. Harmondsworth: Penguin.

Nisbet, R. 1970. History of the Idea of Progress. New York: Basic Books.

Rosenstein-Rodan, P. 1943. 'Problems of Industrialization of South and Eastern Europe' Economic Journal 53, 205-211.

Onibokun, A. 1976. 'Directions for Social Research on Self-Help Projects and Programmes in Nigeria' Community Development Journal 11, 60-69.

Schumacher, E.F. 1973. Small is Beautiful: Economics as if People Mattered. New York: Harper and Row.

Seers, D. 1972. 'The Meaning of Development' in N. Uphoff and W. Ilchman (eds.) The Political Economy of Development. Berkeley: University of California Press, 123-129.

Steifel, M. and A. Pearse. 1982. 'UNRISD's Popular Participation Program' Assignment Children 59/60, 145-159.

Streeten, P. et al. 1981. First Things First. New York: Oxford University Press.

United Kingdom. 1954. Social Development in the British Colonial Territories. London.

United Kingdom. 1960. The United Kingdom Colonial Development and Welfare Acts. London.

United Nations. 1975. Popular Participation in Decision Making for Development. New York.

United Nations. 1981. Popular Participation as a Strategy for Promoting Community Level Action and National Development. New York.

Waterston, A. 1965. Development Planning: Lessons from Experience. Baltimore: Johns Hopkins University Press.

CONTRIBUTORS

DAN A. CHEKKI is Professor of Sociology, University of Winnipeg. He has published several papers and books on family, change, community development, sociology of knowledge and urban policy, the most recent being American Sociological Hegemony.

LEO DRIEDGER is Professor of Sociology, University of Manitoba. He has published several papers and books on religion, ethnicity, and urban community. He has edited a volume entitled The Canadian Ethnic Mosaic.

KRZTYSZTOF FRYSZTACKI teaches sociology at the Jageillonian University, Institute of Sociology, Krakow, Poland. He has done research on Polish communities in the United States.

KIRSTEN A. GRONBJERG is Professor of Sociology, Loyola University of Chicago. She has published several papers and books on public policy, nonprofit organizations and poverty. Her books include Mass Society and the Extension of Welfare; Poverty and Social Change (co-author); The Welfare State: Prospects for the 1980's (editor).

BERND HAMM is Professor of Sociology, University of Trier, West Germany. He has done extensive comparative research on European cities and he has published several papers and books.

MARY JO HUTH is Professor of Sociology, the University of Dayton, Ohio. She has published several papers on housing problems, women in development issues, urban and regional planning in France and Switzerland. She is the author of The Urban Habitat: Past, Present and Future.

THEODORIC MANLEY JR. is Assistant Professor of Sociology, De Paul University, Chicago. He has done research on black communities in the United States.

PETER MCGAHAN is Professor of Sociology and Dean of Faculty, University of New Brunswick, St. John. He is the author of Police Images of a City and Urban Sociology in Canada.

JAMES MIDGLEY is Professor and Dean of School of Social Work, Louisiana State University. He previously taught at the University of Cape Town and the London School of Economics. He has published several books on social work, inequality, social policy and development in the Third World. Comparative Social Policy and the Third World is one of his recent books.

CAROLE E. SILVERMAN and STEPHEN E. BARTON are at the Institute of Urban and Regional Development, University of California, Berkeley. Their research interests include planned development, cooperatives and urban neighborhoods.

INDEX